The Same Difference

by

Deborah Lynn Jacobs

Royal Fireworks Press

Unionville, New York

To my son, Keigh—my first reader, first editor, first critic—who read everything I ever wrote and always said it was good, even when it wasn't.

This is a work of fiction, and any resemblance of characters or their situations to persons living or dead is purely coincidental.

Royal Fireworks Press
First Avenue, PO Box 399
Unionville, NY 10988-0399
(845) 726-4444
FAX: (845) 726-3824
email: rfpress@frontiernet.net

ISBN: 0-88092-465-9

Printed in the United States of America using vegetable-based inks on acid-free, recycled paper by the Royal Fireworks Printing Company of Unionville, New York.

I had always known that my sister and I were the same, yet different.

We were identical twins.

We had the same dark brown hair, the same deep blue eyes, the same clear skin.

The same and yet different.

You would see we were different right away. My sister would not look at you, would not talk to you, would not even know you were there.

She was autistic. I was not.

When we were babies, Mom told me, there were no differences between us. We both laughed at things, like the ceiling fan or the mobiles above our cribs. We both babbled baby talk, cooing and laughing and making bubbly noises. We both learned to sit up and crawl and walk and say our first words at about the same time. Mom said she kept a list on the fridge and added to it each day. If I learned a new word one day, my sister would learn a new word the next.

No difference.

We both cried at loud noises, like the doorbell or the vacuum cleaner. We both were fascinated by the bright border of alphabet letters that Mom had put around our room, and both of us loved venetian blinds and the black and white floor tiles in the bathroom.

It wasn't until we were almost two and a half that Mom began to notice some differences.

I taught myself the alphabet from the border in our room. Mom bought a set of magnetic letters, the kind that stuck on the fridge. I spent hours, she told me, putting them in order, from A to Z, then putting them in reverse order, from Z to A. One day, when I was only two and a half, she found me spelling out brand names on the fridge—Coke, Nabisco, Quaker, Kraft. I had a temper tantrum when I tried to spell Kool-Aid. I needed two *O*'s but only had one. Mom bought two more sets of letters that very same day, to spare me further frustration.

At the same time that I was making words out of letters, I began to repeat things I'd heard—songs on the radio, commercials on TV, parts of dialogue from movies, even bits of conversations. Mom called me "her little tape recorder."

By age four, I was reading. By six, I'd read our entire set of encyclopedias. At age seven, I became interested in world records and recited them to anyone who would listen.

My sister, on the other hand, never learned to read. She never even learned the letters of the alphabet. In fact, by the time she was two, she was losing her speech entirely.

It was as though she retreated into her own little world. Given a car or truck, she would sit quietly, spinning its wheels around and around for hours on end. She developed a strange attraction for one particular dump truck. She slept with it, ate dinner with it, even had baths with it.

The funny thing was that she didn't make truck noises, or push the truck along the floor, or fill it with sand. She just played with its wheels and moved the dump bed up and down, up and down, endlessly.

She began to develop certain preferences then. She would only wear blue. She would only brush her teeth with a pink toothbrush. She only ate certain things—Cream of Wheat, cream of mushroom soup, milk, apple sauce— nothing chewy like steak or crunchy like carrots or apples.

She had tantrums. Often, Mom couldn't tell what set them off. But Chelsea, that was my sister's name, would cry and cry. She couldn't be comforted, Mom said. If you tried to hug her, she stiffened and pulled away.

She was diagnosed as autistic. Mom and Dad hired a special teacher to work with her, but she didn't improve much over the years.

That's why I stayed home with her, rather than going to a regular school. She couldn't function without me. I was the only one who really understood her. The same, yet different.

Mom helped me with schoolwork, and a tutor came to our house three times a week. We had a computer, so the world was at my fingertips through the Net. It was perfect.

Once, when I was ten, Mom thought it was time I went to a regular school. She said I was missing out on "socialization."

I only lasted two weeks. The kids were mean to me. They made fun of me and made me lose my temper.

I bit someone. The principal said it was the last straw. I went back to home-schooling. I was happier at home. Besides, Chelsea had been unhappy without me.

Then I turned fourteen, and things changed.

I'd been noticing for some time that most people my age, people on television or in books, had friends. I had a friend too, my sister, but it wasn't the same. I talked to Mom and Dad about it, and they agreed.

It was time to have friends. It was time to go to school.

Mom said the timing was excellent. Chelsea was older now, and Mom said she could take care of her without my help. We'd just moved to a small town, Clearwater. The high school, she said, was very small and could accommodate people with differing abilities.

I was glad of that. I knew I read faster and knew more things than other people my age. I figured that meant I had differing abilities.

We made an appointment to visit the school.

Mom said that decision was a "turning point" in my life.

It was quite some time before I understood what she'd meant by that.

4

Chapter One

EMOTION IS THE ENEMY

It looked more like a prison than a school.

It had red bricks on four square walls, high narrow windows, and a chain-link fence.

It smelled of lemon floor polish, dust, old wood and people. There was the stinky old cheese smell of running shoes. There was the smell that your winter mitts and scarves get, after they've been stored all summer in a box. A fusty smell, like early death.

The sounds were too loud. People were talking and calling to each other and banging shut their locker doors. There were too many colors, too many things in motion, too many distractions.

It was overwhelming.

I knew I was supposed to go to the principal's office. Mom and I had been there the week before, when I'd come to register. Mom had arranged for me to have a "peer buddy," and I was supposed to meet him there. I looked around for the office, but everything looked different with so many people around. I didn't know which direction to go.

I had just decided to leave when someone came up to me and touched my sleeve. I jumped and he moved back a little and smiled at me. "Hi. Are you Casey?" he asked.

"Yes." I wondered how he knew my name.

"I'm Scott," he said. "Pleasedtameetcha."

"Pardon me?" I asked.

"Pleasedtameetcha," he repeated. "I'm your peer buddy. Name's Scott."

Relief washed over me. "I'm supposed to meet you at the office," I said.

"Yeah, but you didn't show up so I thought I'd look for you. Howareyadoin'?"

I couldn't understand him very well, since he kept running all his words together.

"We have to meet at the office," I insisted.

He smiled again. It was a quirky little smile that lifted one side of his lips, making his face asymmetrical. I wasn't sure if I liked it.

"They told me you were a little unusual," he said. "Sure, let's go to the office and tell Mr. Hoffstetter that I found you."

Scott led the way. We were partway there when a big man stopped us. He had a booming voice, like stereo speakers turned up to the point of distortion. His face was scarred from a bad case of acne. He looked like the harvest moon in September. *Craterface.* I had met him the week before when I'd registered, but I'd forgotten his real name.

"Ah, you found her," he boomed. "Good. We're just about to start the assembly." He nodded to me, then

6

continued walking down the hall. Cigar smell clung to him like a black cloud. "Oh, Scott, don't forget to turn your time sheets in every Friday," he called back over his shoulder.

"No prob, Mr. Hoffstetter," Scott answered.

Hoffstetter. Right. Not Craterface. Hoffstetter. I'd have to remember that.

Scott turned and followed Craterface, I mean, Hoffstetter. "Coming?" he asked.

I hesitated. I didn't like it when plans changed. I was supposed to have met Scott and Mr. Hoffstetter in the office. Nothing was going the right way. My heart started to thump and my stomach felt queasy.

"Come on," Scott insisted. I followed him, trying to keep my anxiety under control. *Emotion is the enemy,* I reminded myself. *Control it. Focus on something else. Focus on Scott. Memorize his name. Scott,* I repeated to myself. *Memorize it. Tack it onto a description so you won't forget. Scott. Grey eyes, flecked with blue and green and gold. Light brown hair, streaked with blond, off center part, bangs pushed up and back, hair longer in back. Wide eyes, wide smile. Quirky smile, lifts up at one edge. Soft voice. Deep voice. Scott. Remember the name.*

We arrived at the gym. Voices echoed off the walls, making it hard to concentrate on Scott's voice. He said something, but I couldn't make it out.

"What?" I asked.

"So, you're new in town," he said.

"Yes."

"Where are you from?"

"Toronto."

"Nice city. We went there once. Ever been up in the CN Tower?"

"Yes," I said, suddenly feeling better. "It's the tallest building and free-standing tower in the world. It stands one-thousand, eight-hundred and fifteen feet, five inches high. It took just over two years to build, and is made of one-hundred and forty-three thousand, three-hundred tons of reinforced concrete. The view from the top, on a clear day, is seventy-five miles."

"Wow. What did you do, memorize the entire *Guinness Book of World Records?*"

"No. Only as far as page three hundred and ten." I was about to continue, but a voice blared out over a set of speakers.

It hurt my ears, so I tuned it out.

"Come on," I heard Scott say. He was walking over to a group of kids by the door. I followed him.

A short, squat, grey-haired woman said, "Follow me." Walking behind her, I decided she looked like a Hobbit, a legendary race of people who lived in the time of elves and trolls.

We followed the Hobbit up a flight of stairs to the next floor. I counted them as I went up, an old habit left over from childhood. Ten steps, a landing, then ten more. Twenty. The steps leading to the rec room in my house numbered only thirteen. Once we got to the classroom, the Hobbit called out our names alphabetically. I kept tuned in this time, waiting for my name.

"Casey Jackson?" she called, looking up over her silver rimmed glasses. She pointed to a desk. I walked over and then hesitated. She had put me behind a girl with blonde hair and a blue shirt. The girl, Blondie, wore so much perfume it was like a thick fog around her. Even when I took tiny breaths, it was like breathing a liquid, like drowning.

"Casey, please sit down," said the Hobbit.

"I can't," I told her. "It's her...her perfume."

A number of people laughed, and I knew I'd said something wrong, but I didn't know what. Sometimes I just blurted things out. It's not that I did it without thinking, it's just that I couldn't find the right way to phrase it.

Someone in front of Blondie turned around and whispered loudly, so that everyone heard, "What did you do? Pour it on by the bucketful?" There was more laughter.

"Are you allergic to perfume?" the teacher asked me.

I thought for a moment. No, I was not allergic to perfume. It didn't make me sneeze or cough or get asthmatic. But it did bother me, to the point of making it impossible to even think straight.

"It gives me a headache," I said.

Hobbit nodded. "Yes, sometimes it gives me a headache, too. Okay, class. For the benefit of Casey, and myself, and anyone else who has a sensitivity to perfume and cologne, please use these products sparingly, if at all. Now, Casey, why don't you sit over there instead."

"Over there" was right beside Scott. That pleased me. He smelled very faintly of deodorant soap and toothpaste. I could handle that.

The Hobbit handed out schedules to each student. There were eight days in each cycle, with six periods in each day. We would begin each day with the first hour in home room. I saw that my homeroom teacher's name was Mrs. Schulz. It was printed in the top right corner of the schedule. *Schulz, Schulz,* I repeated to myself. *I must try to remember her name. Schulz.*

"Did you have a question, Casey?" asked Hobbit, I mean, Mrs. Schulz.

"No, ma'am," I answered.

A light flutter of laughter moved through the room. What had I said wrong this time?

Suddenly, I knew it had all been a big mistake. I didn't belong here.

I was trying to decide whether or not to just go home when a bell rang. I covered my ears with my hands as it pealed on and on, relentlessly. The class emptied abruptly, leaving only me.

"Casey, hurry up. You'll be late for math class," Scott said, poking his head back into the classroom. "We've only been here for thirty minutes," I argued. "Each class is fifty minutes long, with ten minutes to get to the next class."

"Today is an abbreviated schedule so that you can meet all your teachers," Scott said. "We'll be dismissed before noon."

Reluctantly, I followed him to the next class. An abbreviated schedule was another change. It made me nervous. We ran through the rest of the day, staying only thirty minutes in each class and skipping the usual lunch break. My stomach felt like I'd swallowed a ten-pound rock by the time we'd finished.

"See ya tomorrow, Casey," Scott called to me as we left the last class.

"See ya tomorrow," I echoed.

If I come back, I added to myself.

11

Chapter Two

SOMETHING VERY BAD

I rehearsed my route home as I sat on a weathered picnic table near the back door of the school. As I had suspected from the map, there was a clear path through the woods to Sixth Street, a shortcut that appeared to be very popular judging from the groups of students who were disappearing down it. I waited until most of them were gone. I hated crowds.

Walking across the soccer field, I enjoyed the last heat of summer. Already the smaller aspens were turning yellow, their leaves shivering in a light wind. At the edge of the woods were pincherry and pussywillow trees, tanseys, asters, sarsaparilla, mint and raspberry. My "encyclopedia mind" catalogued them effortlessly, running through their vital statistics like baseball scores. Further in were stands of paper birch and poplar, broken up by dark clumps of green balsam and spruce. A mass of undergrowth clogged the spaces between the trees, making it impossible to see more than ten feet in any one direction.

Keeping an eye on my watch, I timed my progress along the winding path. I arrived at Sixth Street after three minutes of careful walking. I jotted the time down in my notebook.

It was one minute down Sixth to Main. I turned right at the post office, then recorded two minutes to reach

12

Tamarack. Left on Tamarack, one minute to George Street. Left on George. It should only take two minutes to reach Clear Bay Road. After three minutes I began to worry. Something was clearly wrong. I couldn't have underestimated the time that badly.

Anxiety washed over me, like a flash flood in a dry river bed. My heart pounded, my mouth went dry, and my stomach felt sick. The feeling that something very bad was about to happen was almost overwhelming. I felt dizzy and disoriented. I couldn't breathe. I tried to, but each breath was like sucking in a wet sponge. I was suffocating. I knew it was irrational, but I felt like I might die, right there, in the middle of the sidewalk, gasping and flopping like a fish deprived of oxygen.

I had to get control. *Control. Emotion is the enemy. Control it.* I repeated it over and over, trying to block out the panic.

That's all this is, I thought. *A panic attack. You've had them before. It feels like you are going to die, but you never do.*

Take ten deep breaths. Control. I must have turned the wrong way. That's it. A simple wrong turn. Left on George instead of right. No big deal. I'll simply have to go back and start over.

Three minutes back to Tamarack, make a right turn, one minute to Main, turn right again, two minutes to Sixth, left on Sixth, one minute to the path entrance and three minutes back to the picnic table at the back of the school.

Once back at the picnic table, I slowed my breathing and willed my muscles to relax. It was okay. I was safe. I hadn't really been lost, not really.

Okay. One more time. Properly, this time.

Heart pounding, I set off again, watching my turns. Right on Main, left on Tamarack, RIGHT on George. Not left, RIGHT.

As soon as I made the proper turn, I felt much more in control. I was sure I wouldn't make the same mistake again.

I had only gone a few steps down George when I noticed the rocks. They were lined up on the grass, paralleling the sidewalk. They were a mix of black gneiss and pink quartz. I picked up one with huge quartz crystals and put it in my knapsack. Chelsea would love it.

Three minutes down George, going the proper direction this time, brought me to the hard packed gravel surface of Clear Bay Road. Four minutes and I was at Fireroad Six, the one we lived on. Forty seconds later I walked in the front door.

Mom came out of the kitchen, wiping her hands on a dish towel. "Casey! What happened? I expected you ages ago. I called the school twice already!"

"I got lost on the way home," I told her. "I'm okay now. I'm going to see Chelsea," I announced, grabbing a fresh banana muffin from the counter on my way out to the deck. This time of day, Chelsea liked to take an artist's pad and pencils to the table outside to do some sketching. I found her sitting at the white plastic table, her back to the sun, her hand busily scratching across the paper.

Chelsea was a natural artist. An autistic savant. The term used to be "idiot savant," from the French words meaning "unlearned" (idiot) and "skill" (savant). Since "idiot" now had a negative meaning, "autistic savant" was used by Chelsea's many doctors to describe her untaught talent.

I sat down beside her quietly and looked over at the sketch. It was a loon, standing partly upright in the water and stretching its wings. Chelsea had drawn it in such detail I could almost hear it calling. Each individual feather was there, each marking, each variation of black and white. It could have been a photograph.

I sat down beside my sister. She did nothing to show that she was aware of me. I didn't expect her to. But, somehow, I felt she knew I was there.

I drew the rock out of my knapsack and very slowly, noiselessly, slid it across the table to Chelsea. Chelsea startled at loud noises or intrusions, so I didn't want to alarm her. That was another difference between us. Sometimes I daydreamed, and a person had to say my name a few times, loudly, before I paid attention. Saying Chelsea's name sharply would cause her to curl up and start rocking, over and over, back and forth.

I knew she saw the rock. I knew she liked it. She said nothing, but I could tell. I waited. She closed up her sketch book and slipped the pencil into its coiled binding. Only then did she pick up the rock. She turned it over and over in her hands, rubbed it against her cheek, and then ran her tongue over it. She loved it. I knew it would join her collection right away.

I used to have collections myself—rocks, feathers, bits of glass, colored papers. I didn't collect anymore, but part of me still understood the satisfaction of having things. Things that you could put on shelves, like Chelsea did with all her rocks. Things that never changed. They were constant, always there in the same place whenever you wanted to look at them or touch them.

"Come on, Chelsea," I said quietly. I took her hand and led her inside. She went to her room and put away her sketchbook. Third drawer, right-hand side of the desk. Everything had a place in her room. Everything belonged somewhere.

O   O   O

Later on, Chelsea and I washed up for dinner. Mom had made meat loaf, with mashed potatoes, carrots and peas. She had mashed some of the carrots for Chelsea, since Chelsea only ate mushy food. I knew there would be apple crisp for dessert. We always had apple crisp with meat loaf. It was my favorite dessert, since Mom always gave me the crunchy topping from Chelsea's share.

"How'd your first day of school go, sweetheart?" Dad asked as he sat down at the table. He said "sweetheart" in his Humphry Bogart accent, pronouncing it "schweet'art." Dad loved movies. He knew just about every actor who had ever been in a film and could imitate just about anyone. It was his hobby, along with gardening and computers.

"Not very good," I told him. "My peer buddy..." I stopped. *What was his name? Quirky smile, grey eyes, deep voice. Oh, Scott.* "My peer buddy, Scott, met me in the hallway instead of at the office. And then, they changed the schedule so that the classes were the wrong length."

"And, she got lost coming home," Mom said, giving Dad one of "those looks" that I didn't understand.

"Listen, the first day is always a little rough," said Dad. "You'll be fine."

"Maybe it's too early..." Mom started to say.

Dad cut her off. "Nonsense. You can't protect her forever. She has to get out into the world like the rest of us. She'll cope. I did."

"Yes, but you weren't..." she started to say.

"She'll cope," Dad said loudly. I wondered if they were having a fight and was about to ask, but Dad went on.

"Casey, tell me. What did you find difficult today?"

"Short classes," I said immediately.

"You were expecting a regular day, right?" Dad asked. "So, tomorrow will be a normal day. Next problem?"

"I can't remember the teachers' names. I get mixed up about what they look like."

17

"Yes, that happens to me all the time," Dad said. "I'll drop by the school tomorrow and pick up an old yearbook for you. You can study the faces and names at home until you know them."

"That would work," I said, feeling much better. Dad always understood how I felt. "Pass the potatoes, please?"

Over dinner, Dad told us about work. His new job was the reason we had moved to Clearwater. Dad had replaced the Head of Records at the regional hospital. Soon, we knew all about the hospital's computerized records system. Dad had a tendency to go on and on about a topic, even if it bored the rest of us.

We watched an old movie after dinner, then I read until bedtime. Just before nine-thirty, when I always turn out the light, Dad came into my room.

"So, did you make any new friends today?" he asked.

"No, no one talked to me except Scott," I answered. I felt disappointed about that, since I'd gone to school to have friends like other people my age.

"Maybe you need to take the first step," Dad suggested.

"What is the first step?" I asked.

"Well, just go up to someone and start talking, I guess," Dad shrugged.

"What do we talk about?"

"Oh—general stuff at first. You know, the weather, sports, movies. Once you know someone better, you might talk about your hobbies or special interests. Often friendships get started with shared interests."

That made sense to me. I decided to give it a try the next day.

Chapter Three

THE FIRST STEP

"It reached 136 degrees Fahrenheit, in the shade, in Al'Aziziyah, Libya, on September 3, 1922. The coldest recorded temperature was minus 128.6 degrees Fahrenheit at Vostok, Antartica, on July 21, 1983."

The group of people I had been talking to looked at me for a moment, then moved away. I tried another group.

"They say lightning never strikes twice, but they are wrong. Roy Sullivan was struck a total of seven times between 1942 and 1977."

"Really?" said a girl with long brown hair. Then she turned her back on me and went on talking to her friend.

Maybe no one is interested in weather facts, I thought. *Dad said sports is a good topic.* I looked around for another group, then decided maybe a single person would be better. There was a boy with a face as long as a zucchini standing alone by the lockers. I tried him.

"The oldest college bowl game is the Rose Bowl. It was played for the first time in 1902, on New Year's Day, in Pasadena, California. Michigan won against Stanford, forty-nine to zero."

"You are really weird," Zucchini Face said. He walked away.

So, sports isn't a good conversation opener either, I decided. *What's left? Oh, yes. Movies.*

A girl was standing alone by the water fountain. I approached her.

"When *Jurassic Park* was released, it had the biggest box office gross of its time, earning 912.8 million dollars world-wide."

"I have to go to class now," the girl said. She walked away, too.

What was I doing wrong? I stood there, unsure of what to try next, when I heard a voice.

"What on earth are you doing?"

I wheeled around. *Light brown hair, wide eyes, deep voice. Remember the name. Scott.* But, Scott had grey eyes, not blue. This person was wearing a blue shirt and had steel blue eyes, not grey. Could it be Scott anyway?

The boy smiled. *It is Scott.* I remembered his quirky smile. Maybe his eyes looked blue today because of the clothes he was wearing.

"I was making friends," I said uncertainly.

"What?"

"My Dad said that I would need to take the first step to make friends. He said the first step was to go up and talk to someone. The weather, sports and movies were good topics for conversation openers, he said."

Scott smiled, shaking his head slowly. "You were too abrupt," he explained. "Too factual."

"Would you teach me how to do it right?" I asked.

He ran his right hand through his hair, pushing his bangs back off his face. "Sure. That's why they pay me the big bucks."

"You get paid to do this? Big money?" I was a little confused. *Isn't all money the same size?*

"Nah…it's really small potatoes. I like doing it, though. I've been a peer buddy for a few years. I like helping people."

I was just about to ask why he was paid with potatoes instead of money but he said, "Oops, better hurry. Mrs. Schulz is a real bear if you're late."

I hurried after him to our first class. I decided I liked Scott, even if he did have some pretty strange ideas about things.

Chapter Four

WHEELS AND GREASE AND RITUALS

We started tutoring right after lunch. I ate the bag lunch I'd brought—cheddar cheese on brown bread, cookies, an apple and orange juice. I watched in amazement as Scott chewed his way through something he called a "foot-long." It was like a hot dog, only it wasn't, because it was much bigger. I wished I had a tape measure. I was pretty sure it measured only eleven and a half inches.

After fifteen minutes in the noisy cafeteria, my nerves felt like they'd been through a paper shredder. I couldn't even pick Scott's voice out of the general confusion. I lip read what I could and guessed at the rest, nodding occasionally as if I understood him.

Scott suggested we go to the library after we ate, and I quickly agreed. Libraries always calmed me down.

"Where should we start?" Scott asked.

"How about with starting a conversation," I said. "That's what I had trouble with this morning."

"Okay, so say you see me in the hall tomorrow and you want to say hello," Scott said. "Show me how you'd do that."

"Hello, my name is Casey. I'm so very pleased to make your acquaintance," I said.

He threw back his head and laughed. "Where'd you get that from?" he asked.

"An old movie. My dad watches them all the time. Isn't it right?"

"It's terrible! Besides, you already know me so you wouldn't say you were pleased to meet me."

"What would I say?"

"You could say, 'How're things going? How are you? What's new? How're you doing?' Something like that."

"Okay," I said. "Should I practice them?"

"Yes, I think that would be a good idea," grinned Scott. He turned his back to me again.

I took a hesitant step forward and said, "How are things going? How are you? What's new? How are you doing?"

"No, no," he said, waving his arms in the air. "Only one at a time."

"Oh," I replied. I paused. "How are things going." Pause. "How are you?" Pause. "What's new?" Pause.

Scott sighed. He ran his hand through his hair. "I meant choose one greeting and say it."

"Which one?" I asked.

"Whichever you like," he answered.

This was getting very confusing. It was much easier to start a conversation the way my Dad had said, by talking about the weather or sports. Of course, those conversations hadn't lasted very long.

"Okay," I told him impatiently. "I'll do it again. Hi, Scott. How're you doing?"

"Fine, Casey. How are you?"

I thought for a moment. "Well, I have a headache from the noise in the cafeteria. There were so many people talking all at once that I could hardly think. It was really hard to..."

Scott was waving his hands in front of him. It reminded me a little of when Chelsea flapped her hands.

"Cease, halt and desist," he cried. "When I ask 'how are you' it doesn't mean you should tell me how you are!"

"Then why would you ask?" I demanded. This was exasperating It wasn't at all logical. Why ask a question if you don't want to hear the answer?

"It's a convention," he answered.

"No, it isn't," I retorted. "A convention is a gathering of people with common interests, to share information..."

"Not that kind. It's a ritual. Yeah, like sort of a greeting ritual. I say 'how are you' and you say 'fine, how are you' and then I say 'fine' and then we talk about something."

"Like the weather?" I asked.

"Sure. Or baseball, or school or anything!"

25

"Then why do we ask 'how are you'? Why not just get down to talking about something important?"

"Because the ritual has to be observed. It's the grease that keeps the wheels turning. It's like saying 'thank you' or 'you're welcome.' It's just polite."

"That's stupid," I exploded. "I don't want to do this anymore. There's no sense in it."

"Fine, leave then," he said. He folded his arms across his chest and glared at me.

I counted to ten. Then, I counted to twenty. It was too hot in the library. I felt like the walls were closing in, trapping me. My stomach was bouncing around on a trampoline, making me feel ill.

"Why do you hate me?" I asked Scott.

"Hate you? Whatever gave you that idea?"

"You're shouting."

"I always shout when I'm frustrated," he said.

"Are you frustrated now?" I asked.

"YES!" He ran his fingers through his hair again.

Frustrated? I knew I got frustrated sometimes, but it had never occurred to me that other people could feel that way too.

Scott took a deep breath and expelled it forcefully. "Look, let's drop it, okay?'

But I didn't want to drop it. I wanted to know more. "Why are you frustrated?" I pushed.

He frowned. "You take everything so literally. I mean, you don't seem to understand figures of speech or anything."

"They don't make any sense to me," I said. "Wheels and grease and rituals. I don't get it."

"Yeah, I figured that much out already. Look, just forget I got mad, okay? We'd better get to class. The bell's going to ring any second now."

All the way back to class, I tried to forget it, but the more I tried, the more I remembered it. Remembered all the times other people had become frustrated with me or told me I just wasn't trying. I was trying, but it was so hard sometimes.

There were so many things I just didn't understand.

Chapter Five

CLOUDS BEFORE A RAINSTORM

Geography class. The teacher, tall and large, with a voice like a foghorn. I tuned it out. It was painful.

For a while, I watched her mouth move, up and down, like a ventriloquist's dummy. Then, I lost my focus and turned inside myself.

The sun poured in through the tall windows beside my desk, lighting up the flecks of dust in the air. They swam in random air currents in front of me. Curious, I reached out to touch one tiny speck. It moved away from my finger, dancing out of my reach.

"Casey!" I heard my name called. I looked over to see the teacher, standing beside me. The whole class was turned around in their seats, watching.

What had I done wrong this time?

"Would you please join us?" the teacher boomed at me.

"Sure," I said. "Where are we going?"

Now everyone was laughing. Except Scott. He had a small smile on his face, but his eyebrows were frowning.

I realized I'd said something wrong, but I didn't know what. "I mean, please stop daydreaming and pay attention," said the teacher loudly.

"Okay," I answered. "I will pay attention."

The class snickered.

"Good," said the teacher. "Now, as I was saying…" Her voice drifted off again. I was glad when the class ended.

Now we were in English. It was easier to pay attention to the English teacher. She was short and thin, with curly black hair and big, round, black glasses. She hopped around the room, like a robin, and spoke in a bright loud voice.

"Your first assignment," said the Robin, "is to write your autobiography."

The class groaned loudly. "We did that in grade four," someone said.

"Yes, but now that you are in grade nine, you'll have a lot more to talk about, won't you?" Robin chirped. "What I'm looking for is four or five pages, typewritten…"

I put my hand up and she paused. "You had a question, Casey?"

"Did you want four pages or five pages?" I asked.

"Either four or five," she answered. "More would be fine, but don't go below four."

"…and does it have to be typewritten?" I persisted.

"No, though I do prefer it. Hand-written is fine, as long as you have good handwriting."

I was beginning to feel anxious. We didn't have a typewriter, and my handwriting was terrible.

"I've written out some questions to jog your memory and help you begin writing," the Robin said. "These are a guideline only, just to get you thinking. Later, you'll have the opportunity to present your autobiography to the class."

There were more groans. "Never mind," Robin said, "it will give you all a chance to get to know each other better, since you all come from different junior highs. Now, remember, have some fun with this!"

Fun? I looked over the list of questions. There were so many! My head began to pound, and my stomach felt like I'd eaten something bad.

"Casey?" It was Scott. I looked up to see his eyes, dark grey today, like clouds before a rainstorm. "Are you okay?" he asked.

"I don't know how to do this," I told him. My voice shook a little, and I was afraid I might start to cry.

"No problem," he said. "Here—I'll give you my phone number. Just call me if you have any trouble, okay?"

"Okay."

The bell rang then. Although I hated it because it was so loud, I was glad to hear it.

It meant I could escape.

Chapter Six

LOST IN THE DETAILS

I set my alarm for early Saturday morning so that I could get to work on the project right away. After gulping down a bowl of corn flakes and half a jug of orange juice, I went out on the deck to work.

Within seconds my attention wandered, focusing instead on the sounds of early morning...a woodpecker making his machine gun noise as he drilled a poplar, a train whistle in town, a red squirrel squealing in a shrill voice at a neighbor...

With a start, I came back to myself. *How long have I been gone,* I wondered? I checked my watch. *An entire hour!* I'd never get my English assignment done at this rate.

Concentrate, I ordered myself.

Okay, one step at a time. Do the first question first. When were you born?

That was easy. January first. I grabbed a black pen and looked over the selection of paper I'd brought out.

Then I was stuck. *What paper should I use? The teacher hadn't told us. Three ring paper? Plain white paper without lines? Colored paper? A lined pad? Foolscap?*

31

Darn it all anyway! *Why can't the teacher be more specific?* *How am I supposed to know what she wants?* My stomach started to ball up, curling in on itself like an armadillo.

Armadillo. *Piglike, with bony armor, found in Central and South America,* I thought.

Stop it! I had to get this done.

Logic. *Use logic.* *Okay, I'll write it on three ring binder paper, then ask the teacher on Tuesday if that's okay.* *If she says it's wrong, I can rewrite it.*

I felt better then. Taking out a clean piece of paper I wrote, "I was born on January first."

There! Now for the next question. What was the weather like on the day you were born?

Now how am I supposed to know? *I have no idea what the weather had been like.* *Do other people remember such things?* I could feel myself getting more and more anxious. I just knew I'd never get through this. I nervously tapped the fingers of my right hand, touching each one in turn to my right thumb in a monotonous rhythm—one, two three, four, one, two, three, four.

"How's it going, schweet'art?"

I jumped. I hadn't heard Dad come up behind me. He sat down across from me and sipped coffee from his favorite cup, the one with Daffy Duck on the front.

"Horrible!" I fumed. "I have an assignment to do for English, and I don't know half the answers!"

"Maybe I can help," he suggested. "What are you stuck on?"

"What was the weather on the day I was born?" I asked him.

"Hmm...let's see," he said. He looked up into the air as if he was seeing an image on a movie screen, his eyes scrunched up with the effort. He began to speak in a low, wispy voice, like Vincent Price in some old horror film. "It was snowing," he lisped. "The first snow of the season, falling all day, on and on. We went off the road on the way to the hospital. You and Chelsea were almost born in a snowbank, but some teenagers pushed us out."

"So, what would you say the weather was like on the day I was born?" I asked. I was confused with all the extra details he'd given me.

"Snowy," Dad answered in his own voice.

I wrote carefully on my page, "The weather was snowy on the day I was born."

"What were the headlines?" I asked next.

Dad scratched the bald spot on the back of his head. "I don't remember. Is it important?"

"I think so," I said. "Why would she ask if it wasn't?"

"True enough. Well, maybe we could go to the library and see if they have old papers on microfiche," Dad said.

"Why are you checking old papers?" Mom asked, joining us at the table. Chelsea came too, carrying her sketch pad as usual.

"I need to know the headlines on the day I was born," I said, handing her the outline.

Mom read it quickly, frowning. "But, Casey, this says the questions are just examples of things you might include. You don't have to answer them one by one."

"I want to answer them all," I insisted. "I don't want to leave any out, in case I leave out the important ones."

"Casey is right," Dad said. "It's safer to follow directions."

Mom stood with her hands on her hips and gave Dad what he refers to as "one of her looks." He says it means she's annoyed with him, though he sometimes doesn't know the reason.

"Maybe you should call your peer buddy and ask him," Mom suggested.

"I guess so," I said reluctantly. I didn't really want to call Scott. I felt I should know the answers on my own. Still, he had offered to help. I found the note from him in my knapsack and dialed his number.

Scott answered the phone. "Hey, Casey, what's up?" he asked.

I knew not to take him literally this time. "I'm trying to do my English assignment and I need help," I said.

"Hey, no prob! Where do you live?"

I wasn't sure what that had to do with my problem, but I answered, "Fire Road Six, off Clear Bay road, just off of George," I said.

"Cool. Give me thirty to shower and eat, and I'll be right over." Click. He had hung up. *Be right over? He's coming over?* I thought he would help me over the phone.

I didn't want him to come over. I didn't want him to know about Chelsea. People didn't like Chelsea very much. They always looked at her with a funny expression and then they quickly went away.

I didn't want Scott to go away.

Chapter Seven

LISTEN WITH YOUR EYES

"You have to get rid of Chelsea," I said to Mom. She was loading the breakfast dishes into the dishwasher.

"Why?" Dad asked, coming in from the deck outside.

"Scott is coming over," I explained.

"He'll meet her eventually," Dad said. "Why not today?"

"I think Casey is right," Mom argued, taking my side for once. "Let's give her the chance to work with Scott without any distractions. Why don't we pack a lunch and canoe out to Brooke's Point? It's a warm day, and Chelsea will enjoy playing at the beach."

"But, Saturday's my gardening day!" Dad protested.

"You can garden tomorrow," Mom said. "Don't be so rigid."

Dad grumbled a little but agreed to go. I anxiously watched them get ready. It seemed to take them forever. I kept looking out the front door for Scott, afraid that he'd arrive before they left.

Finally, they pulled away from the dock in our big canoe, with Chelsea and a picnic basket between them. Chelsea had a paddle too, though I knew she wouldn't use it in the usual way. She preferred to dip the paddle into the lake and watch the drips of water slide down the smooth wood to form expanding rings on the surface of the water.

The doorbell rang, just as Mom and Dad disappeared around the first point of land. It was Scott.

"Hi, Case! How's it going?" he said as I opened the door.

"Fine, Scott," I answered. "How are you doing?"

"Terrific! How's the project going?"

"Fine, Scott. How is your project going?" I replied. I was really pleased with myself for remembering the ritual.

"No, no, no," he said, shaking his head. "I want a real answer this time. Are you having problems?"

I was about to shout, 'How am I supposed to know when you want a real answer or a ritual answer?,' but I stopped myself. Counted to ten. Took a deep breath. Then said, "Yes! I can't get past the part about 'What were the headlines on the day you were born?' Do you think I could just leave a blank for it and then fill it in after I research it at the library?"

He gave me a look I couldn't interpret. "No, Casey, that's not what she's after. Here, I brought my disk over. I can show you what I've done so far. Do you have a computer?"

"Sure, my Dad's a computer expert." I showed him to our computer in the kitchen. Scott slipped his disk in and called up his document.

"Why did you write it on the computer?" I asked while I watched his document appear on screen. "You'll just have to write it out by hand now or do it over again on a typewriter."

He gave me a funny look. "But it will be typed," he said.

"No, it'll be computer printed," I argued. "There's a difference."

"No, there isn't," he said. "A printer is fine. Besides, no one uses a typewriter anymore."

"Then why did she say we should type it?" I really didn't understand. Why hadn't she just said what she had meant?

"Just an expression," Scott said. I bit my tongue to avoid making a sharp response. I hate it when people use 'expressions.' Half the time, I don't understand them.

"Okay, it's ready now," Scott said. "Here, sit down and read what I've done so far on mine."

I pushed my annoyance away, then sat down in front of the screen and read:

MY STORY
by Scott McKinnon

The first thing my mom said when I was born was, "What an ugly baby. He looks like a little monkey." I guess she was in a good position to know, since she had already had two babies before me. They had looked like normal baby boys. I looked like a monkey, with a scrunched up wrinkled face, wizened little eyes and a scrawny little body.

Mom said it was love at first sight.

I think maybe she just felt sorry for me, because I was little and scrawny.

Being scrawny was a problem in elementary school, until I took up tae kwon do. One day, three bullies ganged up on me. I beat all three in a fair fight. Were they ever surprised! The principal gave us all detentions for a week for fighting, but I didn't care. Like Dad said, you have to stand up for yourself once in a while if you are going to earn people's respect.

I sure won the respect of the bullies. They didn't pick on me again after that. I think maybe the principal respected me too, even though he had to give me detention. He always winked at me after that, as if he approved of me.

"What do you think?" Scott asked.

"You didn't answer all the questions in order," I pointed out.

"You don't have to," he told me. "You can tell the story any way you like."

"But the teacher said…"

"Casey! Don't be so rigid. The questions were only guidelines. Besides, I'm only partly done. What did you think of it so far?"

"I guess it's okay. But, why did the principal wink at you?"

"To show he wasn't really angry at me. Sort of saying that he approved of me sticking up for myself and fighting back."

"How do you know that's what it meant?" I wondered.

"It's body language," Scott said. "I mean, about eighty percent of what you say is what you DON'T say."

"Scott, that makes no sense at all!" I said.

"Sure, it does," he said calmly. His low, quiet voice took away my irritation.

"Here, I'll show you what I mean," he continued. "Do you have any videos around?"

"Lots. It's one of my Dad's hobbies," I said. I showed him my Dad's "video library." It was a bookshelf in a corner of the living room, jammed from floor to ceiling with tapes.

Scott whistled when he saw it. "Wow, you weren't kidding, were you?"

"No, I wasn't kidding you," I answered, a little puzzled. Why would I try to fool him about my Dad's hobbies?

"Here's a good one," he said. He put a cassette into the machine and ran it on fast forward. I recognized it as one

40

about a man who had led a rebellion against British rule in Scotland. It was one of my dad's favorites. Some actor was standing in a field, talking to a woman. He wore funny clothes, a sort of old fashioned skirt. He looked silly, a man in woman's clothes, but Dad had told me that's what men had really worn in Scotland back then.

"Okay, here," said Scott, scanning to the part he wanted. "This is one of my favorite parts. What's he saying?"

"Turn the sound up," I complained. "I can't hear." Scott had turned the sound completely off.

"No, listen with your eyes. What is his body language saying?"

Listen with my eyes? Is he crazy? I decided to humor him. "He's asking her to marry him," I said, then told Scott the exact words that were used.

"Hey! You're lip-reading," he said.

"No. I remember the dialog," I told him.

Scott hit his forehead with the palm of his hand then. That reminded me of what Chelsea sometimes did when she got really upset. For a minute, I wondered if Scott were autistic too. *No,* I decided. *He doesn't show any of the other signs.*

"No no no no no no..." he said. "Don't rely on that memory of yours. Read his face. Read the angle of his head, the tension in his shoulders, the tentative way he reaches out to her and then stops. What's he feeling?"

"How can you tell what someone feels?" I asked.

"Put yourself in his shoes. How would you feel?" Scott said.

"Why would I want to wear his shoes?" I asked, really confused now.

Scott hit his forehead again. I was really beginning to wonder about him.

"No no no...I mean, empathize with him. How would you feel if you were asking me to marry you?" Scott asked.

"But, I wouldn't ask you to marry me," I said. This was getting really dumb. "I hardly know you, and we are both too young."

"No no no no..." Those seemed to be his favorite words. "I mean, *look* at him. See that puppy dog look in his eyes? He's afraid she'll say no. Look at the way he holds his body stiff. See, he's holding his breath, waiting for her answer. Okay, now, there...what's that?"

"A smile."

"Right. What's he feeling?"

"Happy," I said.

"Yes. Happy, relieved, joyful, excited...he can hardly believe that she loves him, too."

"But, how can he feel all those things at once?" I asked.

"He just does," Scott answered. He forwarded the tape to another spot. It was the woman from the previous scene. She was tied up, and a man in an orange outfit was holding a knife to her throat. He slit her throat quickly and she died. The other man, the one in the skirt, arrived in time to see her die.

"How does he feel?" Scott asked.

"Angry," I said. I was rather pleased with myself for knowing the answer.

"Come on!" Scott said, waving his arms around. "They just killed his wife! They slit her throat! How does he *feel?*"

"Angry!" I snapped.

"No! Furious. Enraged! Look at him! His face is like stone, his eyes like hot coals. He can barely keep the rage contained, but he does. He burns with it, with a cold, hard rage. He's afraid that if he gives in to the rage it will consume him, so he controls it. Now, here...see the difference. How does he feel?"

It was a battle scene, with the main character, the dead woman's husband, holding a sword and facing a line of enemies. I watched as the actor silently waved the sword, words that I could not hear coming from him as he rushed into battle.

"He's angry?" I guessed.

"No. More than anger. Rage, again, but not a cold rage. This is a hot rage. Look—he's lost control, but that's okay. He's filled with blood lust, with the hot desire to kill, to slaughter. It'll carry him through the battle. He won't feel his body getting tired, he won't feel his wounds...he's working on instinct now, not reason."

43

"Hot rage, cold rage, what's the difference?" I blew up. "Emotion is the enemy."

"Pardon me?"

"Emotion! It's the enemy! It causes you to lose control," I said. *Like Chelsea,* I thought. When she gets angry, she loses control and goes into a terrible tantrum. Sometimes, she even hurts herself, biting or hitting her own body. Or, like me, like when I sometimes used to lose control and bite someone or scream at them or hit them.

"No no no…emotion is the **key**. It drives us all. It's what makes us human," Scott said.

I looked at him. Really looked closely at him, this time. His eyes looked blue today. His hair looked messy, and he was waving his arms around.

He scared me. He was unpredictable. I didn't like that. I liked order, predictability, sameness. He scared me.

"Casey? What just happened here?" he asked.

"We watched a movie and guessed at what people were thinking," I answered. I didn't want to think about the other thing that happened, when he acted unpredictably, and I felt like I'd lost control of the situation.

"Yes, I know, but not that part. I mean when you said 'emotion is the enemy' and then you sort of just shut me out."

"You scared me."

"How?"

"Your emotions. They scared me."

"Why do emotions scare you, Case?" he asked.

"I don't understand them," I said honestly. "I don't know where they come from, or why people act the way they do."

"Would you like to learn to read other people's reactions?" he asked.

"Yes."

"Okay. You can learn by watching movies with the sound off and reading the non-verbal language. Also, watch people carefully at school. Pay attention to their signals."

"Signals?"

"Yeah. Facial expressions, gestures, body movements. Signals. If you have any questions about what something means, just ask."

"Just ask?"

"Yeah, just ask," Scott repeated. "Should we get back to work on the assignment now? We could go out on your deck and get some fresh air while we do it."

"Okay," I agreed. I led the way out to the deck and froze. A canoe was coming across the lake. I could tell it was ours by its red color and the indistinct shapes of three people. "You have to go now," I told Scott.

"What do you mean?" he said. I looked closely at him, to see if he was sending any 'signals.' His face was set in a frown, and he was holding both hands out in front of him. His shoulders were scrunched up. I wasn't sure, but I thought he might be angry. "We've hardly worked on your assignment. Don't you want help writing it?"

"I do, but...my parents are coming back," I blurted out.

"So? They know I'm here, don't they?" he said. He craned his neck to look past me. "Are they in the canoe?"

"Yes." I was feeling frantic now. My heart was racing so hard it was cutting off my breath. I felt light-headed, as if I would faint at any moment. "You really have to go!" I insisted loudly.

He moved past me, opening the door to the deck and walking out. "Who's that in the canoe with them?" he asked. "It looks like a girl. You didn't tell me you had a sister."

"You have to go," I said, my voice getting shrill with anxiety. "You can't meet her. It'll ruin everything!"

Scott tilted his head to one side and grinned. "Oh, I get it," he said. "A younger sister? Afraid she'll tease you about having me over?"

"GO!" I shouted.

"Okay, okay...don't get all hyper on me," Scott said. I let out a long sigh of relief as he went back inside and headed for the front door. "Look, you work on the assignment and I'll call you to see how it's going, okay?"

"Okay." I would have agreed to anything right then, just to get rid of him. It would spoil everything if he met Chelsea.

Everything.

Chapter Eight

BIRDS OF A FEATHER FLOCK TOGETHER

"Hello. How's it going? I'm Casey. What are you feeling?"

"Huh?" The girl with the long black hair and slanted eyes stared at me for a minute, then made a gesture to her friend. She used her finger and moved it in a tight little circle aimed at her head. Her friend, a girl with short brown hair, laughed. They turned their backs on me and walked away.

"Casey! What are you doing?" It was Scott. I observed him closely as he walked up. He was wearing blue jeans and a long sleeved blue and white flannel shirt left open over a deep blue t-shirt. His eyes were pulled together in a deep frown, making a vertical line between his eyes.

He was angry. Or, maybe annoyed. Irritated? I wasn't sure, but I was pretty sure he wasn't happy.

"I'm just doing what you told me to do, Scott," I said. "I watched movies without sound all weekend long, and I'm watching kids at school to learn their non-verbal language. You see, those girls were whispering and giggling together. I did a greeting ritual and then asked what they were feeling."

"Why on earth did you do that?" His jaw was relaxed now, and he had a half smile on his face. I decided he was no longer angry.

48

"You told me to, remember?" I said. "You said, 'If you have any questions about what something means, just ask.'"

"I meant, 'just ask me, and I'll explain.'"

"Then why didn't you say that?"

"I thought you knew what I meant," he said. He was frowning again.

I bit my lower lip. *How was I supposed to know what he meant if he didn't tell me what he meant? Why can't everyone just go away and leave me alone?*

"Casey? *Casey?*" I looked up to see Scott staring at me. "Are you okay?"

"I have to go to class now," I said, walking away quickly.

"Will you cut that out?" he said, pacing me.

"What?"

"Running away whenever things get uncomfortable. Look, I'm sorry I wasn't clear. I meant that if you don't understand someone's reaction, just come to me, and I'll try to explain, okay?"

I kept walking, ignoring him. He grabbed my arm. I hated it when people did that. I smacked his hand away and heard him say "jeez" under his breath. I sped up, marching several steps ahead of him. I was hoping he'd give up and leave me alone, when I heard a voice call from behind us.

"Hey, Scotty boy!" I turned around to see what was happening. Three guys had walked up to Scott. One guy

49

was tall and had the left side of his head shaved. The right side was covered in hair that drooped over one eye. The other boy was short and fat, like a marshmallow. The third person was telephone-pole skinny, with black jeans and a black vest.

"So, who's your retard friend?" asked the one with the shaved head.

"I'm her peer buddy, and she's not retarded," Scott said. He started to walk past them, but the Marshmallow Boy blocked his way.

"Sure she is," said Shaved Head. "Did you see what she was doing today? 'Hello. I'm Casey. What are you feeling?' If that's not retarded, I'd like to know what is." He laughed, and elbowed his telephone pole friend in the ribs. "Talk about crazy!" He laughed, a high pitched laugh that grated on my ears like chalk on a board.

I watched Scott closely to see what reaction he would have. His eyes narrowed and his lips went thin again. "She just doesn't understand, that's all," he said. His voice sounded tight, forced.

"Yeah, I'll say," croaked Shaved Head. "She doesn't understand much at all, does she?"

Scott moved closer to Shaved Head. He had to look up to meet the bigger kid's eyes. "Just leave her alone," he warned.

"Are you threatening me, Scotty, my boy?" said Shaved Head.

"I'm just telling you to leave her alone," Scott repeated. "Now, if you will excuse me, I'm late for home room." He pushed past Marshmallow Boy, and walked over to where I stood watching. "Come on, Casey. Just ignore them. They're jerks."

"Birds of a feather," called Shaved Head as we walked off.

"Guess it's his old man's influence, eh?" laughed Marshmallow Boy.

"Yeah. I guess a retard girlfriend is the best Old Man McKinnon's kid can hope to get," screeched Telephone Pole.

"She isn't my girlfriend," Scott said, in a hard, tight voice. I looked at him and saw he looked white, the color of paper. His body had gone all stiff and he walked with fast, loud steps. I wanted to ask, 'What are you feeling?' but I was afraid that if I did he would think I really was a retard, so I said nothing.

It was halfway through our first class before the color came back in his face.

51

Chapter Nine

LET'S NOT AND SAY WE DID

"I'm not a retard," I told him at lunchtime. We were eating outside, at a picnic table under a big poplar. It was too noisy and crowded for me inside the cafeteria.

"I know," Scott said, taking a huge bite out of his foot-long hot dog. He was looking away, toward the field where some kids were playing touch football.

"No, Scott, look at me," I said. It was a line my tutor had used, a long time ago when I was a kid. 'Look at me.' I must have heard it a thousand times, every time I had switched off and escaped into a daydream. It felt natural to use it now.

Scott turned and looked at me. I noticed the color of his eyes—grey today. I couldn't read his expression. It was too complex.

"I mean it. I'm really not retarded, Scott," I continued. "Retarded is an old term anyway, not used anymore. Like the terms moron and idiot and imbecile. I'm not any of those things. I was tested once, and my IQ was way above average. I'm not a retard."

Scott smiled. "I know that, Casey."

"Then, why did they call me one?"

Scott looked away and became very interested in his hot dog. I watched him carefully, checking for 'signals.' His face twitched a bit, as though trying to find the right expression. He was chewing very slowly, as if he was eating a tough steak instead of a processed wiener.

He was afraid to tell me, I suddenly realized. But why would he be upset? I was the one they were calling names. It didn't make much sense to me.

Finally, he turned to me. "You are a little different, Casey, and that makes people feel uncomfortable."

Different. That was the second time he'd said that. I could feel the anxiety start to percolate through me, like little bubbles in a glass of soft drink.

"What do you mean, I'm 'different?'" I asked.

"Just some of your mannerisms, your voice and stuff," Scott said.

"What mannerisms? What about my voice?" I demanded. My stomach was complaining now, growling that the cheese sandwich I'd just eaten wasn't sitting well.

"Nothing. It's really nothing, Casey. Everyone is different, you know. Everyone is unique. You don't have to change just to fit someone else's expectations."

"But, I want to change. I don't want to be different," I said. "What's so different about my voice?"

"Sometimes, just sometimes, you talk too loud and too fast. You don't always give the other person the chance to say anything. And, sometimes, when you really get going on a topic, you don't seem to realize someone else isn't interested," Scott said. He was looking away again, at the football field.

"I see. And what about my mannerisms?" I insisted.

"They're a little odd," he answered.

"Odd?"

"Yeah, like what you're doing right now. Shaking your arms and your hands like that."

I stopped abruptly, realizing I had been shaking my hands at my sides in an effort to shake out the anxiety. It was an old habit.

"The other thing is you either don't look at a person at all when you talk to him, or you stare at him as if you are studying him."

"I'm trying to learn 'signals,' like you said I should," I protested.

"I know. Listen, Casey, don't make too much of this. It's nothing, really. Just be yourself. Who cares if some jerk calls you names?"

"I care," I said. I realized it was true. I did care, even though I didn't like to admit it. Then, I had an amazing insight. It had never occurred to me to think about how other people felt, but I suddenly realized something about Scott. "You cared too, didn't you?" I asked.

"Yeah. I didn't like what they said about you, or about my father."

"I guess a retard girlfriend is the best that Old Man McKinnon's kid can hope to get?" I repeated. "Who is Old Man McKinnon?"

"My father."

"Is he old?"

"No, not really. What gave you that idea?"

"They said 'Old Man McKinnon.'"

"That's just an expression."

"Oh. So, why is it an insult?"

"They're suggesting that my dad is somehow inferior, and as his son I'm inferior too, and that's why I have an inferior girlfriend."

"I am not inferior," I said, confused. "Am I your girlfriend?"

"No," Scott said quickly. "I'm your peer buddy, that's all."

"Not my friend?" My eyes filled with tears.

"Oh, Case, sure we're friends," Scott said. "We just aren't girlfriend and boyfriend, that's all. You'd understand everything if you met my dad."

"Is he inferior?"

Scott laughed and shook his head. "No, but he is different."

"Like me?"

"Not exactly. Listen, he owns a craft shop and art gallery in town. It's called 'Favorite Things.' Why don't you come with me after school and meet him?"

A warning pulsed through me, as clear as if someone had spoken the words. "I can't," I said. "I have to go right home after school."

"Maybe another day, then?"

"Maybe." I took a few deep breaths to quell the anxiety. I couldn't go to his father's shop after school for one simple reason. I had to take the same route home, every day, without fail. If I didn't...I didn't know what would actually happen, but just the mere thought of changing my routine was enough to make my heart race and a sticky sweat break out under my arms. I changed the subject quickly, before he could suggest that maybe tomorrow would be a good day to go. "Let's work on my voice and mannerisms now," I said.

Scott made a face as if he had swallowed something bitter. "Let's not and say we did," he answered.

"I don't get it," I said in a voice that shook just a little. "Why would we not study but say we did?"

He threw his hands up in the air. "An expression, Casey. Okay, you win. Mannerisms it is."

Chapter Ten

PUT ON THE BRAKES

Late afternoon, and the sun was pouring in through the windows, illuminating the girl's hair, done in a braid, in front of me. I could see each strand of gold and copper and amber, all intertwined in a pattern so perfect it took my breath away. I tried to follow each delicate filament, tracing its path through the complex intertwining of hair. I would lose it and find my attention grabbed by another thin strand of spun gold, and I would follow it instead, until another glowing thread pulled me into another pattern.

"Casey?"

The voice intruded. I shut it out.

"Casey?"

I wanted to be left alone, to lose myself in the pattern, but the voice broke in.

I looked up to see the teacher looking at me. I thought she might be puzzled or angry or sad, but I couldn't really tell.

A sharp pang caught me, like a giant hand squeezing my insides. *I'd done it again. Faded out.* I didn't even know how long I'd been gone.

"Are you okay, Casey?" asked the teacher. The one who reminded me of a robin, with her quick, nervous movements and her bobbing head.

57

"Yes. I guess I was just daydreaming," I told her.

"I see," she answered. "You've been sitting there for the last half hour, hardly even blinking. I was worried about you."

I didn't know what to say to this. It made me anxious to even look at her, since I couldn't read her expression.

"Are you having trouble with the assignment?" she asked. She spoke quietly, so I decided she wasn't angry and dared to look up. Her head was tilted to one side, making her look even more like a robin surveying the grass for a juicy worm. I giggled, then covered my mouth and choked it down.

The room was hushed, with people writing things down on paper. I remembered that the teacher had asked us to work on our autobiographies.

"Yes," I said. "I'm having trouble answering all the questions. I don't really know what my first memory was and I didn't go to school so I didn't do any extracurricular activities and..."

"Whoa, Casey. Put on the brakes," said the Robin. "Let's go out in the hall to discuss this."

As we walked out, I saw that everyone was looking at me. I wondered if I'd been talking too loud again, like Scott said I did.

"Casey, your mom told me you might have some special learning needs..."

Special learning needs? "What do you mean?" I asked. Anxiety washed over me again. *Control it,* I thought. *Control the enemy.*

"Well..." the Robin said. "I mean, is there anything I can do to help you with this assignment, for example?"

"You could clarify the questions," I said.

She smiled. I didn't know why she smiled, but I was glad to see it. It meant she wasn't angry at me. "Okay—I want you to forget about answering all those questions. Just tell me about yourself on paper, okay? Start from when you were born and tell me all about yourself as if you were telling a story. Can you do that?"

"I'm not sure," I said.

"Well, you get started on it, and we'll see how it goes. Why don't you show me what you've done tomorrow at lunchtime? Just come to the staff room and ask for me."

"I can't," I said. Fear made my mouth go suddenly dry. I had lunch with Scott. That was the routine. I couldn't go to the staff room because I'd be having lunch with Scott.

"How about after school then?" she asked.

"I can't." I had to go home after school. I always went straight home after my last class. I couldn't change that either. What should I do? I couldn't keep saying 'I can't,' but on the other hand I couldn't do what she wanted. I was trapped..

Deep breaths, I thought. *Control the enemy. Take a deep breath, let it out slowly.*

59

"Casey? Casey? Are you okay?" The Robin was looking at me with bright black eyes. "Listen. You tell me what will work for you," she suggested.

"Could I show it to you at our next English class?" I asked.

"Of course. That would be fine." She smiled. Then she put her hand on my shoulder. It made me want to run away when she did that. I held my breath until she dropped the hand. "Let's go back to class," she said.

With a sigh of relief, I followed her back in. I managed to keep my focus after that, all the way to the final bell.

On the way home, I picked up another pink rock for Chelsea. She put it with her collection, then spent the next hour re-organizing the entire set of rocks. I think she needed to find the exact right way to make it all fit together.

Chapter Eleven

MONSTER UNDER THE BED

My birthday is January first. It snowed the day I was born. My parents named me Casey. Mom told me they just picked the name because they liked the way it sounded with my last name, Jackson. To me, however, it sounds like a short form of Cassandra, the daughter of Priam, King of Troy. Apollo loved her and gave her the gift of prophecy, but when Cassandra refused Apollo's love...

"Honey, that's a little too much detail," Mom said, looking over my shoulder at the computer screen. She had a small bowl in her hand and was whisking some eggs in it as she read.

"But, it's important to explain where my name came from, isn't it?" I asked.

"Not really. I'd leave out the part about Cassandra," Mom said. "It goes off topic."

Reluctantly, I deleted everything that followed, "with my last name, Jackson."

Behind me, in the kitchen, I could hear Mom scrambling the eggs in a frying pan. My mouth watered. It was Monday morning, and I'd woken up at six, unable to sleep. I had been working since then on my assignment. The strange thing was that I was having trouble remembering much about my childhood. Me, the one who remembered just about every fact she had ever read!

The very first thing I remember is the border in my bedroom. It was the alphabet, done in bright primary colors—red for A, blue for B, green for C, yellow for D and so on. Then, the pattern repeated—red for E, blue for F and so on. I loved that border and would spend hours tracing the letters with my finger.

The next thing I remember is a book that I used to read every day. It too had the letters of the alphabet, one on each page. Each page had big, bright pictures of things that started with that letter. The A page had apples, acorns, antelopes, abacus, ants, aardvarks, alligators, armadillos, and albatrosses. The B page had babies, bats, bears, bananas, bicycles, bridges, and boomerangs. The C page had

"Casey—too much detail again," Mom said. "No one will want to read about what was on every page."

"But, I remember it all. If I describe the memory, I should describe the whole thing, shouldn't I?"

"No, honey. People will get bored reading that. You have to consider your audience when you write," Mom said. "Come on now, breakfast is ready. You'll have to hurry if you want to make it to school on time."

I saved my document and went to breakfast. Chelsea was already there, eating her usual Cream of Wheat with brown sugar and milk. She seemed agitated this morning, and kept hitting her leg with her fist. I had come up with a way to help her calm down. I tapped our special rhythm, that of a heartbeat, on her arm, very gently. She didn't look at me, but she stopped hitting herself. I watched as her fist uncurled and she tapped the rhythm on her leg instead.

I smiled. No one understood Chelsea like I did. The same, yet different. I had worried about her, when I went to school, but Mom said she was doing just fine.

Still, I worried.

Chelsea walked down the hall to the bathroom to brush her teeth, trailing one hand along the wall as she went. It was one of her rituals, always to keep one hand or the other touching a wall no matter where she went. I don't know what she thought might happen if she lost contact with the wall. Maybe she thought it would cease to exist and plunge her into nothingness.

I was running late, but I brushed my teeth the usual full two minutes. I jogged down the lane to make up time, and reached the main road only seconds later than usual. It was a busy morning —a dump truck and a backhoe lumbered by in a cloud of diesel exhaust. I remembered Mom saying that our next-door neighbor was building an addition to his house.

First class was home room. Scott wasn't there yet, so I sat at my desk and looked over the reading assignment from the night before.

"Does anyone know if Scott is coming today?" the Hobbit asked when she got to his name. There was a chorus of 'don't knows' and 'haven't seen him' from the room.

The morning dragged. I missed Scott. It felt wrong without him there. I couldn't concentrate on what the teachers were saying. In math, I got confused and worked on the wrong set of questions in my book. That's when I realized how much I'd come to rely on Scott. He usually went over the teacher's directions for me, explaining them in a way that I could follow.

No one talked to me. It was as if I wasn't there. I walked to classes alone, sat alone and worked alone.

At lunchtime, I sat at the usual picnic table, watching a soccer game and wishing Scott were there. After I ate lunch, I went to the library. I wanted to work on 'social skills,' but Scott wasn't there, so I worked on my English assignment instead. I could transfer it to my home computer later.

I also remember a set of blocks that I owned. They had the letters of the alphabet on them and I liked to stack them, with A on the bottom, then B, then C, then D and so on.

I stopped there, remembering what Mom had said about not listing the entire alphabet.

The most I ever got to was Q. I remember being furious when the stack fell down. I was so mad I threw the blocks across the room, one after another, from A to Z. Their sharp corners made little digs in the wall when they hit.

The first book I ever read was *The Cat in the Hat.* I loved the way it rhymed, and I read it over and over. Then, I read all the other Dr. Suess books. They became my favorites.

When I was little, I made collections of all kinds of things and kept the collections in shoe boxes under my bed. There were stone collections, bottle caps, paper clips, elastic bands, bits of colored paper and little toys I collected from fast food restaurants. Every night, I took out each collection and counted the contents of each. It would throw me into a panic if I was one short of something, like a bottle cap, and I would count again to be sure. I never really lost anything; just lost count a few times.

I used to think monsters hid under the bed and in the closet. I imagined I could hear them, breathing loudly in the darkness. As I grew older, I realized it was only the furnace fan turning on, not monsters wheezing and growling in my room. For years though, I checked under the bed, in the closet and in all my dresser drawers before I went to sleep.

I believed in lots of things as a child. Not stepping on cracks for fear of breaking your mother's back for example. Even now, I try to avoid them. I know it's not true, that my mother's back would really break, but it's hard to get out of the habit.

I was concentrating so hard that I jumped when the bell rang for class. All afternoon I wished Scott were there. Finally, school ended and I rushed home, stopping only to pick up a rock for Chelsea. I knew the route so well now that I didn't have to think about it. Along the path to Sixth, right at the Post Office on Main, left on Tamarack, right on George, left on Clear Bay road, then right on Fire Road Six. I could hear a loud rumble as I approached my house and saw it came from a cement mixer next door.

My heart skipped a beat when I walked into the house. Chelsea was huddled in a corner in the living room, rocking back and forth, hitting the side of her head with her hand and making a noise, a low pitched "ahh, ahh, ahh, ahh," sound.

"Oh, Casey, thank goodness," Mom said as I kicked off my shoes and hung up my jacket. "She's been like this for almost an hour."

"It's the cement mixer, Mom," I said, running down the hallway. "The noise is driving her crazy." I flew into Chelsea's room and grabbed her CD player and her special CD, then raced back to my sister.

"Ahh, ahh, ahh, ahh…" The sound of her low, constant cry made me want to curl up in a little ball myself. Her hearing was even more acute than mine, and I couldn't imagine how she tolerated the roar from next door. I knew, without knowing exactly how I knew, that she was trying to block out the unpredictable, intermittent blast of sound that assaulted her ears.

"It's okay, Chelsea," I said. I knew better than to try to stop her from hitting her head. She needed a safer stimulus to focus on. That's why I'd grabbed the CD. It was a recording of a heartbeat. It always worked. I slipped the headphones on Chelsea's head and turned the sound up.

It didn't take long for her to calm down. First, she stopped hitting her head, then she stopped crying. In a few minutes, she stopped rocking. I pulled all the cushions off the couch and made a little cave for her to hide in. Still wearing the earphones, she climbed in.

I knew she'd be okay now.

"Thank you, Casey," Mom said. She was sitting on the loveseat that matched our couch. "You always seem to know just how to calm her down. So, tell me, how did your day go?"

"Scott wasn't at school today. No one talked to me, and I didn't know what the teachers wanted without Scott there to help explain."

Mom looked worried. "Were you okay? Did anything happen?"

"Nothing bad happened. I was okay."

She looked less worried then. "Maybe you should call to see why he was away," she suggested.

That sounded like a good idea. I wondered why I hadn't thought of it for myself.

Scott answered after five rings. Something in me relaxed when I heard his voice.

"Hi, Scott," I said as soon as I heard his 'hello.' Why weren't you at school today?'

"Oh, Case, you wouldn't believe what happened to me! I was riding to school, right, and this guy, this JERK in a rusty old jalopy was making a right hand turn and he just *cut me off*. I mean, I was riding through the intersection at Main and Sixth, right at the school, and this *idiot* just turned right into me. He said he didn't even *see* me! I've got a neon green helmet, for God's sake. How could he not *see* me? Anyway, I flew off the bike and landed on my right arm. Some other guy in a car saw the whole thing and took me to the hospital and called my Dad and all. I've got a cast on the arm. It's not a real bad break, but I'll be in a cast for about six weeks. Bummer, huh?"

"But, why didn't you come to school?" I asked.

"Dad said I should stay home and recuperate. Actually, I didn't feel so bad at first, but now my arm really aches."

"You should have come," I told him.

"Yeah, well, I'm sure I didn't miss all that much, did I?" he said.

"No, but I missed you. I need you there to help me. You should have tried to come," I insisted.

There was a long silence on the other end. "Casey...isn't there anything else you want to say?"

"I don't think so," I said. I started to drum my fingers on the counter. *What does he want me to say?* I didn't understand. His voice had gone funny. *What's wrong?*

"Don't you even care how I'm feeling?" he asked slowly.

My anxiety level rose. *Feelings again.* I hated when people mentioned feelings. *What does he want me to say?*

"Fine. Terrific," said Scott. "Sorry you missed me. Well, catch you later." His voice sounded flat, expressionless.

Then, all I heard was a dial tone.

What had I done wrong?

Chapter Twelve

PUT YOURSELF IN MY SHOES

It was one of those dreams where everything is mixed up. I was at school, walking down the corridor. I was in my underwear. A group of kids gathered, pointing and laughing at me. Then, Scott arrived. He pulled me by the arm, away from the laughter and took me to his locker. Inside it, he had an extra pair of jeans and a shirt that he gave me to wear.

The scene changed. I was in the classroom. It was the English teacher, but this time she was a real robin, a bird as big as a person. She kept looking at me, her head sideways, her beady eye fixed on me. Then, she swooped down on me and began to pull on my head as if I were a worm that she had to yank out of the ground.

Then, Robin changed into my old teacher, the one who came to our house when I was little and helped me with school things. Every time I got an answer right, she fed me a brown, wiggly worm. They tasted like Smarties.

"Look at me, Casey," she'd say. "Good girl." Then, she handed me a Smartie. It was a blue one. I hated the blue ones. I threw it across the room, where it made a dent in the wall.

I went over to get a better look at the dent. On the wall was a corkboard. There were pictures on the board.

"Put the pictures in the right order to tell a story," the teacher said. Her name was April.

There were three pictures: a picture of a nest with eggs in it, and a picture of the bird feeding baby birds in the nest, and a picture of a bird building a nest. I put them in order.

"Good girl, Casey," April said, handing me a red smartie. I ate it.

"Now put these pictures in order," she said.

I stared at them. There was one of a girl crying, one of a grown-up putting a bandaid on the girl's knee, and one of a girl falling off her bike.

That was easy. I put the girl falling off her bike first, followed by the adult putting a bandaid on her knee.

"What about this one?" asked April. "Where does it go?"

I looked at the picture she handed to me. It was the one of the girl crying. "I don't know," I said.

April frowned. "See? The girl is crying because she scraped her knee. What is the girl feeling?"

"Her knee hurts," I said.

"Yes, but what is she feeling inside?" April insisted.

I didn't know. It wasn't fair for April to ask questions when there were no real answers. I yanked the pictures off the board and ripped them into tiny shreds, then stomped on them with both feet.

71

"What am I feeling, Casey?" April asked. Only now, it wasn't my old tutor, April, it was Scott. His right arm was bloody and mangled, hanging at an odd angle from his body.

"What am I feeling?" he repeated. He held out a handful of Smarties in his left hand.

"I don't know," I said, starting to feel anxious.

"Try," he insisted. "Put yourself in my shoes."

"Your shoes are the wrong size!" I cried, looking down at his feet. He wore foot-long clown shoes, red with striped laces.

"Then, my clothes must be the wrong size too," he said. "I want them back now." Tears ran down his face and mingled with the blood on his shirt.

I handed back his jeans and shirt and stood there in my underwear. We were in school, and I was up on the stage. All the students in the school were gathered on the gym floor. Someone began to laugh, and the sound rippled through the crowd until they were all laughing and pointing at me and pelting me with handfuls of blue Smarties.

The laughter changed in pitch and became a loud buzzing in my ears. I watched in horror as the students turned into giant bees. They swarmed around the room as if they had only one mind between them and then headed straight for where I cowered, my arms wrapped around my nakedness.

○ ○ ○

My alarm clock was buzzing. I was lying in bed with my arms wrapped around my shoulders and the sheets twisted tightly around me. Groaning, I untangled myself and groped for the alarm.

My face was wet with tears, and my heart was hammering like the water pipes do when air gets into the system. *Just a dream, just a dream.* I kept repeating that to myself as I staggered into the shower. *Can't hurt you. Just a dream.*

April. Funny, I'd forgotten her name until then. What had she been saying in the dream? Something about Smarties? The more I tried to remember the details, the more elusive the dream became. All that was left was the oppressive feeling of anxiety.

It was a dull, overcast day with heavy rain clouds in the sky. The school looked gloomier than ever and smelled of musty, damp clothes. I ran up to my locker on the second floor, counting the twenty steps as I went up the staircase. My locker was in the green section, at the end of the hall by the windows. I put away my lunch and the books I wouldn't need until the afternoon, then yanked my lock three times to make sure it was closed.

Scott was standing in front of our home room when I arrived. He was wearing black pants and a white sweatshirt with some black writing on it. A bunch of kids were gathered around him. They seemed to be writing things on the cast that covered the lower part of his right arm.

73

I was so glad to see him. I had felt so incredibly alone the day before; so left out. It had been like falling overboard from a cruise ship and having nobody notice. Seeing him again was like being thrown a life ring.

"Hi, Scott," I said, when I got close enough. "I'm so glad you're back. I have a dozen questions to ask you about the homework assignments we got yesterday. I didn't understand the instructions at all."

Scott looked up at me. "Maybe later, okay Casey?" He turned his attention back to the person who was writing on his cast. She had short red hair and green eyes. As she finished writing, Scott put his head close to hers to read the inscription and they both laughed.

I stood on the sidelines, drowning.

○ ○ ○

We had history first class. I checked my schedule to find out the teacher's name. Mr. Stadnyk. He was a short, muscled man with black hair cut uniformly short. He reminded me of a black bear.

"Okay, who did the assigned reading last night?" he asked.

I raised my hand. Only a half dozen other people raised theirs. Scott wasn't one of them.

"Very good, uh..." He checked a clipboard in his hand. "...Casey. Could you tell us what you remember from your reading." He looked up from the clipboard and waited.

"Yes, I can," I answered.

74

He waved a hand in my direction. *What does that mean?* Anxiety ran through me, turning my nerves into high tension wires. I glanced at Scott for direction, but he was looking in his textbook.

"Maybe Casey's memory has failed her. Ah...Jason, perhaps you could tell us what the chapter was about?"

"My memory didn't fail me," I interrupted. "I remember everything I read. Do you want me to tell you everything?"

"Please do..." said the Bear. He made the funny gesture, the hand wave, again.

"The second world war was initiated by the invasion of Poland by Germany on September 1, 1939," I said. "However, this was not Germany's first warlike act. Between 1931 and 1939, Germany, as well as Italy and Japan, had taken over new territories, heedless of the protests of the United States. "

"Very good, Casey," the Bear said. "Now, then, Jason, can you tell me who else..."

"Wait. There's more," I said. "Two days after Germany invaded Poland, England and France demanded they retreat. Germany refused, and England and France declared war."

"Excellent, Casey. Now then, Jason, please tell us..."

"I'm not finished..." I started to say.

"Yes, I realize that Casey," interrupted the Bear. "But, I think someone else should be given the opportunity to show that they also read the chapter, don't you agree?"

I didn't agree, but something in his manner made me stop. I had the feeling he was annoyed, but I didn't understand why. First he asked me to tell him what I'd read, then he made me stop before I could finish. It didn't make sense.

I didn't volunteer any more information for the rest of the class, afraid that I might make another mistake.

When lunchtime came, I went out to the picnic table near the playing field to wait for Scott. The air seemed heavy, weighed down with rain. Our school sat high on a hill, giving me a view of the main street and the harbor. A few seagulls bobbed uneasily on the nearly purple water, occasionally taking to the air with their complaining cries.

I checked my watch. Scott was five minutes late. *Maybe the lineup for foot-long's is especially slow,* I decided. I could feel a headache coming on, probably caused by hunger, so I opened my blue lunch bag and pulled out my cheese on brown bread. I'd finished it, and my cookies, orange juice and apple, and there was still no sign of Scott. A cold wind had begun to blow from the lake, chilling me in my jean jacket. The first splatter of rain hit me, fat sloppy drops that would soak through my jacket in no time at all.

I hesitated. *We always meet at the picnic table. Why isn't Scott there? Should I leave, or go inside to find him?*

I **hated** this. If there was a set of rules, I'd never heard of them. Whatever decision I made, it always seemed to be the wrong one.

Finally, the rain decided for me, soaking through my clothes and making my hair stick uncomfortably to my forehead. My running shoes made squishy sounds on the wet walkway as I ran toward the school.

"Too stupid to come in out of the rain." I heard the comment as I pushed open the glass door into the foyer. It was the shaved head guy who had made Scott angry the week before. Scott had said to ignore him, so I did, squelching wetly past without looking at him.

I found Scott in the cafeteria. He was sitting at a table with five or six other guys, all talking and eating and laughing. Again, I hesitated. *Go in? Wait here? Who is to know?*

Finally, the bell rang and Scott came out.

"Where were you?" I blurted out. "I was waiting for you."

I knew by the look on his face that I'd blown it, yet again. Why couldn't I put things in nice language like other people? Why did I just open my mouth and let stuff spill out?

"I do have other friends, Casey. I can't spend all my time with you," he said, and began walking towards the lockers on the second floor.

I didn't understand. Did that mean he'd only eat lunch with me some of the time? How would I know which days? Or, had I done or said something to annoy him? Maybe it had been in history, when I'd gone on for so long about the war. Maybe, he'd wanted to contribute too, and I'd made it difficult for him.

Or, maybe we weren't as good friends as I had thought.

Maybe we weren't friends at all.

Chapter Thirteen

THE STORES ARE FULL OF CARDS

Dad was digging in the front garden when I got home. He was wearing headphones and had a tape player clipped to his belt. I watched him pull gladioli out of the ground, snip off their yellowing leaves and shake the dirt off the bulbs. He worked precisely—pull, snip, shake. Dad always said that once he figured out a system that worked, why change it?

He was like that about work, too. Up at 5:30, a bowl of corn flakes with bananas for breakfast, and at work by 6:30. Dad said he could get half a day's work in before the rest of the computer records people straggled in at 9:00. He ate lunch at his desk, in front of his computer, then left work promptly at 3:30. By 3:45 he was home, and by 3:55 was changed into work clothes and was in the garden. Dinner was at 5:00, followed by reading the paper and working on the computer or watching an old movie.

You could set a clock by my father.

A truck rolled past on the dirt lane, raising a cloud of dust despite the rainstorm earlier. I heaved a sigh of relief to see it go, and hoped it was the last day it would be at the house next door. Now I could hear Dad humming along with the music. I groaned. *My Fair Lady.* It looked like Henry Higgens and Eliza Dolittle would be joining us for dinner again.

I sat cross-legged beside Dad and tapped his shoulder. The reaction was immediate.

"Ahhwooo," he yelled in a thick accent. "Wot's the idear of sneakin' op be'ind me loik that? Give a pour gurl a 'eart attack, that's wot you'll do!"

Eliza, I thought. "Hi, Dad," I said.

"Hi, schweet'art," answered Humphrey Bogart. "Uh-h-h-h-h, what's up, doc?" Bugs. I wished he'd pick a character and stay in it for once. I was too tired today to follow all the switches.

"Nothing much is up," I answered, "except that Scott isn't talking to me."

"Whadja do? Fink on him?" Dad asked in his best James Cagney gangster voice.

"Dad, get serious," I groaned. "I don't know WHAT I did. That's the whole problem. I don't know why he's so angry with me."

"Hmm, well, you're looking at the wrong guy for answers, sweetheart," Dad said in his own voice. "You know me—classic computer geek if there ever was one. I don't pretend to understand people. That's your Mom's department. Why don't you go talk to her?"

I found Mom inside, making dinner as usual at this time of day. "Dad said I should talk to you," I told her. "First, I have to give Chelsea her rock."

80

Chelsea was sketching, also as usual. I pushed the rock, a beautiful one with white and black layers, into her field of vision and watched with satisfaction as she examined it.

Mom came out with muffins and milk. "How was she today?" I asked.

"Just fine, honey. No cement truck today," Mom said, smiling. "I was more worried about how you were today. Was Scott back?"

"Yes, but he didn't want to be with me," I said. "He was angry, but I don't know why."

"Did you tell him you were sorry that he hurt his arm?" Mom asked.

"Why would I do that?" I asked, mystified.

Mom sighed. "He's your friend, isn't he?"

I was about to tell her I wasn't sure anymore, but she went on.

"Friends do things for each other. They care about each other. I mean, how would you feel if you broke your arm?"

"It would hurt," I said.

"Yes, it would hurt, and you would like your friends to make a little fuss over you. You know, to sign your cast and carry your books and maybe give you a get well card."

"I could do that," I said. "Could we go buy him a get well card right now?"

"Casey, I'm right in the middle of...okay, honey, sure. Let's have a little talk before we go, okay?"

"But we are talking."

"No, I mean... Listen, Casey, maybe it's too soon for you to go to school. Maybe you should stay home another year. I'm worried about you, honey. You seem pretty agitated. Maybe it's just too much for you to handle right now."

Leave school? Mom was right that I was agitated. I felt agitated all the time, in fact. It would be nice to stay at home with Chelsea. I missed her.

Then I thought about Scott. I missed him, too. I wanted him to like me and be my friend. I wanted to be just a normal person.

"I'm fine, Mom," I lied. "I'm having fun at school. I can handle it."

Mom gave me a long, searching look. I couldn't read her expression. I wished I could snap a picture of it and then ask Scott what it meant.

"Okay," Mom finally said. "But if it gets too much for you, you just tell me."

I decided right then that she would be the last to know if it got too much for me. I didn't want her to pull me out of school.

"Well, let's go buy that card now," Mom said. "I'll drive you into town."

That made me feel better. I had a plan. I'd give the card to Scott and then he'd be my friend again.

If I'd known it was so easy, I thought, *I'd have made lots of friends years ago.*

After all, the stores were full of cards.

Chapter Fourteen

BRAD, SCOTT'S FATHER

A bell jangled above the door as I walked into "Favorite Things." I noticed the smell first. I always do. Cinnamon, bayberry, sandalwood. The smells came from candles, an elaborate collection of them on tiered pine shelves to my right. There was a old man fishing on a dock, his hat pulled low against the sun, a dog sleeping under a willow tree, dwarfs, dragons, trolls…all in wax, all so realistic I thought they might talk if I could only break the spell.

In the back of the store, there were paintings and sketches lining the walls. Some reminded me of Chelsea's bird sketches. Others were in color, mostly of animals or natural scenes. All were so realistic that they could have been photographs.

"Anything special that I can help you find?"

I jumped. I had forgotten I was in a store, and that the owner would eventually appear. I turned around to see a man, taller than Scott but shorter than my father, with wavy light brown hair and grey eyes. He had Scott's smile.

"Yes, wh…" I caught myself just in time, just before I blurted out 'where's Scott.' "May I talk to Scott, please," I said. "If he's in?"

"Sure, he's working in back. I'm Brad, Scott's father."

"Nice to meet you, Brad, Scott's father," I said.

He laughed. "You've got to be Casey," he said. "Scott's talked a lot about you. He said you had an unusual sense of humor, but he didn't tell me how pretty you are."

I wasn't sure what to say to that. Then I remembered what my teacher, April, had said about accepting compliments graciously. "Thank you," I said.

Brad, Scott's father, led me to the back of the store. Another man was there, a tall person with short dark hair and a mustache. He was framing a painting of a bald eagle. Scott, his arm in the sling, watched.

"Someone here to see you, Scott," said his Dad. "Casey, this is Ray, my partner," he added, nodding to the mustached man. "Hi, Casey," Ray said. "Heard a lot about you. Scott, I can handle this alone. Why don't you get lost?" He winked at Scott. I wondered what it meant, but didn't think about it too long. I was watching Scott's reaction too closely.

I swear I saw at least three emotions on his face before he decided on an expression. I thought they were surprise and pleasure, and something else, but I couldn't be sure.

At least I hoped it was surprise and pleasure.

Then his voice told me. "Casey! How're you doing?"

I knew it was a ritual question, so I didn't tell him that my heart was doing the tango with my stomach.

"Here," I said, shoving the card toward him. "I wanted to give you this."

I saw Ray nudge Brad, Scott's father, and they both grinned.

"Thanks, Casey," Scott said, taking the card. "Let's go read it outside, and get away from Mutt and Jeff here."

Mutt and Jeff? I thought they were Brad, Scott's father, and Ray. I was about to ask him what he meant, but he'd already started toward the front of the store. "Goodbye," I said to Brad, Scott's father, and Ray, pleased that I'd once again remembered my manners.

Outside, Scott leaned against the rough grey stone of the building and read the card.

"Hey, this is great, Casey. Thanks," he said. He was grinning. His eyes looked light grey today, with flecks of green and gold. "Look, I'm sorry about today. Leaving you alone was pretty irresponsible. I was mad at you."

"I knew you were angry," I said. "But I didn't know why. My mother explained it to me. I have trouble understanding how other people are feeling sometimes."

"Yeah. They told me about that when I took the peer buddy job. Look, let's get a frozen yogurt and forget about it, okay? My treat."

"It would be a treat for me too, Scott," I said.

Scott laughed, but I didn't know why. Just the same, his laugh made me feel warm inside.

We ate our yogurts down at the harbor, sitting on a bench. Scott had paid for them, and I realized what he meant by "his treat." It was an expression.

The earlier mist had lifted, and the sun shone low in the sky. It bounced off the crest of the wavelets on the water like a whole galaxy of suns.

"So, what did you think of my father?" Scott asked.

"I liked him," I said. "He looks like you." I watched as Scott smiled crookedly. Same smile.

"And what did you think of Ray?" Scott asked.

"What should I think of Ray?" I asked, rather confused by the question.

Scott ran his fingers through his hair. "He's Dad's partner, you know?"

"No, I didn't," I said. "They own the store together?"

"Yes," Scott said, drawing the word out slowly. "But they're also partners, if you know what I mean."

I didn't know what he meant at all. He was blushing, which I knew meant embarrassment, but I didn't understand why.

"Scott, I don't get hints," I said. "You've got to spell it out for me."

"Ray lives with us," he said, turning even redder. "My Mom and Dad got divorced because of him."

"So?"

"He and my Dad are…that is, they share a room," he managed to say.

"You mean they don't share the whole house?" I asked. *What kind of weird arrangement was this?*

"Jeez, Casey. You really make this hard. They share a...like, they have the same bedroom. They're, like, married almost."

I burst out laughing. *This has to be a joke. Men don't marry men! Not unless they are...*

Then, I finally got it. I stopped laughing, realizing from the look on Scott's face my laughter hadn't been appreciated.

"You mean your father's a homosexual?" I asked.

"Yeah. He's gay. That's why some of the kids at school make fun of me. They think I'm gay, too."

"Are you?" I asked bluntly. Too late to take it back, I groaned, wishing I'd phrased it a little more delicately.

"Does it matter to you?" he asked.

"No," I said, realizing it was the truth. "I like you, no matter what your..." I hunted for the words. "...sexual preference."

"It's not a preference, Casey," he said, almost angrily. "My dad didn't choose to be gay. He didn't choose to be different. There's evidence of a 'gay gene,' an actual genetic cause. And, autopsies of gay people's brains show a difference in brain structure. Of course, no one knows if being gay causes your brain to develop differently or if gays are born with different brains, but still..." He paused and ate more of his yogurt. "I'm sorry. I get carried away

88

when someone calls it a 'preference.' I didn't mean to lecture you."

"That's okay," I said. "I enjoyed hearing it. All facts are fascinating."

"Yeah, not so fascinating when you take the heat all your life. You know, like when I walk down the hall at school and someone goes into a limp wrist routine for my benefit, or minces around with little girlish steps. Not all gays are effeminate, you know. In fact, most you can't tell at all. Did you think my dad was effeminate?"

"Well, I know what the word means, but I'm not a good judge of 'body language' yet, remember? I'm still learning."

"Yeah, I forgot," he grinned. "Anyway, to answer your question, no, I'm not gay. I don't think so anyway. It scares me sometimes, when I'm with another guy and I feel, like, any sort of affection or anything. I guess that's why I don't have many friends. As soon as I start to feel close to someone I get really scared and so I back off."

"But, you have lots of friends," I said. "Everyone knows you and talks to you."

"They aren't close friends, Casey. I mean, yeah, I have a bunch of friends that I do stuff with, but no *best* friend. No one I can really talk to about things. I'm afraid that if I want to be good friends with another guy, he'll think I'm queer, and if I try to have a girlfriend, she'll think I'm going out with her just to prove I'm not gay."

"I thought I was the only one who found relationships difficult," I said.

"Huh. I wish," he grunted. "You know, I've never told anyone this but you, Casey. You're different from other people, you know?"

I froze. *Different? I don't want to be different.*

But Scott wasn't looking at me. He was looking at the sun, a reddish disc on the horizon. "Like, I don't feel as if you are judging me. You seem to take everyone at face value, Case. You're not like my other friends."

"You're welcome," I managed to say. My insides were churning. Scott had called me "different," not a good thing at all, but then he'd called me his friend, which was a very good thing.

"Hey! Look at the time! After six! I'd better get you home!" Scott said, checking his watch.

A tidal wave of anxiety hit me. *After six.* Mom said she'd hold dinner, but I'm sure she didn't mean for a whole hour. It wasn't until I'd left the harborfront area, crossed the park and walked half a block towards home on the brick sidewalk that I realized Scott had followed me.

"Where are you going?" I asked.

"I'm walking you home," he said, as if the answer were obvious."

I stopped. "Scott, I know the way home." What I didn't add was that it made me anxious to have him there. I was used to walking alone, back and forth to school, and so I

90

felt I should walk home the same way. I knew it wasn't logical, but it was the way I felt.

"Yes, I do have to walk you home, Casey," Scott said. "My dad would skin me alive if he knew I let you walk all that way alone at dusk. Besides, I'd worry about you."

I wasn't sure whether to ask what "skin me alive" meant (surely that had to be just another saying) but I did like it when he said he'd worry about me. Friends worry about each other.

"Okay," I agreed.

For a while there was no sound, except the wind rustling the dry yellow leaves of the trees and our footsteps on the sidewalk. My anxiety began to drain away. Nothing bad was happening, even if I was breaking my habit of walking alone.

We turned down Clear Bay Road and our feet crunched on the gravel surface of the road, marking a comfortable rhythm. The sky was turning a deep blue, and I saw the first star wink on as if someone had thrown the light switch. I felt more content than I had felt in a long time.

Then, Scott did something that totally ruined everything.

He reached out and held my hand.

Chapter Fifteen

SANCTUARY

"Casey, I'm glad you're home. I was getting worried about you," Mom said as I came in. "I put your dinner in the fridge. Your father didn't want to wait. You can nuke it, okay?" She followed me into the kitchen and sat down at the counter while I warmed dinner in the microwave. "So? How did it go?" she asked.

"Fine," I said. "He liked the card. We went for a frozen yogurt and then he walked me home."

"Great!" Mom said. "I knew it would all work out. I'm going to check on your sister, okay?" I glanced at her and nodded. Her expression, as she left, looked happy. If she was so pleased for me, why was I feeling so anxious?

Because he had held my hand as we walked along the road. I could still feel the touch of it. Bigger than my own, the fingers wider and stronger, the grip warm.

It scared me. But why? Was it normal, or was I weird?

I had never liked being touched. Mom said that even as a baby I hated being held or rocked. One of my earliest memories was of someone, an uncle I think, picking me up and holding me. His voice was so loud that my eardrums shivered in pain. I thought they would burst. He smelled so strongly of aftershave that I almost threw up. His chin was rough with stubble. When he tried to kiss my neck, I screamed. It was like being rasped raw with heavy duty sandpaper. I screamed and screamed, even after he put me down. Screaming was the only way to release the horror of what I felt.

And that's how I'd felt, all over again, when Scott took my hand. Like screaming.

Now surely, that wasn't normal.

What was wrong with me? Why did the mere touch of his hand make my guts feel like I was on roller coaster? Was it just that I didn't want to be touched? Or, was it that Scott had just complicated things? Did holding my hand mean we were girlfriend and boyfriend like in the movies, or were we just friends?

It was overwhelming. *Emotion. The enemy. I have to control it.*

I closed my eyes and concentrated on my breathing, waiting until the urge to scream passed. My hands were shaking as I scraped my uneaten dinner into the garbage can.

"Casey, how did it go with Scott?" Dad asked as I walked past the living room. "Are you friends again?"

"Yes, thanks," I answered quickly, heading for my own room. Heading for my sanctuary.

Sanctuary. That's how I always thought of it. The one place where no one talked to me, or asked anything of me. I shut the door and flopped down on my bed.

I used to think there was a monster under the bed. A slimy green one, flattened out like jello in the sun, waiting

93

for me to come close enough for it to reach one tentacle out and snag my ankle. It would pull me under and slowly digest me with its stomach acid.

I shook my head. *Stupid childhood fear. There are no such things as monsters. There is nothing under the bed. I will not look,* I told myself. *I refuse to look.*

But I had to look.

I flipped up one edge of the pink ruffle that ran around the bottom of the bed and saw...

...My collection boxes. That was all. No slimy green jello monster.

I pulled out the one marked minerals and gems, and lifted the lid. Inside were all my old friends, labelled and neatly separated, each in a small open box, like the sort that you use for jewelry. I picked up each one, remembering. Quartz. Hardness seven. I picked up a cool piece of rose quartz and ran my finger across its faceted face. I had amethyst too, my favorite because of its beautiful purple color. I touched it next, feeling each perfectly formed spire. My citrine sample was particularly clear, a pure yellow unpolluted by other minerals. I had always regretted, though, not finding a rutilated quartz, or aventurine.

Still, my mineral collection did include agate and garnet, feldspar and mica, talc and chalcopyrite. That was a comfort right there. Not to mention my sea-green aquamarine, from the same family as emeralds, but less valuable. Or, my azurite, which had come from Utah. And then, there was the marble, the malachite, beryl and a particularly large piece of chalcopyrite, also known as fool's gold.

"Casey—are you all right?" Mom's voice called through the door.

"Yes, I'm fine," I answered.

"I called you three or four times, and you didn't answer," she said, walking into the room. "It's ten o'clock, honey. Have you been looking at those all night?"

I froze. *Ten o'clock.* I remembered glancing at the clock when I came into the room. It had only been seven. It had only taken a few minutes to check for monsters which meant I'd been looking at my mineral collection for almost three hours.

Looking, feeling, rubbing, even tasting the specimens, I realized. Classifying, reciting the facts to myself—where each was found, its hardness, whether it was rare or common, all of its uses.

Lost in my own little world.

Just like my sister.

Mom's words came back to me. *Maybe it's just too much for you to handle right now. Maybe you should stay home another year.*

I couldn't tell her the truth, even though I wanted to. I had to let her think I was handling it.

So, I lied.

"Oh, no, Mom. I've been studying. I just pulled these out to take a look. We're studying minerals and gems in science class." I scooped up the rocks and carelessly tossed them in the box, then shoved it under the bed.

Is that relief on her face? "Are you sure, honey? You're sure you're okay?"

I forced a smile. "Just perfect, Mom."

She left reluctantly, a small frown on her face. Once she was gone, I pulled the box back out from under the bed. Lifting the lid, I methodically put each mineral back in its proper resting place. Then, and only then, did I slide it back under the bed.

I crawled into bed, but I couldn't sleep. I kept imagining monsters. I lay there for hours, eyes wide open, heart pounding, ears straining for sounds in the night.

Finally, I slipped out of bed and carefully opened my bedroom door. It was dark. Mom and Dad must be asleep. I crept down the hallway, keeping one hand on the wall, until I got to Chelsea's room. I eased open her door and looked inside.

She was sleeping on her side, the covers pulled up to her chin. It was like looking at myself in a mirror.

Very quietly, so I wouldn't wake her, I slid into the bed. I curled up on my side, not touching her but close enough to feel the warmth of her body.

At last I was warm and safe.

At last I slept.

Chapter Sixteen

A NEW FRIEND

I woke long before Chelsea did. My dreams had been disturbing, made up of incidents from early childhood. They faded away as soon as I opened my eyes.

I checked the time. Five o'clock. Too early for a shower. Not even Dad was up yet. Sneaking like a burglar down the hall, avoiding the cracks created by our ceramic tiled floor, I made my way to the kitchen. I had a lot of work to do, since I'd wasted the night before looking over my rock collection.

History didn't take long. I read the assigned pages, then answered the list of questions the teacher had given us. Since most of the class didn't seem to be reading the chapters, he said, we would have to hand in our answers at the beginning of each class.

After history, I did math, then English. I was supposed to show the Robin my autobiography today. I read over what I had written so far, ending with the entry about my collections and worrying about monsters under the bed.

Why was I reverting back to old childhood patterns? I wondered. I hadn't checked for monsters in years, but last night, there I was, checking under the bed, just like I had when I was six. And my mineral collection. I hadn't looked at it in years, or even given it a second thought.

Why now? What was happening to me? Was it the stress of starting school, as Mom thought?

"Hi, schweet'art," said a voice near my ear. I startled so badly that my hands froze on the keyboard, leaving a long line of gibberish on the screen.

"Dad!" I said. "Don't sneak up on me like that!"

"Ya gotta keep a sharp eye out for varmints, little lady," Dad said. It was his John Wayne voice. He stuck his hands in his waistband and pretended to hitch up his pants. "How's about I rustle us up some grub?"

"Sure, Dad," I said. "Scrambled eggs would be nice."

"You got it, little lady," he said, swaggering over to the fridge and bringing out eggs, cheese, green onions and hot sauce. Texas eggs, he called them. Good thing Mom would be cooking supper, otherwise we'd probably get Dad's "cowpoke dinner": baked beans and black coffee.

I went back to the English assignment. Robin had said to just tell my life story, but I wasn't sure where to go from here. I looked back at her questions list, hoping for a clue.

Tell about an accomplishment. Well, I'd memorized most of the *Guinness Book of Records* and I'd memorized five hundred Web addresses. Did that count?

"Come'n git it, before I feed it to the dawgs," Dad drawled at me. He set the eggs, toast and juice on the table.

I grabbed the cutlery and glasses and joined him. The eggs were good. I hadn't realized I was hungry until I took the first bite.

"So, what where you doing up so early?" Dad asked, talking around a mouthful of food.

"Homework. I got a little distracted last night and didn't get it all done," I admitted.

"I know the problem," he said. "Sometimes I get so wrapped up in what I'm doing that hours can go by without me knowing it. Just yesterday, I was working on this program..."

"Dad, why did I have a special teacher when I was younger?" I interrupted. "I just remembered her the other day. April."

He was in the kitchen now, scraping our plates and putting them in the dishwasher. "Oh, you just needed a little help with schoolwork," he said.

"What kind of help?"

"Oh, I can't remember right now, schweet'art. Maybe you should ask your mom," he replied. "Gotta go to work. See you later."

He grabbed his lunch bag and was gone. The funniest thing was I had the feeling he was being evasive. Don't ask what gave me that feeling. Maybe I was getting better at picking up on signals.

After Dad left, I did a little more homework, then had my shower and left for school.

I was walking up the concrete steps to the front door of the school when I heard someone call my name. I turned around. *Oh, no,* I thought. The guy with one side of his head shaved and the other side with long hair. Shaved Head. The one who had called me a retard.

"Casey? That is your name, isn't it?" He came closer. He stunk of cigarettes.

"Yes," I said, walking away.

"Hey, wait Casey. I only wanted to say I was sorry for calling you names the other day. I saw how smart you were in history class. You must have memorized the whole book, word for word!"

I looked at him more closely. He was smiling.

"Listen my friend, could you do me a favor?" he asked.

"What kind of favor?"

"Well, you see, I have this real problem, Casey," he said, lowering his voice and coming closer. "My mother is in the hospital and I spent all night there. I didn't get my history questions done. Could I borrow yours, just to see how you answered them?"

I thought about it. He'd called me his friend. Mom said friends did things for each other.

"Okay," I said.

"Great! You're a lifesaver!" He smiled again. "Oh— and could I borrow your math homework, too?"

"I guess so." I set my knapsack down on the steps and took out my binder. I handed him both sets of homework.

"Thanks, Casey," Shaved Head said. "Hey, you know, I'd appreciate it if you didn't tell anyone about this. I don't want them feeling sorry for me, about my mother dying of cancer and all."

"Okay," I agreed. Then, I realized I didn't even know his name.

"What's your name?" I asked, as he walked away.

"Carl."

I walked to my locker feeling very pleased. I'd made a new friend. I hadn't even had to give him a card.

Chapter Seventeen

FRIENDS DO THINGS FOR EACH OTHER

I counted the steps to the second floor, as usual, then counted each locker until I reached my own. Scott was already at his, across the hall and ten lockers down from mine. His back was to me as he one-handedly grabbed books from his top shelf.

I hesitated. *Should I go over and do a greeting ritual?* Part of me wanted to, but part of me remembered how he had taken my hand the night before, and that part of me was scared.

Just what I was scared of, I didn't exactly know. That he might touch my hand again? Why should that make my heart thump and my hands sweat? It made no sense.

I pretended I didn't see him and busied myself getting my morning books out of my locker.

There was a loud crash, then the sound of Scott swearing. I turned around. There was a pile of books at his feet and he was holding his cast to his chest with his other arm. Had he hurt himself?

"Scott. Are you okay?" I asked, dodging kids wandering by in the corridor to reach him.

"Yeah, just great," he said, gritting his teeth. "The stupid books avalanched off the shelf. My science book whacked my cast but good on the way down."

"Did you break it again?" I asked, alarmed.

"No, just bumped it. Can you help me out, Case? Put the books back up there, and grab science, English and math for me?"

"No problem," I said, using a phrase he had used the day before. I picked up the jumbled stack of books and binders at his feet and chose the ones we needed, then neatly stacked the others in his locker. I slid his lock on, shut it, then yanked three times to be sure it was secure.

"Here, just put the books on my left arm," Scott instructed. He awkwardly held out his arm to receive them.

Friends do things for each other, I remembered. "No, I'll carry them for you," I said, my face getting red.

Scott looked at me strangely but nodded a reply.

When we got to math, I found my math homework and history notes were waiting for me on my desk. Carl must have returned them. I thought he might say something, but he was sitting at the front of the room with his back to me.

I loved math. The answers were always the same, time after time, no matter how many times you did the question. Each time the teacher asked for an answer, I put my hand up and answered. I noticed that after several answers, the teacher didn't seem to see my raised hand. He looked all around the classroom, looking for other people to call on, but ignored me.

"I know the answer!" I called out finally, frustrated.

The teacher still ignored me.

I was about to say something again, in case he hadn't heard me the first time, when I felt someone pull on my sleeve. I looked over at Scott, who was tugging at his left ear. It was a signal we had arranged at one of our tutoring sessions. It meant I was talking too much.

I nodded to show I understood. I put my hand down and let the teacher call on another student for the answer.

In the next class, science, we were doing a unit on the environment. The teacher was tall and had ears that stuck out from his head like an elephant's. I nicknamed him Dumbo.

Dumbo was explaining about a class assignment. Choose an environmental issue, explore it, write a report and give an oral presentation. He said we could work in groups if we wished.

Scott was trying to get my attention. I looked over. He pointed to me, then himself, then raised his eyebrows.

Now, what the heck is that supposed to mean?

"I don't understand..." I started to say, but Scott's frantic tugging at his ear stopped me. He jerked his head toward Dumbo. *Oops.* Dumbo had stopped talking and was glaring at me. I guess talking in class wasn't allowed.

Dumbo started droning again, about length and other requirements. I began to feel a little panicked. Wasn't he going to give us the instructions in writing? Somehow, I could remember facts just fine, but got all confused when someone gave detailed instructions verbally.

The bell rang then, and I covered my ears to block out its painful volume.

"I was trying to say, how about we pair up for the project," Scott told me as soon as we were outside the class.

"That would be great, Scott. Maybe you could explain the requirements to me."

"No prob. We'll hit the library on Saturday."

"Come to my house, instead," I suggested. "We've got three electronic encyclopedias. We could do a websearch, too."

"Cool!" Scott's eyes opened wide. They looked sea green today, against a deep green sweatshirt he was wearing.

We had English next.

"Now, I expect you are all about half finished with your autobiographies," Robin said, bobbing her head and bouncing up and down between the rows of desks. "Presentations start in a few weeks. Now, earlier we talked about beginning your stories with a narrative hook. Can anyone tell me what that is?"

I glanced at Scott. He nodded. No ear tug. I raised my hand and answered the question.

For the rest of the class, I took my cues from Scott. Before I volunteered an answer, I glanced at him, looking for a nod or head shake.

I also learned what a hand woggle meant. That's when someone holds a hand out horizontally, then waggles it side to side, turning at the wrist. Maybe, possibly, doubtful...it meant all those things. I checked it out by passing him a note when he used it. I remembered my tutor, April, who told me it meant *'comme ci, comme ca,'* literally 'like this, like that,' a revelation which had not helped much at the time.

All my life, I had felt like a stranger in the world. I knew the language, but I did not understand the subtleties of meaning. Finally, I felt like I had found a special guide, like a tour guide in a foreign country. Just as a tour guide might explain the money system, the local customs, the local foods, Scott was guiding me through the experience of high school.

For the very first time, I felt indebted to another person. Without him, I would be lost.

Sitting there in class, the meaning of my dream hit me. I had been wandering the school naked, in danger of ridicule, and he had given me clothing. He had protected me and cared for me.

I needed him. I had never needed anyone else before. Not even my parents, not really. I had never needed them for love or affection, cuddles or kisses or bedtime stories. I had needed my things, my collections, my books. Knowledge, facts, information. That's what I had needed.

Even the need to be normal, to have friends...I had needed the idea of normality, the image of friends. Not the real thing. I'd never confided in anyone, never done a favor for the joy of doing it, never really, really needed someone.

Until now.

The very idea terrified me.

Chapter Eighteen

THE CENTER OF ATTENTION

I was waiting outside at our picnic table for Scott to arrive, when Carl sauntered up.

"Hey, Casey, what's happening?" he said.

"Hey, Carl, what's happening?" I responded.

"I need another little favor, Casey," he said, reaching into his jacket pocket for a cigarette. Acrid smoke wafted over to me, and I shifted away. "With my mother in the hospital, I won't have time to research my science assignment. I wondered if you could dig out some of the facts for me?"

"Okay," I said. After all, friends do things for each other. "What topic did you pick?"

"Endangered species. Could you do it over the weekend for me and have it to me by Monday?" He put one foot up on the bench of the picnic table and blew smoke toward me.

"Sure." I was hoping he'd go away. The smoke was making my head spin.

"Thanks, Casey," he said. He smiled. "Oh, by the way, I'll need our history reading questions done by Monday, too. And could you whip off an extra set of answers for me in math?"

I hesitated. It was beginning to sound like a lot of work. But, he was my friend...

"Sure," I told him.

"Good. And remember, it's our little secret, okay?" He butted out the cigarette on the top of the picnic table, then left.

Disgusted, I flicked the butt away. I wished he wouldn't smoke around me. Then, I saw Scott coming, along with a few other people, and forgot my irritation.

"What did Carl want?" Scott asked, setting down a hamburger and fries.

"Nothing much," I answered, feeling very uncomfortable. Friends don't lie to each other, and saying 'nothing much' was close to lying. On the other hand, Carl had asked me not to tell anyone about me doing his homework. I felt trapped.

"Well, just watch out for him, Casey. His only ambition in life is to use people," Scott said, sitting down beside me. He introduced the other people who had joined us— Jeff, who I had already met, Carol, and Jim.

I ate my cheese on brown bread, listening to the conversation rather than joining in. Now that I knew that I sometimes talked too much, and dominated the conversation, I felt self-conscious about saying anything at all.

They were talking about movies, something I knew a fair bit about. Jeff was saying that he watched the newest

Dracula movie on cable the night before. He said it was the best ever made, much better than the other three that had been produced earlier.

At that point I just had to say something. "Dracula, or his direct descendants, have actually been portrayed in one hundred and sixty-one films, not four," I said.

I glanced at Scott. No ear tug.

"Hey! Scott told me that you're a walking encyclopedia," Jeff grinned. I watched his signals closely. He was leaning towards me, smiling. "So, tell me, what else do you know?"

"Ask me a question," I said back.

"What's the record for the tallest person?" Jeff asked.

I glanced at Scott. He nodded his head up and down. I took it as an okay signal.

"Alive or deceased?" I asked Jeff. *This is going to be fun.*

"Both," Jeff said. He was grinning. I bet he thought he could stump me. *Ha! Nobody can stump old encyclopedia brain!* "Living: Haji Mohammad Alam Channa of Pakistan and Sandy Allen, Chicago, are both seven feet, seven and one quarter inches tall. The tallest person ever was Robert Pershing Wadlow, born in 1918 in Illinois. He reached eight feet, eleven point one inches."

"Shortest person," said the girl beside Jeff, the one named Carol.

"Twenty two and a half inches, Gul Mohammad, born 1957; shortest woman, Pauline Musters, born 1876, measured twenty-four inches at death, weighed nine pounds at her heaviest."

"Wow," said the other guy, Jim, "that's amazing. What about the fattest man in history?"

"Jon Brower Minnoch, born 1941, died in 1983, reached a maximum weight of one-thousand, four-hundred pounds."

"Heaviest woman?" asked Carol.

"Rosalie Bradford, born 1944, reached an all time high of one-thousand, two-hundred pounds in 1987. By 1994, she had dieted down to two-hundred and eighty-three pounds. She's going for a target weight of one-hundred and fifty."

"Bet she'll gain it all back again," said Carol. "Diets never work!"

Everyone laughed. By now, there was a small crowd surrounding us.

"Oldest person on record?" someone asked from the crowd.

"Easy," I answered. "Shigechiyo Izumi of Japan, born 1865, died 1986 at the age of one hundred and twenty years and two hundred and thirty-seven days."

"Youngest person on record?" someone else asked.

Huh? Youngest person on record? I didn't understand the question and was about to ask for clarification. Then, everyone laughed, and I realized it was a joke.

"Very funny," I said. "Anyone have a REAL question?"

A short, fat girl asked, "What's the record for greatest number of children born to a single woman?"

"You mean an unmarried woman?" I asked.

More laughter. I wondered what was funny.

"No," said the girl. "Any woman!"

That was easier to answer. "The wife of Feodor Vassilyev, a peasant from Russia, was pregnant twenty-seven times. In all, she gave birth to sixty-nine children—sixteen pairs of twins, seven sets of triplets and four sets of quadruplets."

There was a lot of groaning. "What was her first name?" someone asked.

"Mommy," answered someone else, and they laughed.

This felt good. I was the center of attention and it felt good. They liked me. They were laughing, but it was because I was amusing them.

Then I checked my watch. *Oops. Two minutes late for tutoring with Scott.* "Come on, Scott," I said. "Time for tutoring."

"Let's skip it, Casey, just this once," he argued.

"Nope. It's your job. Let's go," I said. It wasn't really because it was his job, but because I hated to break the pattern we'd established. I didn't want to tell him that, though. My mom always said I was too inflexible, just like my Dad, and I didn't want Scott to have the same criticism of me.

"Sorry folks," Scott said, waving his good arm at the crowd. "She's a slave driver."

Scott's friends and some of the other's who had been hanging around said goodbye. They even said goodbye to me. It felt good.

Don't expect it to last, said the voice of doubt inside my head. *It's only a matter of time before you do something to mess up.*

Just a matter of time.

Chapter Nineteen

IS THE IRON OFF?

I didn't have friends when I was young. Some of the time, I just preferred to be alone. People seemed like an unnecessary distraction when I was playing with my collections or organizing all the books in my room into alphabetical order. Sometimes, people got in the way, disrupting the things I had so carefully arranged.

Like the time Mom invited a "little friend" over to play. I was skeptical about the whole thing, even more so once the girl arrived. We were in my room. My carefully arranged room. She saw my dolls, the ones from all the countries of the world. Instead of playing with them the right way, she took them all down off the shelves and mixed them up on the floor, so that Bolivia was next to Uruguay, instead of next to Chile the way it should have been. She made them talk to each other, making up the words and saying them for the dolls.

"Here, Casey…take this one. Let's pretend her name is Allie, okay, and my doll is called Cindy, and they're best friends and they're going on a picnic, okay?"

I didn't see the point of it. Why give them names? They already had names—Miss Bolivia and Miss Uruguay. I didn't understand why we would want to pretend to talk for them, speaking in high little voices as if we were the dolls.

It made me angry to see my dolls scattered around, lying on the floor where they didn't belong. I picked them up and started to put them back on the shelf, in order, the way they should be. The girl wouldn't give Miss Bolivia back. Then she began to take Miss Bolivia's jacket off. That's when I grabbed hold of the girl's blond hair and yanked. She let go of the doll then, and ran from my room. Glad to be rid of her, I arranged my dolls properly on the shelf. Their clothes weren't meant to come off, no more than the dolls themselves were meant to talk.

○ ○ ○

I stopped typing and remembered. Mom had been so angry with me that she wouldn't say a word the whole time we were driving the girl back home. Later that night, she'd had a talk with me about friends. Friends share their toys, she told me. Friends do nice things for each other, she said. None of it made much sense at the time.

Now, finally, I was beginning to understand. Friends do nice things for each other. I had a lot of friends, suddenly, at school. There was Carl. I had done a lot of things for him in the last week, ever since he had asked for help with his endangered species project. On the weekend, I had looked up endangered species on the Internet for him. There were fifteen hundred entries, so I didn't finish reading them all right away. I kept at it all weekend, then all the next week, whenever I had time.

Of course, there wasn't a lot of free time, since I had been doing Carl's other homework for him as well—his history questions, math homework, his geography assignment, his French essay. His mother was still in the hospital, so he didn't have time to do it himself.

Carl introduced me to a lot of his friends, and they became my friends too. They said "hi" to me in the halls. Many of them were not able to do their homework, either. Within another week, I was doing three sets of history notes, five of math problems and had written ten French essays. I was staying up until two or three every morning, but that was okay. Friends help each other.

When I wasn't doing homework, I was studying the latest *Guinness Book of Records*, or the newest almanac. People kept coming up to me at school and asking me questions. So far, I had answered them all, but I had to keep ahead of the game.

Ahead of the game. That was a phrase I had learned. Scott was still teaching me at lunchtime. He said I needed to pick up more expressions. He gave me a new list each morning, and I tried to use as many expressions as possible during the course of the day.

My speech was becoming more natural, Scott said. Less stilted. It made me feel good to have him looking out for me that way, so I looked for ways to make his life easier. The broken arm made it hard for him to carry his books around between classes, so I carried them for him. Since he was right handed, and had broken his right arm, it hurt him to take notes in class. I couldn't actually take notes for him, since I never could listen and write at the same time, but I made use of my good memory by typing out the content of our lectures once I got home. Scott told me I was a lifesaver. Another expression.

TGIF, I said under my breath as I sat at the computer before school. Thank God It's Friday. An expression. I was exhausted from staying up so late with schoolwork each night, and was looking forward to the weekend. My parents would be out of town on Saturday with Chelsea, shopping, and they said I could have Scott over to work on our science project. Mom said we could order a pizza for dinner.

I hadn't seen Scott the weekend before, the weekend that I spent looking up endangered species for Carl. Scott worked in his father's store on Saturday, and on Sunday he was at a birthday party for his grandmother. Scott invited me to the party, but I told him I had too much homework to do. This was partly true, since I was helping all my new friends at school with their work, but it was partly a lie. A white lie. That's an expression I had learned, too.

The truth then. I was too anxious to go to the party. The anxiety had been building all week. It wasn't the heart pounding, stomach clenching type that I usually endured. It was a slow poison in my body, eating me from the inside out.

I created little rituals to control the anxiety, but I didn't dare tell anyone about them. Especially Mom. She would

117

say that school was too much for me to handle. She would make me stay home.

The rituals began innocently enough. On Monday evening, I went downstairs to the laundry room to iron a skirt for the next day. When I came upstairs, Mom asked if I had turned the iron off. I was pretty sure I had, but I ran downstairs to check. It was off.

On Tuesday night, I checked the iron, but then I wondered what else might have been left on. I checked the stove and made sure no one had left the kettle plugged in.

On Wednesday, I checked the iron, the stove, the kettle and the toaster.

By Thursday night, I checked the iron, made sure the stove was turned off, pulled the plug for the toaster and the kettle, then checked that the fridge door was securely shut. Then, I made sure the front door was latched and the windows shut. I checked that the TV, computer, VCR and stereo were all shut down and that the lid of the deep freezer was closed. Only then could I go to bed.

The mornings were almost as bad. I was late for school because I went back to make sure I had shut the front door properly. Then, I worried that Dad might have left the hose running after watering his garden, so I went back to check that, too. I was glad we didn't own a dog. I'm sure I'd have gone back to make sure it wasn't running loose.

What made things worse was hiding the rituals from my parents, especially Mom. I didn't want her to know I was falling apart. She'd say school was too much for me.

The scary thing was that I'd developed the rituals to help me cope with the anxiety, but now the rituals were taking over my life, and causing even more anxiety. They were making it harder for me to cope, not easier. Each day that went by I felt less and less in control.

And the less control I felt, the more I needed the rituals.

It was a vicious circle.

That's an expression too.

Chapter Twenty

ENDANGERED SPECIES

"Casey—you got them notes for me?"

It was Carl, waiting just outside the school grounds, smoking a cigarette. His hair was growing back on the shaved side of his head, but hung long and lank on the other side. He looked like a bison shedding its winter coat.

"Yes, I do," I told him. "History, math, French."

"Good girl," he said, dropping the cigarette to the pavement and letting it burn. "Just give me everyone's copy and I'll distribute them, okay?"

"Sure. No problem," I said. The burning cigarette smoldered in the dry fall grass. I ground it out beneath my foot.

"So, you got my science project researched yet?" Carl asked.

"No, not really," I said. "I've been having a lot of trouble with it. I searched on the World Wide Web under endangered species and came up with fifteen thousand entries. There were web sites all over the world—grizzlies in Yellowstone, butterflies in Australia, pink dolphins in Hong Kong, birds of prey in Lebanon, salmon on the West Coast...I didn't know what to read about first."

"Jesus, Casey, can't you just get the stupid list of endangered species? Is that too much to ask?" He closed in, standing so close that the stench of cigarettes on his clothing made me feel ill. He kept flicking the long side of his hair away from his face, but it fell back in greasy strands.

I wanted to run away, but my feet had grown roots. Just as I was beginning to panic, I heard Scott's welcome voice. "What's going on here?" Scott asked. In his blue denim shirt and jeans, his neatly brushed hair and clean white arm sling, he was a sharp contrast to Carl.

"Nothin', punk," Carl answered. "Mind your own business, okay?"

Scott carefully set his knapsack on the ground. In a soft, low voice, he said, "Casey *is* my business, Carl. Now, maybe you'd like to answer my question. Just what is going on here?"

Carl spit on the ground. "Nothin,'" he snarled. "Casey's just doin' me a little favor, that's all." He turned to walk away, the homework clenched in one hand.

With his good hand, Scott grabbed the papers from Carl. His eyes widened as he flipped through them.

"What kind of a racket do you have going here, Carl?" he said slowly. "Are you charging for these?"

"What if I am? What's it to you?" Carl said. "So, I made a little off the deal. It's a free world, jerk. Now give 'em back, before I give you a new face."

"I don't think so," Scott said evenly. "She may not know when someone is taking advantage of her, but I do. Back

121

off." Slowly, deliberately, he ripped the pages in half, then handed them back to Carl.

Carl's face went red and his eyes bulged. He threw the papers down on the ground, then lunged toward Scott, catching him in the throat with his arm and slamming him into the fence. Scott tried to speak, but only a choked sound came out.

"I'm going to make you pay, big time," Carl growled.

I turned and walked away.

Chapter Twenty-One

WHERE IS THE RULE BOOK?

My heart was racing so fast and hard I was afraid that
I might be having a heart attack. I rested my forehead on
the cool metal door of my locker, trying to slow my
breathing down. A giant hand was squeezing my head,
squeezing so tight I thought it might burst and spray my
brains all over the place.

*Why had I walked away? Friends help each other,
right?* But I hadn't known how to help, what to do. Where
was the rule book?

"Casey!" Scott marched towards me, his good arm
swinging at his side, his face red, his blue eyes cold as
lake ice in January. "What's the big idea? Why'd you
just leave me there?"

Oh, no, I thought. I knew enough about signals now to
read his. Blue eyes blazing, chin jutted out, jaw tight,
shoulders back. *Rage.* I wasn't sure if it was a cold rage
or a hot rage, but somehow I didn't think it much mattered
right now.

"I was scared," I said shakily. "I couldn't handle it. I
had to get away."

"You were scared? How about *me?* How do you think
I was feeling, Casey?" He stared at me, his chin jutted
out, his breathing fast and noisy. "Try putting yourself in
my shoes, for once."

"They don't fit," I whispered, remembering my dream, the horrible dream where Scott had been wearing foot-long clown shoes, red with striped laces.

"Ha, ha. Very funny," Scott gritted out. "Well, for your information I was scared spitless. Carl's not the kinda guy you mess around with. I thought he was going to break my good arm, for cripes' sake. If a teacher hadn't walked by right then, who knows what would have happened!"

"A teacher?"

"Yeah. He told Carl to take a hike. Why the heck were you giving Carl all that homework anyway?"

"He's my friend. He said he couldn't do the work himself because his Mom is in the hospital, dying of cancer," I answered.

"Just because he talked to you doesn't mean he's your friend, Casey! He was lying to you. His mom works in the school cafeteria as one of the cooks. She's there right now, making the meat loaf or chili or who-knows-what for lunch. How could you let him fool you like that?" He was waving his good arm around, making me even jumpier.

"I don't know!" I shouted back, frustrated with myself as well as with Scott. "How am I supposed to know who's a real friend and who is taking advantage of me?"

"Use your brains! Work it out! Don't just walk around like some stupid..." Scott punched the locker beside me and I jumped.

"Some stupid what? Retard? Is that what you were going to say? Yeah, you're right, Scott. I'm nothing but some stupid retard who can't even tell the difference between a friend and an enemy!"

I slammed my locker door, yanked my lock through the hook, snapped it shut and viciously jerked it three times to make sure it was locked. Turning my back on Scott, I squared my shoulders and walked away.

Chapter Twenty-Two

THE PRETTY ROCKS

So close to losing control.

Emotion. The enemy. It was all around me. I was breathing it in and out with every breath. *Emotion.*

My heart pounded sickeningly. It felt like it was trying to break through my ribs and fly free. My pulse raced, leaving me dizzy and disoriented. I couldn't think straight. I couldn't answer when a teacher asked me a question. The bell rang and I jumped, letting out a scream before I could control it. I was Humpty Dumpty, in a million pieces at the base of the wall. I had to get away. I had to leave.

I stood up and walked out. I didn't even know what class it was, or which teacher I was walking out on. I was pushing open the heavy glass doors, leaving, going, when Scott caught me by the sleeve. I slapped away his hand.

"Casey, where are you going? You can't just walk out."

"I have to go home. I can't stay," I told him.

"Okay, okay. You have to get a dismissal slip at the office first. Here, I'll take you."

I let him lead me there. He talked to the secretary in the office then to my mom on the phone. Then he hung up and steered me toward the fresh air, away from the office and the noise of phones ringing and the clatter of keyboards and the smell of the principal's ugly cigars.

He tried to go the wrong way and I pointed to the right route home. We had to go the right way, or else I'd have to retrace my steps and go back alone. I walked ahead of him, pretending he wasn't there. He shouldn't be there, because I always walked home alone.

Partway home, I picked up a rock for Chelsea. I had been bringing her home a new one every day. She had quite a collection now, pink with quartz crystals.

"Casey? You can't just take that," Scott said as I slipped the rock into my knapsack.

"What? Why not?" I struggled to focus on his face. Why couldn't I take the rock?

"Because it belongs to someone," he said in a strange voice. He pointed to the neat line of rocks at the edge of the sidewalk. "Look—it's part of a border around this flower garden. This is someone's private property."

I swallowed hard. I hadn't noticed. I'd been taking a rock each day. I hadn't really looked far enough to see the flowers, purple asters and yellow chrysanthemums, or the neatly tilled black earth, or the small white stucco house that stood behind the flower garden. I hadn't noticed. I had only seen the rocks.

"Scott, I honestly didn't know. I sometimes pick up on details and miss the larger picture. I didn't know..."

"It's okay, Casey. Look—there's an old woman watching us from the window." He nodded in the direction of the house. A woman, her white hair tied up in a bun, her green and white flowered dress half hidden by a white apron, stood at the window. She smiled and waved.

"Oh, for cryin' out loud," I said. "Look at her. She thinks I'm mental, doesn't she?" I felt like dying. I wished I could sink beneath the black earth of the garden.

The woman disappeared. The front door opened. I got up to run away, but Scott grabbed me firmly by the arm and steered me toward the old woman.

"It's all right, deary," the old woman trilled in a high, wavery voice. "Your mom called me and explained. You can take all the pretty stones you need, child. I have a whole box of them in the basement."

My mom called? What's going on here?

I turned to look at Scott, searching for signals. Shock showed plainly on his face. It must have mirrored my own.

Chapter Twenty-Three

THE WALL COMES DOWN

"What did you tell that woman?" I demanded as I threw open the front door.

Mom walked out of the kitchen. "Casey, are you okay?" she asked, her face tight with worry. Then she saw Scott. "Oh, Scott. Thank you for bringing Casey home. I was so worried when you called from the school. What happened?"

Scott glanced at me, then back at my Mom. "It was all my fault, Mrs. Jackson. We had an argument before class and I called her stupid and...she started to fade out in class, you know? Staring off into space and rocking back and forth, humming to herself? Then she walked out, so I followed to make sure she'd be okay."

I cut in before Mom could reply. "What did you tell that old woman?" I asked again.

"Now, Casey, don't get all upset," Mom soothed. "I just told her that you liked to collect rocks, for Chelsea. I told her you sometimes forgot to ask permission, that's all."

She wasn't telling me the whole truth. I was about to ask, but then Scott said, "Chelsea? Whose she? Oh yeah, your little sister."

"Little sister?" Mom said to me. "You mean you haven't told him yet?"

"Told me what?" Scott asked, his eyes darting between Mom and myself.

"You have to go now, Scott," I said. "You should get back to school." I planted a hand on his back and pushed him toward the door. I had to get rid of him. I was on overload now, barely in control, and I had to get rid of him.

He swivelled around to face me. "No," he said. He tried to fold his arms across his chest, forgetting the cast, then settled for a half fold. "Not until you tell me what's going on here."

I wanted to yell, **get out**, but then someone beat me to it. Just as I was opening my mouth, filling my lungs with air, a screeching cry came from the kitchen.

Chelsea. I forgot about getting rid of Scott, forgot about the panic that was starting to blow me apart. Chelsea was in trouble.

"Now what?" Mom said in an exasperated voice. She turned and ran towards the screaming that kept on and on, rising in intensity and volume. I followed.

Chelsea was in the kitchen, frantically looking for something, a trail of opened drawers marking her progress. She came to the last one and yanked so hard it pulled out and fell on the floor. She sat down beside it, rocking and crooning, hunting through the spilled contents.

"What is she looking for?" Mom asked me.

I looked around, feeling like a detective at the scene of some crime, searching for clues. Chelsea's sketches were on the kitchen table, spread out around where she had been sitting. Her erasers and pencil sharpener were there too, lined up like soldiers in perfect rank. There should have been a row of pencils too, yellow with pink erasers, lying side by side, all sharpened to a deadly sharp point.

There was none. Nothing but a sad little stub of a pencil, its eraser rubbed down to a mere pink shred, its lead rounded and useless.

"Pencils," I answered. "Dad bought some last night. I bet he walked in the door, then got distracted and put them somewhere different. They should be here, in the top drawer where he always stores them, but they aren't."

Where would Dad have put them? I tried to think like Dad, walking in with new art supplies, then losing track of what he was doing. On an impulse, I checked the shelves above the computer desk. That's where I found them, three new boxes, neatly stacked where Chelsea would never have thought to look.

As soon as I handed Chelsea the box, she stopped rocking and took her seat at the table. She pulled out a pencil, sharpened it, and resumed her drawing of a great blue heron in flight.

Scott had followed us into the kitchen. He'd seen the whole thing. *So, now he'll turn and go,* I thought. *I'll never see him again, except maybe in passing at school.*

Chelsea's odd behavior made people nervous. They didn't like to be around her.

"What's her name?" he asked me softly.

I examined his expression closely before I answered, looking for the shock, the revulsion, the instinctive drawing back.

There was none. He looked surprised, yes, and curious, but also a little amused.

"Chelsea," I answered in a choked voice. I cleared my throat and lifted up my chin, meeting his gaze straight on. "Her name is Chelsea."

"Your younger sister, huh?" he asked. He was wearing his quirky grin. "You're twins, aren't you Casey?"

Amused? He's amused? I thought back, trying to trace the origin of his emotion. Oh, yes, I remembered. When he had been over before and I had tried to push him out the door because Mom and Dad and Chelsea were coming back in our red canoe. He had guessed that I had a younger sister in the canoe, one who would tease me about having a boy over to visit. At the time, I hadn't corrected him.

"Yes. But I'm two minutes older, so technically she is my younger sister," I defended myself.

"I see that," he grinned at me. The grin faded. "What's wrong with her?" he asked.

"Autistic," I said. "Lost in her own world."

"The rock is for her?" Scott asked, pulling it from my knapsack.

"Yes."

He walked over to the table, carrying the rock, and sat down beside Chelsea.

"Don't touch her," I warned. "She freaks out if you touch her." I was getting anxious again. I wanted him to leave. He didn't belong here. Chelsea belonged to Mom and Dad and me, not to Scott or the outside world.

"I wasn't going to," he said, looking into my eyes. Then he took the rock and slid it over the table so that Chelsea could see it. She picked it up and examined it closely. She turned it over and over, checking each angle, holding it to the light, then putting it under the table and peering at it there. Finally satisfied, she set it down on the table, within sight, within reach. Ever so briefly, so fast that you might have missed it if you weren't looking, she glanced at Scott, then glanced away.

"She knows I'm here," he smiled at me.

I sat down across from him. "She almost never does that, Scott, even to us." Something inside of me relaxed. It was like I had built a wall, made of huge field stones and dried mud, to keep the worlds separate. The wall had just fallen, and Chelsea was there and Scott was there and I was there and nothing bad had happened. Chelsea had let Scott in, into her own private universe, and nothing bad had happened. There didn't need to be a barrier between the worlds to keep Chelsea safe or to keep me safe.

133

It was a monstrous relief. I felt giddy with joy. I felt like I was a helium balloon, lifting off into the sky.

"She's awfully talented, Case. These sketches are as good as the ones Dad sells at the store. In fact, would you like me to show some to Dad? Maybe he could sell them on consignment for Chelsea."

"Who'd buy a sketch made by an autistic kid?" I asked.

"Who'd need to know?" Scott countered. "Besides, what difference would it make if they did know? She may be autistic, but that's not the sum total of her being, any more than my Dad being gay is the sum total of who he is. Chelsea is a talented artist. Her work speaks for itself, Casey."

"I guess it would be okay, if my parents agree," I said.

"Good," said Scott. "Are all autistic people this talented?"

"No," I answered, feeling much calmer now that Scott had accepted Chelsea. "Some are profoundly retarded, some have musical talents or a talent with numbers. One kid memorized all the call numbers of all the radio stations in the U.S., another can tell you the exact day of the week if you give him a year and month and day to figure out, some are human computers, able to do complex equations in their head."

"Wow. Amazing. I guess the mind compensates, huh?" he commented, watching as Chelsea sketched the heron's wing feathers.

"For the lucky ones," I said. "The unlucky ones can't even be toilet trained. Some bite their arms, pull out their hair, bang their heads. Some live in institutions because their families just can't care for them."

"I'd never do that. Hide someone away just because there's something wrong with him," Scott said. He reached across the table and squeezed my hand. It made me tremble, but I didn't pull away. After all, if Chelsea could let Scott into her world, I could let him set foot in mine.

There was a funny kind of silence that stretched on until I thought maybe someone should say something.

"Well, time for lunch," Mom said, breaking the awkwardness. "Chelsea, wash up now." She turned to Scott. "Would you like to stay, Scott?"

"Thanks, Mrs. Jackson," Scott smiled, "but I think I should get back to school."

Mom nodded. Chelsea gathered up her artwork into a neat pile and began to put everything away.

"How'd you teach her that?" Scott asked, watching her.

"Behavior modification," I explained. "You break the behavior into small steps, then reward her for each step."

"Rewards?"

"Yes. Positive reinforcements. Chelsea would do almost anything for arrowroot cookies."

"Wow. It must have been hard for you to teach her all that," he said.

"Not me. My parents did most of it, following the program put together by special tutors. Early on, the tutors came to the house to work with Chelsea, then my parents took over."

Scott asked if I wanted to come back to school, but I said I needed a break. He just nodded and said he'd come by the next day at one o'clock. I watched him walk down the three steps of our front porch and start down our stone driveway. Sudden fear gripped me. He was walking out of my world and I wondered if he would ever come back.

"Scott?" I called.

"Yeah?" He half turned to look at me.

"I'm different from her, Scott," I said. "I'm not like my sister."

He paused, just for a fraction of a second. I think my heart stopped as I waited for his reply.

"I know, my friend," he said. "I know." Then, it was as if he read my mind. "Listen, I'll be over at one tomorrow." He waved goodbye and was gone.

Chapter Twenty-Four

A MASTER OF RITUALS

It was one-thirty. He wasn't coming. I could feel it in my bones.

That pause, yesterday, a split of a split of a second, a nanosecond.

An eternity.

He knew. He knew everything.

And that's why he wasn't coming.

I sat on the porch, on the top step, my head in my hands. So very tired today. Up until three the night before, unable to sleep. Going through my collections, checking, checking...

Checking the house...the windows, fridge, stove, oven, toaster, kettle, iron, freezer, doors...checking every part of the house. Going through the entire ritual, knowing it was nothing but a stupid ritual, but unable to stop myself.

Just like Chelsea. She had rituals and routines, too. Keeping one hand on the wall as she walked through the house, only drinking from her old, cracked Bert and Ernie cup, only eating from the plate with the pink flowers around the edge, only using the black towels, tapping her fork three times on the plate before spearing a piece of food...my sister was a master of rituals.

I was becoming like her.

I was becoming like Chelsea and Scott somehow knew that and that's why he wasn't coming.

"Case! Wake up. I'm here!"

I jolted upright. Had I really fallen asleep? Scott skidded to a stop in front of me, spraying gravel all over the porch.

"Man, am I ever sorry!" he panted, standing awkwardly on one foot and booting his kickstand open with the other. "Dad made me re-arrange a whole stupid display of candles to make room for a shipment of soapstone. I woulda called, but I didn't realize the time till I started over here."

"That's okay," I told him.

"No, it's not okay," he said back. "I see it in your face. You thought that I wasn't coming, right? I hate it when you do this, Casey."

"Do what?" I asked.

"Hide your feelings! You're annoyed with me, but you won't say it. How can we be friends if you won't be straight with me?"

"We have to get to work," I said, ignoring his question. "We have a lot of research to do. I logged onto the Net already, so all we have to do is initiate a keyword search." I turned and entered the house. "I'd recommend we search 'ozone depletion' rather than 'ozone layer,' since..."

Scott followed me in and grabbed my arm. "Cut it out. If you're angry with me, just say so!"

I yanked my hand free. "I can't!" I choked out the words. "You don't understand, do you? I can't show my anger because if I do I'll lose control. Just like Chelsea!"

"So?" he shrugged. "Everyone loses it, now and then."

"Not like Chelsea," I argued. "What you saw yesterday was nothing. You have no idea what she can be like."

How could I show him? I didn't have the words to describe it. Then, I had an idea. "Follow me," I said, walking down the hall to my parent's bedroom. I remembered the tapes Mom had made of Chelsea's training sessions, a long time ago. She had shown me parts of them once. If Scott saw them, if he saw how truly bizarre Chelsea could be, maybe then he'd understand what scared me so much.

He stood up and followed me down the hall.

Chapter Twenty-Five

BLUE SMARTIES

"I know they're here somewhere," I mumbled, pushing aside boxes of loose photos, Mom's wedding gown, a set of moldy drapes, old tax records and a box of childish artwork. Finally, I found them in an unlabelled filing box at the back of the shelf.

"Here," I grunted, handing it down to Scott. "Mom is incredibly disorganized, but at least she labelled these with the year."

Back in the living room, I put in one of the tapes and hit the play button.

"Hmm, I don't think I've seen this one yet," I told Scott. It was Chelsea, at about age two, wearing a blue dress with little white daisies, seemingly oblivious to the camera. Her arms were held out from her body, hands up. She spun in the centre of the room, twirling on tip toes, face uplifted in rapture. She spun until she fell drunkenly on the deep blue carpet, giggling in a high pitched tone. Then, she stood up and spun. Spin, fall, giggle; spin, fall, giggle; the same pattern, repeated over and over.

"What does she do that?" Scott asked.

"Self-stimulation," I answered. "Autistics often engage in repetitive movement—rocking, flapping their hands in front of their faces, spinning, swinging on a swing—that sort of thing."

140

"Why?" Scott asked.

I shrugged. It was something Scott had taught me to do when I wasn't sure.

"Casey, I'm amazed! Something you haven't read about?" Scott said in mock horror.

"I guess it's too close to me, Scott. I've never really wanted to learn too much about it."

"Could we do a web search then? Find out more?" Scott asked. "This is really fascinating. Did I ever tell you that I want to be a psychologist someday? Either that or an actor. Can you imagine playing the part of an autistic?" He stood up and put his arms out, imitating Chelsea. He spun around, head uplifted...

"Cut it out!" I ordered. The sight of him acting like Chelsea really bothered me. It was bizarre. "Okay, come on—I'll do a stupid web search for you."

"Why are you so upset?" Scott asked, following me into the kitchen. We left the tape running and I could hear Chelsea giggle in the background as if Scott had said something wonderfully funny.

"I'm not," I replied.

"You're hiding your feelings again," he accused.

I grimaced. "All right! YES, it upsets me. Happy?"

"Uh-huh. I'm ecstatic. Why?"

"Why what?"

"Why does your sister's twirling upset you?"

"Because we're the same! Identical twins! With the same genetic code! So, don't you think I've asked myself, why is she like that and I'm not?"

"You're the lucky one, Case," Scott said. "Just because you have the same genetic make-up doesn't mean you'll turn out the same. When one twin is a homosexual, for example, the other twin has only a fifty percent chance of being gay as well. Environment is important, too."

"But we were born into the same environment. Same parents, same house, everything," I argued.

"By that argument, identical twins would always have identical personalities, right?"

"Yes. I suppose so."

"But, they don't. One likes to wear blue; the other likes pink. One twin loves broccoli; the other can't stand it. One is adventurous; the other more timid. Genetics only determines part of it. What happens after birth dictates the rest." He paused. "Jeez! What's that?"

"That is my sister," I said dryly. "See what I mean about loss of control?" Loud screeches were coming from the television. We craned our necks around the corner to see the screen. Chelsea was screaming on the tape, bloodcurdling, heart stopping screams. It sounded like someone was holding her hand over an open flame. I turned the sound off and we watched the silent movie unfold.

"What is she doing?" asked Scott.

"That's one of the teachers that taught us to use behavior modification with Chelsea. Her name is April. She tutored me with school subjects, too. Right here, she's trying to get Chelsea to sit in the chair. Mom told me that was the first step. To get her to sit still and make eye contact."

"Jeez," Scott said in a hushed tone. "What a battle."

That was putting it mildly. April, a slim girl with blonde hair tied back in a ponytail, gently set Chelsea on the chair. Chelsea, her mouth opening in a scream, slid down off the chair and landed on her bottom. April picked her up and again sat her down. Chelsea slid to the floor, screaming.

"I think this goes on for a while," I told Scott. "Let's do that web search and keep the tape running. We can check later to see what's happening."

"Okay. So, how's this work?" Scott asked, sitting down at the computer. I dragged another chair over to sit down beside him.

I showed him how to connect to the Net and do a search under "autism."

"This is awesome," Scott said, following my instructions. A long list of documents appeared on the screen.

"Now, choose a document and click on it," I instructed.

"Hey! Here it comes." Scott was almost bouncing up and down in excitement. The document, originating from a research institute for autism, appeared on screen.

"Did Chelsea ever talk?" Scott asked, staring at the computer and reading.

"Yes. She started at the same time as me, but by about age two she started losing words," I answered.

"Did she prefer to play alone?'

"Yes."

"Inability to form meaningful social relationships," Scott said. "How about this one? Seems indifferent to the presence of others."

"Yes."

"Asks for help when she was upset or hurt?"

"No, never. If something upset her, she'd go into a tantrum. Trying to hold or comfort her made it worse."

"Okay. How about inappropriate emotional responses. You know, like giggling for no reason, or being aggressive towards herself or others?"

"Yes, both," I answered.

"Any repetitive body movement?" Scott asked.

"Like rocking, twirling, hand flapping?" I said. "Yes, she still does, in fact."

"Unusual responses to sensory stimuli?" Scott continued.

"What does that mean?"

"I don't know. Senses—like sound, sight, touch, I guess. Any odd reactions?"

144

I had to think about that one. "Well, she hated loud, unexpected noises, like a train whistle or police siren. She'd run and hide in the closet and sit there, rocking back and forth, humming in this strange, monotonous voice."

"Yeah, that's it," Scott said. "This article says autistics may be oversensitive to some stimuli, like sounds or sights. In fact, it's thought that they engage in repetitive movements to block out a barrage of stimulation...it gives them one, steady, predictable thing to focus on."

"So, that's why she twirls or rocks?" I asked.

"Maybe," Scott answered. "It sure is bizarre."

"Yes," I agreed. The tape had ended in the living room. I inserted a new one. "Hey, Scott, come here. Here's a tape with me on it."

Scott sat beside me on the couch.

"I'm about two and a half here," I said excitedly. "Mom told me about this, but I had no idea she'd caught it on tape. Told you I learned to read at an early age."

I was standing in front of the fridge playing with brightly colored alphabet magnets. I watched as my younger self spelled out words—Nabisco, Quaker, Kraft, Coke. Words I saw every day. I reached up with a pudgy hand and put a K on the fridge, followed by an O. Plopping down on the floor unceremoniously, I looked in a shoe box of letters for the next one. I began to whimper as I searched more and more frantically. Finally, I threw the box across the room, screaming in frustration.

145

"Casey, what's wrong honey?" said a younger, darker haired version of my mother. I kept screaming, ignoring her question. I lay down on the floor and began to bang my heels on its hard surface. I was thrashing around, tossing my head from side to side, screaming and screaming.

"Talk about the terrible two's," Scott said in a hushed tone that approached awe.

"I remember this, Scott! I wanted to spell Kool-aid, but I couldn't. I only had one set of letters. Once I calmed down, I took a package of Kool-Aid out of the cupboard and gave it to Mom. She ran out the very same day and bought two more sets of letters so that I wouldn't get frustrated again. I remember."

A new segment appeared. "Back to Chelsea again," I said.

"But, she's in a pink dress," Scott said. "You told me she only wore blue."

"She must have developed that preference later," I said. "It's definitely her. Look at her. She's staring off into space, not even looking at April. It's got to be Chelsea." April was talking. "Put the pictures in the right order," she said.

"Hey! April used to do that with me, too!" I said.

Chelsea stood in front of a bulletin board, arranging pictures. "Good girl!" April said, and handed her a treat.

"What'd she give her?" Scott asked.

"Don't know," I said in a distracted voice. A feeling of 'déjà vu' came over me. Had I seen this tape before?

"That's right," April said to Chelsea. "The bird builds the nest first, then lays the eggs, then feeds the baby birds."

The memory danced mockingly just out of reach. Why did this seem so familiar? The birds, the nest... Ah ha! I had it! My dream! April had used the same picture sequence to teach me about... About what? Sequencing? Story telling? I wasn't sure.

New tape segment, some time later. Another set of pictures. "Good girl!" April said. "The child dropped her doll. The doll broke. She took it to Mommy to get fixed. That's right! Now, tell me, how did the girl feel when the doll broke?"

Chelsea hesitated. I could almost feel her anxiety as if it were my own. Sweat trickled down my face. The blood pounded in my temples. The room was too hot, too close.

"What did the girl feel?" April insisted.

"I don't know," Chelsea answered.

"She was sad," said April.

"Sad," echoed Chelsea. She turned away.

"No!" April ordered sharply. "Look at me."

Chelsea turned back and looked at her.

"Why was the girl sad?" April asked.

"I don't know!" Chelsea said, much louder. You could tell she was getting agitated. Her hands rose in front of her, flapping, flapping, like the wings of a captive bird.

"No!" said April calmly. "Control yourself! Tell me why the girl was sad."

"I don't know, I don't know, I don't know..." Chelsea screamed. She began to pound on the bulletin board in her fury, her fists slamming it again and again.

"Stop! Get control," April commanded. Struggling with her anger, the wild girl, the crazy, bizarre, autistic girl, dropped her arms and turned away from the board. She turned towards the camera.

"I thought you said she lost all her words, Casey," Scott said. I looked at him. His eyes were dark grey, worried. "She did," I told him.

"Then why...?" He left the question hanging. I felt my heart slow and then stop. It turned to glass and then I felt it shatter into a million tiny shards. The girl on the screen was rocking back and forth, shaking, flapping her hands and then stopping, then flapping again, stopping...finally she got control of herself.

"Good girl," April praised her warmly. "Here's a Smartie. Good girl for calming down. Very good control."

April handed the girl a treat. A round colored candy. A Smartie. The girl looked at it. Abruptly, she screeched and threw the Smartie at the wall.

"Why the heck did she do that?" Scott asked.

"It was a blue Smartie," I whispered. "I always hated the blue ones."

Chapter Twenty-Six

THE SAME DIFFERENCE

"Casey? *Casey!* Don't shut me out like this. You're scaring me."

"Go away, Scott. I want to be left alone."

"*No!* Don't you see that's the worst thing for you right now? Come on, Casey...I'm not the enemy here!"

"Well, you aren't my friend, either," I said. "Autistics can't make friends, remember? Inability to form meaningful social relationships."

"Casey, you aren't autistic." Scott sat down beside me. I was outside, sitting on our big three-person swing overlooking the water, trying to shut out the world.

"Oh, really, Scott?" I said. "Just what am I then? You saw the tape. That was *me*, not my sister. *Me!*"

"*So?* So you had some problems. You overcame them."

"You don't 'overcome' autism, Scott. You read the articles. There's something wrong with my brain. Once an autistic, always an autistic."

"*No!* That's what I'm trying to tell you. Look, while you've been out here rocking..."

"Classic self-stimulatory behavior..." I interrupted.

"Shut up, Casey! You don't fit the description. You have Asperger's Syndrome, not autism!" He said the words triumphantly, as if they meant something important.

"It doesn't matter what you call it, Scott. I've got it, and it's been getting worse. Would you like to hear about my own rigid adherence to routine, my own little rituals? I check under my bed for monsters each night, you know."

"Me too," Scott said. He took my hand in his. I snatched it away.

"Liar."

"It's true. I used to, anyway."

"'Used to' doesn't count. I still check under the bed, in the closet, in my dresser. Then, I go around the house, checking every single door and window, the stove, the iron, the kettle, the toaster, the VCR, the computer. *everything!* I touch each thing and repeat to myself 'this is turned off' or 'this is unplugged.' And the worse thing is, if I get out of order or miss something, I have to go back and *do it all over again!*"

"Lots of people check that the house is secure before going to bed, Case," Scott said, sounding a little less sure of himself.

"Yeah, sure. And do lots of people have to take the exact route home every day? Do they? Do they time themselves exactly on each leg of the trip? Do they color code their subjects at school and tug their locks exactly three times, no more and no less, when closing their lockers?"

I hated the rising hysteria in my voice, but I couldn't seem to control it. *Aggression,* I thought. *Inappropriate emotional responses. Autistic as the day I was born.*

"Casey, *look* at me!" There was real anger in Scott's voice. Like the day I'd left him at the edge of the school yard to face Carl alone. I looked at him.

"Just listen, for one minute," he said.

"Hurry up," I replied coldly. "Clock's ticking."

"You see?" He shouted at me. "You never would have said something like that, even three weeks ago. You may have been born with a problem, but you *can* overcome it. In fact, it says so, right here. People with Asperger's can learn social skills just like someone learns to play a musical instrument. Here, look at this! I printed this stuff from an article about Asperger's." He thrust a pile of papers at me. I waved them away.

"Fine…I'll tell you what they say. Here's the description from the *Diagnostic and Statistical Manual of Mental Disorders,* fourth edition," he said.

"Oh great. Mental disorder. Isn't that nice."

"Shut *up!* Okay—impairment in social interaction, as shown by at least two of the following: lack of non-verbal behavior, for example, eye contact, facial expression and gestures; inability to form age-appropriate peer relationships; lack of sharing interests with others; lack of social or emotional reciprocity."

"Well, that explains why I didn't react with the appropriate show of caring when you broke your arm," I grimaced.

"Agreed."

"Thanks for the vote of confidence," I said in a grating voice.

"No prob," he replied, ignoring the sarcasm. "Now, listen. The second category has to do with restricted, repetitive and stereotyped patterns of behavior, interests and activities," he continued.

"No need to go on. I've got that one covered, big time," I said.

"Shut..."

"Yeah, yeah...*up,* " I added.

"Right! Okay—the diagnosis calls for one of the following: preoccupation with one or more restricted patterns of interests..."

"Like memorizing the entire book of world records," I said. "Do you think that counts, Scott?"

He ignored me. "Routines or rituals?"

"Guilty as charged," I said. "You ought to see the 'going to bed ritual.' It's a beauty."

"Pre-occupation with parts of objects," read Scott.

153

"Not guilty," I shot back.

"Repetitive movements," he said.

"Like Chelsea flapping her hands? Definitely not guilty!"

"Uh...actually, Casey, you do."

"Do what?" I snapped.

"Repetitive movements," he said, looking sheepish.

"Name one!"

"Look at your hands."

"What?"

"Look at what you are doing with your hands," he said, reluctantly.

I looked down at my right hand. I was touching each finger in turn to my thumb, index, middle, ring, baby, over and over. "A nervous habit," I defended myself.

"You do it all the time," he said quietly. "People have commented on it to me. It's more than just a nervous habit."

"*Fine!* All this proves is that I *am* autistic, which is what I've been trying to *tell* you."

"Not autistic. Asperger's Syndrome."

"What's the difference?" I yelled at him.

"Well...no one seems quite sure. Some articles I read said that a person with Asperger's Syndrome is just functioning at the upper end of the autistic spectrum. Others claim it's a different disorder altogether. The important thing is that there are major differences between someone diagnosed as autistic and someone diagnosed as having Asperger's."

"Name one!"

"I'll name several," he said. "No language delay, right?"

"True."

He nodded. "Okay—so autism involves a delay in language, or, like your sister, a total lack of language skills. Now, it's estimated that seventy to eighty percent of autistic kids are retarded. You are not."

"Right. Tell that to the kids at school," I snorted.

"You are *not* retarded. Like many Asperger kids you have no delay in cognitive development. In fact, people with Asperger's are often very successful. They are seen as extremely smart, somewhat eccentric, absent minded and socially awkward. Like your father."

I sat bolt upright and looked him straight in the face. "What do you mean, 'like my father'?"

"You said he was a computer genius, right?"

"Yes. He told me he was a computer nerd at school."

"My point exactly."

"And what exactly *is* your point?" I shouted.

"It's genetic! Most people with Asperger's disorder have a parent, almost always the father, who meets some, or all, of the criteria for a positive diagnosis. You said he keeps to a rigid schedule, right?"

"So what?"

"Sounds a bit rigid in his routines to me, kiddo," Scott said. "And the passion for gardening? His intense preoccupation with old movies?"

"So? Lots of people watch old movies," I defended.

"Yeah, right. And do all the voices, and know all the dialogue by heart and all the songs? I bet he has your memory, too."

"I guess so."

"Well then…" Scott said maddeningly.

"Will you quit doing that?" I exploded. "Well then *what?*"

"I proved it!" he said, waving his good arm around. "You have Asperger's, like your Dad. You are brilliant, single minded, focussed in your interests, possess a phenomenal memory and will probably excel at any occupation you choose, as long as it doesn't involve a lot of people contact."

"Oh, great," I snarled. "Just dandy. I am also socially inept, unable to make friends, the laughing stock of the whole school, completely unaware when someone is taking advantage of me, too sensitive to sounds and sights and smells, easily distracted, totally dependent on rituals to

156

make it through the day, absolutely overwhelmed by anxiety most of the time, and unable to control my *emotions!*"

"Well, no one's perfect," he grinned.

"Easy for you to say!" I shouted. "Nothing's wrong with you. You have things easy! You can't even imagine how I feel!"

"Give me a chance, Casey. I want to understand." Scott touched my arm and I pulled away.

"Remember? We autistics don't like to be touched," I said sarcastically. "I want you to go now."

"I'm not going until your parents come home," Scott shook his head.

"Suit yourself. Just don't expect me to talk to you. In fact, don't expect me to talk to anyone, ever again. We autistics have trouble with communication skills, remember?"

"Fine. Have it your way. Play the part for all it's worth, Casey. Poor little autistic girl. Just don't expect me to be there when you finally come to your senses."

I couldn't stand the mocking tone in his voice. It hurt, deep down where I didn't want to hurt. I wanted to hurt him back but I couldn't think of the words.

So, I hit him, catching him square across the face.

That's when he left.

Chapter Twenty-Seven

LIKE FATHER, LIKE DAUGHTER

The loons were keeping me company, as I sat on the bench swing in our gazebo near the water. There were two of them, floating by on a glass-like lake, throwing their heads back and sharing some fine avian joke. Maybe they were laughing at me. Maybe they were just crazy.

"This is a fine mess you got us into, Ollie," said my father in his Stan Laurel voice. He sat down beside me on the swing.

I didn't answer him.

Autumn fog hung low over the water, like the veil that had covered my past. Mom came out, bringing a platter of pizza for dinner, then left us alone.

"You were so beautiful when you were born," Dad said. He spoke quietly, as if to himself. "You and your sister. We called you our little angels."

"We loved you both, so very much. Especially me. Your mom had always taken it for granted that she would do the usual thing—you know, get married, have a career, have babies." He made a funny sound, like a choked laugh. "Though, I guess she lost out on the career part, once the problems with Chelsea started."

Back and forth moved the swing. Shaded by the gazebo, we watched the setting sun break apart on the waves.

"Me, though…for me it was different," Dad was saying. "When you were born, it was a miracle. I know that's what you're supposed to say, but for me it was true. I had never dared to hope for the normal things like marriage or children."

He offered me the pizza and I took a slice. Being upset had never hurt my appetite.

"Did I ever show you my high school yearbook picture, Casey? Lordy, lord. Big, square black-rimmed glasses, center parted hair that always fell into my eyes, spaced out expression…they must have invented the word 'geek' just for me.

"What your mother ever saw in me, I don't know. She said I was crazy, always talking in voices…she thought it was funny. I've never told her that I didn't have real speech until I was about six years old. I repeated everything I heard, though, using phrases and bits of dialogue and song to get my point across. My parents thought I was unusual, but that's about all. They were proud of me, of the way I taught myself to read when I was only four."

His voice changed. It wavered and almost broke on the next words. "I'm so sorry, sweetheart. I would have told you earlier, but your mother said no. 'If she believes she is normal, she will become normal,' your mother said. You progressed so much with special teachers and behavior modification. Not like your sister. She'll never be whole…"

His voice went funny, and I knew he was crying. I would have comforted him, but I didn't know how.

The tears flowed in silence down my cheeks, tears for my father and my sister and myself.

Chapter Twenty-Eight

SHARED HEARTBEATS

I spent the next day, Sunday, with Chelsea. It was a warm Indian summer day, so we spent most of our time down by the water, at our tiny sand beach.

Chelsea spent an entire hour watching little waves lap onto shore. Only I knew what she was seeing. Most people would glance down and see only waves. But Chelsea felt the calm rhythm of the clear water moving back and forth across the sand. She saw each grain, grey and white and orange and clear. Like snowflakes, no two were alike. The water flowed over them, rolled them against each other, carried some in and some out, infinitely patient, infinitely unvarying and constantly variable.

In a way, her world was intensely beautiful and calm. It wasn't such a bad place to be.

In the afternoon, Chelsea sketched while I brought out all of my collections. There were rocks, gems, beads, dried flowers, bird's feathers, bits of glass, scraps of wool, ripped shreds of wrapping paper, buttons, and, last but not least, my shoelace collection. They called to me with their dusty voices, demanding to be set free. I pulled them all out of their boxes and arranged them neatly on the table I shared with my sister.

Chelsea reached over and picked up a blue jay feather, placing it beside the sketch she was doing. I glanced at the sketch. It was a blue jay, sitting at a bird feeder, cracking a sunflower seed. It occurred to me that my twin wasn't as oblivious to the world as everyone thought. She just interacted with it differently.

After dinner, I played a spinning game with Chelsea. We took a coin and spun it on the table, watching as it twirled, ever different, ever the same.

Just like my sister and I.

I slept with her again that night, observing the way my breathing changed to match her own.

It was almost like being together again, in the womb.

Our shared heartbeats rocked us to sleep.

Chapter Twenty-Nine

FREE

There was a freedom in being autistic. I felt the freedom in the beating of my heart and in the blood that ran like quicksilver through my veins.

When I woke up, it was to a new world. The anxiety was gone. I didn't have to fear being like my sister because I WAS like her. I didn't need the rituals to keep my world in order because I'd made a new order of the world. I didn't have to worry about being liked, or fitting in at school, because I knew I'd never fit in and would never be liked. I no longer had to worry about losing Scott as a friend because I'd already lost him.

I felt like a canary with an open cage door.

I went to school, because I liked to learn new things, not because that's what normal kids did. I didn't have to show off my knowledge, or speak to anyone. If I wanted to get lost in the contemplation of a dust mote in the sunlight, I could. In fact, I got lost in a lot of things, listening to the rhythm and pitch of my teacher's voice rather than the words in English class, doodling in Math class and counting my breaths in History class.

The teachers didn't bother me. Mom had probably called to explain what was going on.

Scott approached me Monday at lunchtime, to ask in a tentative voice if I wanted a tutoring lesson. I ignored him and he went away.

On Wednesday, my English teacher asked if I had finished my autobiography. I looked down at the floor and counted on my fingers, one, two, three, four, while she talked. Then she broke in, saying my name sharply, just like my old teacher April used to do. I wondered if Mom had told her to do that.

She asked again if my autobiography was done, so I showed her the folder with my typed notes. She said the work was fine and that she hoped I could do my presentation in class on Friday, as planned.

I didn't have to answer. I think she already knew that I didn't plan to do it. I left the school and started on the route home, feeling curiously light.

Free.

Chapter Thirty

EMOTION IS THE KEY

I took the path behind the school as usual, leading to Sixth Street. The trees had changed almost overnight and shone yellow against a blue fall sky. I stood for a moment beneath one, looking up to lose myself among the changing pattern of leaves in the breeze.

A voice, coming from a short distance behind me, brought me back to earth. A whiny, grating voice that made the hairs stand up on my arms. *Carl.*

I picked up my pace, hoping to reach the safety of the street before he caught up with me. The path led through the forest, over a small rocky creek, up over a rock cropping and onto Sixth Street. It was only a three minute walk, but today it stretched endlessly in front of me.

As usual, I had waited until the rush hour was over and the other students were long gone. Now I regretted it and wished there were a crowd of people with me. I suddenly felt very alone and vulnerable.

Whirring of gears. Bikes. Voices, Carl's and two or three others. Heart pounding, I ran.

"Casey!" Carl called as he pedalled within sight. "Wait up. I want to talk to you."

His voice sounded friendly. I hesitated, confused. That was a mistake. He caught up and pushed past, skidding

165

to a stop a few feet ahead of me. I looked back. Telephone Pole and Marshmallow Boy blocked the way.

For a crazy moment, I wrestled with the impulse to curl up into a ball and pretend they didn't exist. I had done that when I was little, imagining that if I only tried hard enough I could make the world disappear for awhile. Chelsea still did it. I had a feeling, however, that it wouldn't work for me. Not this time.

Carl leaned his bike against a birch tree and sauntered up to me. His hair fell in greasy strands over one eye. He was smiling, but I didn't trust him.

"You've been avoiding me, haven't you?" Carl said. His voice grated on my nerves, like chalk on a blackboard. I tried to go around him, to continue on my way, but he reached out an arm and blocked me. I jumped back to avoid contact.

"I thought we were friends, Casey," he whined. "What happened?"

I didn't have to answer. But, he wasn't going to let me go unless I did. I considered just standing there, like stone, until he went away, but then my anger got the better of me.

"We were never friends, Carl," I spit out. "You were just using me. You only talked to me because I agreed to do your homework."

"You have it all wrong, babe," Carl said in an oily voice. "Is that what Scott told you? Don't you see what's going

166

on here? He just didn't want you to have any other friends, that's all. He wanted to keep you all to himself."

I stared at the ground, trying to make sense of what Carl said. *Can he be right? Can Scott have been jealous of my other friends? How well do I really know Scott, anyway? Everyone knew I'm a lousy judge of character. Maybe Scott has only been my peer buddy and never my friend.*

Then, something Scott had said came back to me. *Trust your feelings, Casey. Trust your emotions.* My emotions told me I didn't like Carl. He made me feel bad inside.

"Listen, babe," Carl was saying, "you just agree to go back to our old arrangement and nothing bad will happen to you, okay?" He moved very close, so close I could smell the reek of smoke on his breath. I wanted to scream.

"Nothing bad WILL happen, Carl, as long as I'm here," said a voice from behind me. It was Scott. Had he followed me home to keep an eye on me, or was it a coincidence that he had arrived just now? Either way, I was glad to see him. He pushed past Carl's friends, Telephone Pole and Marshmallow Boy, and came to stand beside me. He took my hand in his own and for once I didn't pull away.

"Leave her alone, Carl," Scott said evenly. "Let her go now."

"You gonna make me, queer?" Carl sneered. He reached out and pushed Scott. Scott stumbled, thrown off balance by his arm in the sling. His face was red, his jaw set in

167

anger. His eyes were fixed on Carl as he said to me, "Casey, I want you to go now. Just turn around and walk home, okay?"

"But what about you?" I asked, confused.

"I'll be along in a little while," he said. "Carl and I have something to talk about first."

I walked away slowly, looking back once or twice before the twisting path obscured my view. They were standing almost chest to chest, Scott glaring up at the taller Carl. Neither of them was saying anything.

Something felt wrong. I was shaking from the rush of adrenaline, my legs trembling so hard that I could barely walk. I didn't understand what was going on. Why did Scott tell me to go home alone? Why did I have a feeling of dread, of something very bad about to happen?

Something bothered me about walking away and leaving Scott there with Carl and his two buddies. Something about the situation was *wrong*.

Emotion. Control it, I thought. *The enemy, clouding the mind, eroding rational thought. Emotion.*

But emotion is the key. Scott had said that.

Trust it, he had said.

I turned and started back. I heard a sound as I got closer, a dull thud, followed by a grunt. Another thud, another grunt. My heart began a runaway rhythm. I rounded a turn in time to see Carl punch Scott in the stomach. Thud. Grunt. Scott's arms were pinned behind his back by

Marshmallow Boy and Telephone Pole. Telephone Pole tightened his grip, pulling Scott upright, and I saw Scott's face twist in pain as his injured arm was yanked tight behind him.

Carl punched him again. Thud. Scott grunted.

I wanted to run away. I wanted to run away and hide. They were hurting Scott, and Scott was my friend, and I wanted to run away so that I wouldn't see.

The emotions were too overwhelming. Rage and fear washed over me. Carl was a coward. He was beating up on a person who had one arm in a sling and had his arms pinned behind his back. He was calling Scott names, bad names, saying he was weak and a coward. But that was wrong! Carl was the coward, not Scott.

I lost control. I couldn't help it. I felt reason leave me, felt myself act without thought, watched myself launch my body down the path, leap onto Carl's back and wrap one arm around his neck. With my free hand, I clawed at his face, as hard as I could.

Carl yelled and threw himself backwards so that we fell awkwardly, with me hitting the ground first. He twisted quickly, full of a strength that caught me by surprise. Another quick movement, and Carl had both my hands pinned in one of his. I tried to wriggle free, but his hand was like a band of iron around my wrists. He pulled his free hand back and slapped my face.

It hurt! I was furious at the sudden pain and the humiliation. *How dare he? That slime bucket, that low-life excuse for a...*

I screamed my rage. Yanking my hands toward me, I bit deeply into his wrist, the one holding my hands together. He roared and tried to push my head away, but I bit deeper, grinding my teeth together, tasting blood.

He let go of my wrists, howling in pain and sucking at the blood that ran down his arm.

I wanted to kill him. I wanted to kill him for touching me, for holding me against my will, for hitting me. I grabbed a rock that lay in the path, and threw it like a baseball, aiming at his head. He ducked it, screaming something about crazy retards. He backed up, stumbled over a tree root, and fell, swearing. I watched him scramble for his bike, and took a fierce satisfaction in heaving another rock at him. It hit him square in the back and he yelled again, but kept pedalling.

Scott! I had forgotten all about him. I grabbed up a rock and wheeled around, ready to defend him. But, it appeared he didn't need my help.

I'd forgotten about the tae kwon do. It seemed that the use of two arms was not necessary when both legs were free for action. Marshmallow Boy, I mean Jason, was already getting on his bike. I jumped aside, into a raspberry bramble, as he pushed past me on the path. Scott aimed a kick at Kyle, Telephone Pole, catching him in the side. Telephone Pole howled and dropped, scuttling backwards, crab-like, to escape. Scott let him go, and Telephone Pole followed his buddies through the bushes to safety.

Scott was breathing hard. He sunk down onto a rock and I rushed to join him.

"Are you okay?" I gasped.

"I'm fine," he grinned back. "When you bit Carl, they were so surprised they relaxed their grip on me and I got loose. With Carl out of the way it was more of a fair fight. Thanks for coming back, Casey."

"No problem. It didn't feel right to leave you."

"Didn't feel right? Feelings, Casey? You trusted your feelings? Not very logical of you."

"Shut up!" I said. Scott laughed. I did too, but then for some strange reason my laughing turned to crying. Once I started I couldn't stop. I was out of control again, sobbing like a little kid. It was like a storm had taken possession of me, like a hurricane that had to be endured because it could not be stopped.

It terrified me. I'd done the thing I'd promised myself I would never do. I'd lost control, not once but twice. *Just like Chelsea,* said a voice in my head.

No, not just like Chelsea, I fought back. *Different.* Even though I was gasping and crying and hiccuping, there was a small part of me that was still rational, still logical. It was possible to let go completely, to be swept away by a storm of violent emotion and still maintain a small measure of control.

I was different. And that difference meant I could do things my twin would never do, like have a friend to watch over me and for me to watch over.

Scott sat with me in the hard packed dirt, rocking gently, comforting me with the strength of his arms and the warmth of his body and the sound of his beating heart.

Chapter Thirty-One

YOU SHOULDA SEEN THE OTHER GUY

"Casey, what happened? I *knew* I shouldn't have let you go back," Mom exclaimed when she saw us limping down the gravel lane to our front door.

"Hey Mom, stop sweating. You shoulda seen the other guy!" I called to her. For some reason, that struck Scott and me both as extremely funny. I knew it was just an expression, a really old expression at that, but it seemed so perfect somehow. We both howled with laughter. Scott slapped me on the shoulder, and I slapped him right back, laughing all the more. He grimaced, and I winced.

"Oh, Scott. Did I hurt you? I'm sorry. I forgot about the arm. Are you okay?" I was babbling, and I knew it, but I really hadn't meant to hurt him. His arm must be throbbing like mad, after being twisted like that behind his back, and here I was, like some idiot, slapping that shoulder and jarring it...

"No prob, Casey," Scott grinned at me. "I'm one tough character. Not as tough as you, but I'm no baby myself."

I smiled back. His face looked open and happy now, his eyes warm, grey with shining gold spokes in them. He was looking at me now, with those eyes, with admiration and caring. I could see it clearly. I didn't know how I could have missed it before.

"What is going on here?" Mom demanded. "Casey, your shirt is all dirty and torn. You're arms are covered in scratches. Are you okay?"

"Sure, Mom," I said cheerfully. "I guess Carl pushed me into some raspberry brambles, and I scratched myself."

"Who is Carl?" she asked, her voice rising an octave.

Scott took over then, explaining briefly and factually, leaving out the part about me losing control completely, trying to brain poor stupid Carl with a rock and then falling apart into a million tiny pieces once the fight was over.

"I'm calling the police," Mom announced, heading for our front door.

"No, please, Mrs. Jackson, don't," Scott pleaded. "That might just make it worse for us at school."

"But, I can't just let him go," Mom protested.

"Don't worry, Mom," I reassured her. "Carl won't bother us again, right Scott?"

Scott grinned and gave me a thumbs up sign with his good hand.

"Good thing Scott was there to save you," Mom said. "If he hadn't happened by…"

"I didn't save her, Mrs. Jackson. Casey did all the saving. She was amazing!"

Mom looked alarmed. "What did you do to him?"

"I bit him," I said, not even trying to keep the satisfaction out of my voice. "He was beating up on my friend. I couldn't let him do that, could I, Mom?"

Mom's face kept shifting, like a chameleon. Wonder, fear, joy, amazement...she didn't know which to settle on.

"It's okay, Mom," I said. "I'm okay." Then, I did a thing I had never done before. I wrapped my arms around her in a big hug. Then, she did a thing I'd never seen her do before.

She cried.

Chapter Thirty-Two

ONLY WHEN I LAUGH

Reaction set in a little later, when I was out in the gazebo with Scott, drinking lemonade and eating ginger snaps. I wondered if prize fighters felt this way after victory. A feeling of letdown. It was paradoxical.

I talked to Scott about it and was surprised to find out he felt the same. Sort of sad. Tired. Wanting to sleep.

"Listen, Scott," I said. "About the other day. When I hit you..."

"It's nothing, Casey," he waved away my halting apology. "It's already forgotten."

But I couldn't let it go. "Scott, I didn't know how much it hurt, not until Carl hit me. I mean, you see it all the time, in movies, where someone slaps someone else, and you don't, I mean I didn't, think anything much of it. But, when I hit you, and your head snapped to the side like that, and I heard the sound of my hand hitting you...I didn't know that's what it was like, Scott, honest."

"It's okay, Case. I understand," Scott said.

"No, let me finish. I didn't know it would hurt you so much."

"Casey, even you don't slap that hard!"

176

"No, I mean hurt your feelings. I saw the look in your eyes, Scott. Like you'd been betrayed. I chose to ignore it at the time, but I want you to know I saw it, and I'm sorry for putting it there."

He set down his cup of lemonade carefully on the bedrock beneath the swing and took my hand. I shivered, but didn't pull away. "I accept your apology, Casey," he said softly. "I'm just glad I have you as a friend and not an enemy."

"Me too. I'm glad to have you for my friend, Scott," I said. I watched as the color rose up his neck and into his cheeks. Then, I did a thing that amazed me. I reached up and put my hand on his cheek, just to feel the heat of the blush. It made him go even redder.

Footsteps on the gravel path to the gazebo. I snatched away my hand and Scott let go of my other one, and we sat there like blushing idiots as Dad rounded the side of the structure.

"So, pilgrim, I hear ya' taught the bad guys a real lesson," he drawled, planting his thumbs in his belt.

"John Wayne," I whispered to Scott. He nodded.

"Are you okay, sweetheart?" Dad then asked in his own voice.

"Never felt better, Dad," I said. "Just kinda tired right now."

Dad nodded. "And you Scott?"

"Only hurts when I laugh, sir," Scott said. I giggled. Another old line, but in this case it was true. Every time

Scott laughed it hurt his diaphragm, where Carl had landed several heavy punches. Scott started to laugh too, then groaned and clutched at his middle.

Dad just shook his head. I suddenly realized he didn't get the joke. He didn't understand.

But I did. Scott had taught me.

"Listen, sweetheart," Dad said, "your Mom and I have been talking. I think she's right. Maybe school is a bad idea, for right now at least. We wouldn't want anything like this to happen again."

My reaction surprised me. "Wrong, Dad. School is exactly where I belong. With other kids, like myself." Then, I hesitated. "Well, sort of like myself."

"Exactly," agreed Scott. "Different isn't always a bad thing. Sometimes different is just different."

I knew then that Scott really was my friend. Maybe he always had been and I just hadn't known how to recognize one.

Chapter Thirty-Three

LIKE MUSIC TO MY EARS

"I was born on January first. It was snowing."

I looked up at the class. They were bored. I could tell. They were looking down at their notes or at their feet or leaning back with their eyes closed. Bored. It gave me a thrill to look at them and know how they were feeling.

Scott winked at me. We had worked for hours the previous night, writing out cue cards for my speech, working on my gestures and rehearsing. I was scared, but ready.

"I was one half of a set of twins," I continued. Several people looked up, interested.

"You are probably wondering why I am at school and my twin is not," I said. That was a line Scott had given me. He said it was an 'attention getter.'

He was right. Half the class was looking at me now.

"Here is my twin," I told them. I slipped a tape into the VCR and hit 'play.' It was Chelsea, at the age of three. I had chosen a session with her teacher, one where the teacher was trying to establish eye contact and Chelsea was not cooperating. She looked at the floor, flapped her hands, screamed and squirmed—in fact, did just about everything except look at the teacher.

I turned the tape off. Every single set of eyes in the classroom was trained on me now. Most of them looked interested, except for Carl, who wore a sullen, angry face.

"I had always been told that my sister and I were different. I grew up believing that my sister was autistic and I was not.

"This was only partly true. My sister is autistic. She was born that way. She has learned a lot of useful things, mostly through behavior modification, but she will never be normal. She will never hold up her side of a conversation or ask you how you are doing today. In fact, the people in her world are objects, no more alive to her than a piece of furniture.

"I guess, compared to her, I am pretty normal."

I paused. Scott nodded at me. The class was silent, leaning forward in their seats.

"But compared to you," I continued, "I am very different. You see, I see things differently from you. For example, look out the window. What do you see?" I asked.

"Trees," someone shouted.

"Clouds," came another response.

"Telephone poles." "Buildings." "An airplane." "People." "Cars." "A bus."

"Anything else?" I asked.

No answers.

I smiled. Scott told me I had to smile during the presentation, so I had put it down on my cue card. 'Smile.'

"I see the frame of the window," I told them, "made of old dark wood. It glows a deep red where the sun hits it. I can see every line of the grain. I see the glass of the window, and the wooden strips that divide it into squares. In one square, there is a branch of quaking aspen. The leaves have turned the color of a school bus. They twist on the branch, and I see one side is shinier than the other. There's a bird on the branch, a grackle. His eyes are the color of the leaves; his feathers look like oil sliding over a puddle of water."

I looked back into the classroom. "What do you hear?" I asked them.

This time they were more specific.

"The drone of the airplane." "A bird, singing." "The ventilation fans." "Someone playing a video in the classroom next door."

When they ran out of things, I told them what else there was to hear. "If you listen, you will hear the hum of the florescent lights," I told them. "There is the scuffing sound made by one of you moving a foot beneath your chair. I hear breathing. Someone just sniffed; someone just cleared his throat. Outside, I hear the wind running its fingers through leaves on the aspen. It sounds like the rubbing sound you hear when a fat woman wearing pantyhose walks past. I hear many other things as well," I said, "all competing for my attention. Sometimes, the sound of my own heart is so loud it distracts me. Sometimes, the sounds I hear are so distracting that I do not hear you call my name. I do not even know you are there.

"So, it's both a gift and a curse, to hear things that a normal person does not hear and see things that a normal person does not see."

"Sometimes," I went on, "I get lost in what I see and hear. Sometimes, I don't understand what you've just said to me, because I've been listening to the sound of your voice, not your words. Sometimes, you think I'm not looking at you when you talk to me. I am, but I'm looking at some unimportant detail, like the way your earrings flash when you nod your head, or the way your forehead wrinkles when you lift your eyebrows.

"Sometimes, you think I am stupid. And, in some ways, you are right. I do not understand expressions very well, and gestures, like shaking your head when you mean 'no.' I'm changing some of this—with the help of my friend Scott—but most of the time I still feel like a tourist in some foreign country where I do not know the language or the customs or the laws.

"This makes it easy for people to take advantage of me, like Carl did when he made me do many copies of homework and so he could sell them. Sometimes, people think they can hurt me and I won't fight back. But I am learning to fight. Scott taught me. You can fight back even with a broken arm, even when there are two guys beating you up, right Scott? And even a retard can defend herself against a bully."

I winked at Scott, then looked at Carl. He had turned pale. The only color on his face came from the scratches I had put there. It gave me a strange pleasure to see that his right wrist was bandaged.

"Carl," whispered someone loudly, "you told me you got into a fight with a street gang. Some gang!"

A lot of kids laughed. The teacher, Robin, bobbed over to Carl, looking angry enough to peck him to death. She asked him to stay after school.

Scott and I smiled at each other. We had rehearsed the whole thing the night before. Then, he raised his hand, in an obvious signal.

"Oops," I said to the class. "That's Scott's signal to stop. I guess I shouldn't have said that stuff about Carl, huh? We retards have no sense of what is appropriate to say, right Carl?" I smiled sweetly at him. He turned red and seemed to slither further down under the protection of his desk.

Of course, this was a lie. Scott's 'shut up' signal was still an ear tug, not a raised hand. But no one knew that, except Scott and I.

I continued to talk, feeling more relaxed by the minute. "Actually, I am not retarded at all. Besides, the correct term is developmentally delayed. I'm not that either.

183

"I taught myself to read when I was four. I know the entire book of world records by heart. I can tell you who won the World's Series for every year since it was first played. I know the current record for every Olympic sport, and many that are not played at the Olympics. I know the length of the Great Wall of China, or the distance from the earth to Alpha Centari."

Brief pause. "I even know what you had for dinner last night."

There were some startled looks, then laughter.

"That was just a joke," I explained. "Scott told me to put it in."

"Although I have memorized many, many facts, there are some things I do not know," I added. "There are many things you learned effortlessly, that I had to be taught by a tutor. Would you like to see the tape?"

There was head nodding and some replies of "sure" and "yeah" and "why not" so I put on the second tape.

I was seven years old. My tutor, April, was teaching me about emotions. She would show me a picture and ask, "What is she feeling?" Most of the time, I couldn't answer, so she had to tell me. Some of the time I got upset, and began rocking or hand flapping or finger counting. Then, she stopped me with a sharp, *"No."* I ran through several short segments of tape. There was a lesson on taking turns, where April would throw me a ball and then say, "Your turn to throw," then toss it back to me with, "My turn now." It was much like you would do with a two year old.

184

There were short segments on the concepts of the "same vs. different," and "which comes first," and a section of tape where I answered the questions "who, what, where, when, why" after listening to a very short story.

I stopped the tape. I tried to figure out the expressions on the faces in front of me. I think there was sadness on one, and disbelief on another, but I couldn't really tell. The teacher, Robin, was shaking her head.

"Casey, I had no idea," she said. "You've worked very hard to get to where you are now. Are you autistic, like your sister?"

"Sort of," I answered. "Scott and I did some research, and we think I have Asperger's Syndrome, even though I was initially diagnosed as autistic when I was very young. Asperger's is seen by many researchers as a different disorder than autism, and by others as merely a higher functioning type of autism. It's characterized by social impairment with extreme egocentricity, limited interests and pre-occupations, repetitive routines or rituals, peculiarities in speech or language, non-verbal communication problems and..."

Scott was tugging his ear. "Just a minute, Scott," I said, "there's more."

"Casey, you brought the printouts in case anyone wanted to read about it, remember?"

"Yes, Scott, but I haven't told them about the implications for..." Scott was tugging again. I sighed. "Okay. You're right. You see, people, that's another thing

185

I do. Go on and on about facts, even when no one is listening."

"Sounds like a lot of our teachers!" commented someone from the back of the room. Everyone laughed.

"Maybe some of them have Asperger's Syndrome, too," I said, and people laughed again.

"That's all I wanted to tell you," I concluded. "Except for this. I know I am different. I know it causes problems. I know that sometimes I lack sensitivity to what you are feeling. It's not that I don't care, it's just that I don't understand feelings very well yet. I'm learning though, and you can help me by explaining what you are thinking and feeling. I can't pick these things up from your expressions and your gestures, the way other people can.

"I know I bore you sometimes, going on about the things I know. It's because I'm still learning to take turns in conversation. It's okay to tell me to shut up.

"I know that I get distracted sometimes, and don't really listen to what you are saying. It's okay to ask me to listen more closely.

"And I know that I don't get your jokes or share your sense of humor. Maybe you can teach me that, too. I really want to have friends, but sometimes I'm not sure how to do that.

"There's one thing that Scott taught me, though, that I want to share with you. Scott said that 'different' isn't always worse. Sometimes it's just different.

"Thank you for listening."

I gathered up my notes and tapes and went back to my seat. Scott winked at me and gave me a 'thumbs up' signal.

There was no sound in the room, except for the hum of the lights and the buzz of the fan. Then, someone began to clap. Another person joined him, and then they were all clapping, except for Carl.

I wanted to run away from the sound. It was too unexpected, too unpredictable, too loud. Then, Scott leaned over and whispered, "You're a hit, kiddo! That was terrific!"

The sound took on new meaning. Applause. They liked me. They accepted me. At least, right now, for this particular moment in time, they accepted me.

I picked up the rhythm and pattern of the clapping and it sounded like waves slapping against the rocks. It warmed and soothed me.

It was like music to my ears.

That's an expression, you know.

Praise for *Not by Accident*

"The descriptions Dunn conjures of her euphoria riding horses are lush and weightless. . . . For readers who don't ride horses, Dunn's decision to, quite literally, get back on her horse is hard to fathom. But it is precisely that persistence that drives Dunn to share her honest and beguiling story."

—Sara Ivry, *San Francisco Chronicle*

"Dunn is a terrific writer. She strikes just the right tone of vulnerability, introspection, and reflexive black humor. She is self-deprecating, intelligent, stubborn, and endearing. In other words, she makes for a winning narrator. The book itself avoids the memoir pitfalls. It is at no time cloying or muddled, and instead marches along breezily because of Dunn's expert organization of the narrative and clear prose."

—Chelsea Cain, *The Portland Oregonian*

"Wise, gripping, cinematic, and entertaining, *Not by Accident* is one ripping read." —*Yoga Journal*

"A thoughtful meditation on the consequences of choice in everyday life. With intelligence, compassion and wit, Dunn delivers a poignant memoir remarkably devoid of sentimentality." —Pam Ullman, *The Missouri Review*

"Samantha Dunn pulls no punches in this tough, witty, and deeply personal memoir of a brave woman's moment of crisis, as she examines the parts played by elements of risk, identity, and the unexamined life in her own catastrophe. A beautiful, necessary book."

—Janet Fitch, author of *White Oleander*

"Full of candid wit and insight."

—Ara Taylor, *Bellingham Herald*

Not by Accident

Also by Samantha Dunn

Failing Paris

Not by Accident

Reconstructing a Careless Life

S A M A N T H A   D U N N

AN OWL BOOK
HENRY HOLT AND COMPANY
New York

For my mother and my grandmother

Henry Holt and Company, LLC
Publishers since 1866
115 West 18th Street
New York, New York 10011

Henry Holt® is a registered trademark of
Henry Holt and Company, LLC.

Library of Congress Cataloging-in-Publication Data
Dunn, Samantha.
    Not by accident : reconstructing a careless life /
Samantha Dunn.—1st ed.
        p. cm.
    ISBN 0-8050-6586-5 (pbk.)
    1. Dunn, Samantha. 2. Conduct of Life. 3. Leg—
Wounds and injuries—Patients—California—Biography.
4. California—Biography. I. Title.

CT275.D88226 A3 2002
979.4'053'092—dc21
[B]   2001046355

Henry Holt books are available for special promotions and
premiums. For details contact: Director, Special Markets.

First published in hardcover in 2002 by
Henry Holt and Company

First Owl Books Edition 2003

An Owl Book

Designed by Kelly S. Too

Printed in the United States of America

1 3 5 7 9 10 8 6 4 2

[I]

THOROUGHBREDS ARE BY
DEFINITION NERVOUS HORSES.

It begins with a jerk and click, as if a projector is being turned on in the middle of a film. A winding canyon trail lies in front of me. Live Oak leaves tough and green mottle the late afternoon light that filters down. I ease the leather of well-oiled reins between my fingers.

Today I arrived a little later than usual, not up for the concentration it takes to work in the ring. Was on the phone all day, forgot to pay the electric bill. Two realtors showed up, unexpected. The landlord is going to sell the house, a thirty-day notice, thanks a lot. I'm impatient to escape into the hills where the mustard weeds are still blooming, a sea of yellow that comes up to my horse's belly. This trail is supposed to lead up to a waterfall. Everybody at the stable comes back with reports of its beauty, but for some reason my horse and I have never been up there. Not that far, maybe five miles round-trip. The usual route at the beginning, a very narrow track along the edge of an arroyo that rises steeply to the top of a ridge. I tilt forward in the saddle as we climb, take my weight off his back. The sun and the incline soon make him sweat, darkening his bay coat.

We come to the turn for the waterfall where the trail slopes down into the canyon. The trees grow taller, the brush more dense. The path twists, it's impossible to see what lies around the next bend.

All at once we're facing a narrow creek, unexpected in the dryness of southern California. My horse freezes as if we have come upon a giant anaconda rather than the simple flow of water. He shakes his head, every muscle taut as a metal spring, and chews on his bit, foam from his mouth flying with every toss of his head. This is his way of saying: You didn't warn me about this! Why didn't you warn me about this?

I ignore him. Thoroughbreds are by definition nervous horses; mine is no exception. I can feel his back round, the shift of his weight onto his haunches. He wants to jump this obstacle and take off; I just want to make it to the top of the trail before dusk.

I slip my feet from the stirrups and dismount. It will be faster to guide him through this than to negotiate a settlement. "C'mon Harley," I say as I begin to lead him to the creek, "don't be a sissy."

His head descends toward the creek to sniff the water, creating an arch with his neck. His large brown eyes, the color of malt balls, can't gauge the depth of the water.

"Relax sweetie," I tell him, reaching far up above my head to smooth my hand over his coat. The first touch is like the skin of an eel, then of a mink, oiled and slick. As I lead Harley, I realize that I'm wearing my new paddock boots. I don't want to get them wet, so I skip over the water.

It is small motion, really.

All at once I have a sense of being flung. Then the surprise as the bony force of Harley's knee suddenly pushes into my back. A kind of nausea. My 2,000-pound horse has reared back. He is now jumping forward. And he is landing on top of me.

Dirt in my mouth as I'm pushed to the ground. The odd beauty of the angle formed by my arm as it pops out of my shoulder. I feel no pain right now, aware only of how mammoth my horse appears as he stands over me, blocking all sun. He snorts, not able to see me under him but knowing by scent I'm there. His muscles quiver. His sweat drips onto my face; perhaps it is my own.

"Harley, easy boy, easy."

But his body pulls away and I see the flash of the steel-shod hoof as it strikes downward. I hear the crack of something, loud as gunfire, and look to see my left leg snapped apart like dry kindling.

His hind hoof has just sliced the middle of my left shin, cutting like a dull shovel straight through the bones, the muscles, ligaments and veins, leaving a hinge of calf muscle and sinew.

It can't be as bad as it looks, I think. It really can't be this bad.

I try to stand, or at least I have the intention. Maybe I pass out. Grains of dirt roll against the enamel of my teeth. I lick my lips.

I have to remove my lace-up paddock boot. I have to, I have

to, I have to. Last month when I fell down the flight of stairs and badly sprained this same ankle, the area ballooned, making the process of removing my shoe complicated. And then what about that young mare last year. Slammed me against a gate, smashed my right side, and my right foot swelled. Had to wear my boot for a few hours and that hurt like hell. That fallen horse, the gelding, what was his name? Romeo. His hoof struck my toe as he struggled to his feet. What was wrong with Romeo? I couldn't bother with the boot then. When I finally got around to taking it off, there was so much swelling the laces had to be cut to spread the leather wide enough.

I reach to untie the laces. The dead weight of my own foot feels like meat. With each beat of my heart, blood flows out of my body into the ground like water from a garden hose left running on the lawn.

I lie back in the dirt, exhausted, boot still on. Forget it. My horse grazes as if he has never eaten, quickly tearing the grass with his teeth. His reins drag across the ground as he mows from clump to clump. What if he steps through his reins, becomes tangled and breaks a leg? He can't break a leg. They shoot horses with broken legs.

The loudest sound is my own breath. Everything is perfectly ordered, the quick rise and fall of my chest. The ground, the chlorophyll sweetness of grass, the squawk of a scrub jay, the rush of breeze in the oaks overhead. People have died to these sounds for thousands of years.

But people can't die this way today.

I can't die this way today.

———

I am picturing the time I was in my living room with my sprained foot propped up, talking to my friend Lucia. But as I think of her she changes, her African skin becomes a leopard, her black almond eyes turn orange and watch me. I am lamenting a string of bad luck that has seemed to come my way these past months: the tumble down the stairs, a fall from Harley in which I sprained my back, cracked my tailbone. She is not sympathetic.

"God touches us with a feather to get our attention," she growls. "Then if we don't listen, he starts throwing bricks."

The same breeze, the same grass. I cannot say if a moment or an hour has passed since the last time I saw the light coming through the oaks. My blood pools around me. Harley stops grazing and puts his nose to my face. The inside of his nostrils are plush as old velvet.

He takes a step nearer to me, snorts loudly, sniffing the overripe scent that is the smell of blood escaped. I push his head away, afraid of him for the first time in my life. Hooves of a beast. At the core we are both animals, propelled by fear and basic impulses.

"Get, get!" I shrill at him, "Don't step on me again! Please, damn it, just get away!"

Then a voice starts yelling in my ear with a tone and pitch exactly my grandmother's, says, *What the hell's the matter with you?* My grandmother is dead ten years. The voice is coming from the inside of my head but sounds as if she's standing right in back of me. *You're not dead yet. You can still scream. Sam, scream. For chrissake, scream.*

I prop myself up on the uninjured arm. I take a deep breath. I open my mouth.

I have never heard my own voice truly scream. It is ugly, not unlike the sound a rabbit makes when caught by a pack of coyotes. I raise goosebumps on my own skin.

A rustling from up the trail. Coyotes, damn them, or could it be deer? A dog? No, the sound in the dirt has a one-two-one-two rhythm. Feet.

A blond man running reaches me. But he steps back, clearly afraid to go any farther. By the look on his face, it seems he might throw up.

"I'm fine," I say, although the way he recoils means the situation is even worse than it looks to me. "Please, just get my horse. He's going to step through those reins."

"Right," he says. "Right. I'm sorry. You stay there."

"Right," I answer. Where, exactly, would I be going with half a leg?

Probably he meant to say that help is on the way. It arrives seconds later. Another man, this one with dark hair, runs through the dry brush and stands over me. He is an actor whose face I recognize, a disorienting fact that makes me consider perhaps I am already dead and have been sent to a special purgatory for Los Angelenos.

"Can you hear me? Can you hold on?" I think that's what he says. I know for sure that he kneels beside me without hesitation. I remember him in a role from a movie with

Goldie Hawn I've seen on cable. Maybe I truly am dead. Maybe this is St. Peter revealing himself as an actor with a good tan and even smile. His voice is deep and does not betray any sense of panic. Around his neck is a choker with a tooth or claw in the center. I have a sudden desire to fluff my hair and wipe the dirt from my face.

"I've had a little accident," I tell him.

"I can see." He asks me if I can move my arms, if my head is hurt.

"My leg is kind of messed up," I tell him. "And I think I might be dead."

"You're very much alive, and you're going to stay that way," he says. "We're going to get some help. What's your name, sweetheart?"

"Sam," I say. I want to be polite about this but politeness takes time. "I know you're an actor, can you please tell me your name? I'm sorry, I feel like I should know it—"

"Edward Albert," he says, "and please, don't—"

"*Green Acres*? You're not that old—"

"That's my dad. I've been in a few movies, but don't worry about that."

Of course I'm not dead because I can still feel embarrassed. The idea is comforting. "I'm sorry, I should have—"

"Please, you've got a few other things going on right now." His voice resonates like an iron bell. "Are you hurt anywhere else?"

"My shoulder."

"Let's see," he says, looking me over. He touches my left shoulder. "I'm trying to remember anything useful from the times I've played a doctor."

SAMANTHA DUNN

"I feel better already."

"Ssh. You don't have to talk, just relax," he says.

"But I need to talk," I say.

He tells me that they'd been coming from their barn, he and Dave, the blond man, they'd been working the horses. They heard a screech. He says he was going to ignore it, he thought it was the cry of a bird, sometimes the red-tailed hawks make this kind of sound, but his daughter said, No, Dad, I think it's someone yelling for help.

I hear Edward tell someone, it must be Dave, I wonder if he threw up, We probably can't get a signal here on your cell phone. Can we? No? Run back and call 911. Hurry. Lead the horse back to the house and tell Tai to call.

What follows must include a call to paramedics, questions about whom to call in case of emergency. I remember a telephone number, but I can't recall what it's to.

"Is Harley OK? Do you think he'll be all right?" I need to know.

"He's great. He's sorry about the accident," I think Edward says.

"That's OK," I say, "he didn't mean to."

"He didn't mean to," Edward echoes.

He smoothes my hair back from my forehead in a rhythmic motion. I keep trying to raise my head to look down to where my leg lies, but the pressure of his palm against my forehead becomes more insistent and I realize he's purposely preventing me from lifting my head. I am aware of how green his eyes are, but I cannot see his hands. There is no tourniquet.

He says, "I'd carry you, but I'm afraid—" He does not

complete his sentence. I know what he will not tell me. Since only muscle and skin prevent the leg from being completely severed, the dead weight would likely tear the rest of the leg off if he tried to lift me.

And then, what to do with all this blood? I don't know how he stays with me here in the dirt. Help takes a while; shadows slant more sharply through the oaks, that crystal time of day just before dusk when the light draws the world in perfect relief. The breeze seems colder by degree.

Sometime later I hear a young woman's voice shouting down the trail, "Dad! The paramedics can't find you!"

The paramedics can't find us, and that breeze is getting so cold. I want to move my arm to get comfortable, but no such angle exists that will bring comfort.

"Well, go get them," Edward shouts back, the first time I hear the tinny ring of tension in his voice. But then he turns to me, smiles. "That's my daughter, Tai." He tells me she was born into his arms, and that his was the first face she saw. This explains him. Here is a man who has seen a woman bleed before.

He tells me many things about his life; he asks me about mine. The way two people talk when one is keeping the other from bleeding to death makes for its own category of conversation.

"Do you think I'll ever dance again?" I ask him, out of nowhere. I don't even know how to dance. But now I'm thinking it's something I would want to do if I could. "Why haven't I been dancing all my life? Doesn't it seem dumb that I don't?"

"You'll dance," he says.

I shut my eyes and his voice surrounds me just as a blanket would. It talks to me about Ireland and the exact color of heather. The voice, which seems to be the only voice, ever, asks me, Have you ever been there?

No.

You must go.

Now?

No, when you're better. Surely your family is originally from Ireland, surely with auburn hair and freckles.

Yes.

The Irish are fine horsemen.

As fine as the Spanish.

My mother was from Mexico.

Fine horsemen they are, too.

The paramedics materialize out of the dry brush. The looks on their faces provide no reassurance; I realize that somewhere I held the notion they would tell me the situation wasn't that dire, that it's nothing more than a broken leg. Many people break their legs. It happens every day. I was even afraid of inconveniencing them—"We came all the way out here for this, lady?" they'd say.

Instead they talk on walkie-talkies, they've seen this kind of thing before in the canyons but this is a bad one, horses are dangerous animals, why would anyone want to get on a horse? Do you have insurance? Yes? What kind? Do you happen to remember your social security number? No, but I can remember the first phone number we had when I was a child, 435-4351, that doesn't help, does it?

But I have insurance, so there will be a medi-vac helicopter to take me to UCLA's trauma center. They will have to cut away the rest of my breeches, do I mind? They're pretty well torn, I say, they're old anyway. But my boots are still good. Did I mention to you guys that I didn't want to get them wet? I have on black cotton underwear with stretchy lace, my mother would be proud. The paramedic with a mustache asks, Where can the helicopter land up here? Is there level ground within a mile? You can't possibly be asking me that question. No one seems to know.

I think they also ask if I have pain anywhere else, or maybe one of them touches the arm that is pulled out of the socket. Somehow it ends up that one of them pulls my arm straight and then moves it slightly. The joint pops back into place, my body like the box of doll parts I had as a child, a collection of Barbie legs, a head, arms, torsos of varying sizes.

I think I must cry out as he does this, because suddenly I am again looking up through those leaves.

"Can't you give her something?" Edward's voice again. He holds my hand. "Valium, anything?"

They're sorry but no, not until X rays. There could be head injury; there could be who knows what.

Edward keeps holding my hand. "Squeeze when it hurts," he says.

"But your fingers are turning purple."

He tells me not to worry, that worry implies the absence of faith. Here, in this dirt, is exactly where I need to be. The Chumash tribe considered this very ground sacred, he says. He knows some Chumash, they still believe it. "Your life will change because of this," he tells me, "in ways you can't imagine now."

I try to focus on his eyes; they seem farther away, and I

have a peculiar sensation of looking up through a hole that is getting deeper and more narrow. A drain. If I were to feel water fill my lungs at this moment it would not be a surprise.

"It's here," the paramedics say. To reach the helicopter landing site they'll need to hike out with me on a stretcher, but to do that they will have to gather up my leg to form some semblance of a straight line.

"Is that all right?" says the one with the mustache.

"All right, yes. Considering the other options," I say. "You look a little like Randolph Mantooth on that old show, *Emergency*. Do people tell you that?"

"This will hurt," he replies, and I tell him it can't be much worse than what has already happened.

I am wrong.

All at once it seems I am above myself, observing the way blood forms a kind of adobe as it flows into the earth, the opalescence of exposed bone, the leg slung out to the side of the woman's body, which I recognize as my own. I keep asking myself, How can this be reassembled? How can this be reassembled?

People often say things like, "I was in shock when he told me it was over" or "I was in shock over how much they wanted for that piece of crap," when of course what they mean is that they were simply surprised.

Shock, on the other hand, is not a state of mind but a real, physical syndrome. When doctors or paramedics say you're in shock, they are telling you that the oxygen supply to the tissues of your body, and the flow of blood returning to your heart, have been upset, cut off, disturbed.

Blood loss over time becomes the central equation. It is good to know that many parts of your body can survive for a long time without blood. Legs, for instance. During ortho- pedic surgery, the blood flow is clamped off for up to three hours with a hemostat (a device which looks something like shiny, needle-nosed pliers that lock), yet the cells that make up the tissue of a leg continue living. Longer than that, how- ever, the cells begin to die, tissue becomes "nonviable," mak- ing the leg a dead thing, a condition called *ischemia*, an absence of oxygen. Your heart can exist for ten minutes without blood before the tissues start to die but your brain can last only five minutes without a fresh supply.

Because of this order of importance, your body compensates for blood loss by prioritizing just what needs how much, shutting off the flow to parts that aren't vital for survival. Those nonvital parts include the hands and feet, legs and arms, which turn cold and blue while what blood remains on tap gets poured into the heart, the brain, and the kidneys (even though, during the course of your day, the practical function of an arm or leg may strike you as more vital than a kidney's). If you keep bleeding, eventually you will "bleed out," more specifically the word is exsanguinate, but even doctors use the lay term. However it is said, it still means there's not enough blood to support even the vital organs, and so your heart stops. But Nature is an exquisite system, measuring and balancing all factors to produce the best possible outcome. In this particular case that means you are spared the pain of cardiac arrest, because your brain is already comatose.

Shock is proportional to the extent of injury. The greater the injury, the greater the degree of shock. Every injury is accompanied by some degree of shock and so should be treated promptly. This is true if it is a bee sting, or a paper cut, and especially true in cases of a crushing injury and compound fracture, where there is often extensive blood loss and your body is not able to maintain circulation. Emergency workers know not to move a patient experiencing shock unnecessarily, questions should be kept to a minimum, as the risk of cardiac arrest is high, even in someone relatively young, someone with good health. A physician should be called promptly. Blood transfusion will likely be required. The *Tabers Cyclopedic Medical Dictionary* clearly states, "Constant kindly, tactful encouragement and extreme gentleness in all procedures are of importance."

I think I know why most descriptions of God involve a being from above, why angels are said to fly down to humans from the heavens. It is because when you are seriously wounded you are usually lying prone and see the world from that vantage point. Your sense of proportion has changed, so the people who come to your aid appear larger, descend toward you out of you-have-no-idea-where, and they are powerful, so powerful, so able to do for you that which you are unable to do for yourself.

Then there is the sky, which in the case of Malibu on a September late afternoon contains not one cloud; it is a blue so smooth it seems ceramic. A tint like pink or orange is quickly diluting the color. I am able to turn my head to see hands holding the stretcher and I realize this is the way pall-bearers hold a coffin, and it does feel like floating, something like bobbing in an inner tube along a glassy river.

And then there is the loud clomp-clomp-clomp-whirl of what I know is a helicopter, because it sounds exactly like the helicopter always sounds in movies about Vietnam, soldiers trying to talk through the noise. I think I should brace for the force of air, that's what they have to do in the movies, but not that much wind hits my skin. Someone puts a hand to my forehead, holds my hair back so it doesn't fly in my face. Measures of comfort have relative value; what in other times would seem just a courtesy now becomes nothing less than evidence of humanity's central beauty.

Inside the helicopter I can't hear the paramedic, but I can see his mouth moving. His face is directly above me. His eyelashes are blond. He has on a helmet. The words he mouths are, Can you hold up this bag? And I realize it is for an IV, and I say yes because I am forgetting that my left arm is hurt. That doesn't matter because right then my body starts to shake, my teeth chattering so much I think I might break the enamel. I say, I'm sorry, but I'm just too cold.

He mouths, That's OK, here, let's get you some blankets. He pulls them up to my chin as if tucking me in. I would sleep if there were not the feeling of being gnawed upon, bitten into, through every part of me but the last eighth, a sixteenth maybe. The lack of pain there even more terrible. I close my eyes but I see again the picture of Harley's stomach above me. The V shape of muscle on the underside, the never-seen side, is tattooed on the inside of my lids. The skin quivers, the hind leg cocking up, then striking down. It occurs to me that when this was happening, it already felt like a memory. I knew the blunt force that was to come, a remembered weight; some primal recall from the reptilian part of my brain. Our species is, after all, fleshy, no exoskeleton, used to being struck underfoot.

From here on I try to keep my eyes opened to that space above me, the one through which help keeps arriving. I try not even to blink.

"I've never been in a helicopter," I say, although I might only think it.

The blond paramedic comes into view. He gives me a thumbs-up, shouting, "We're over the water. Almost there." He means the helicopter is flying over Santa Monica Bay, and within minutes will reach inland to Westwood, and then to the roof of UCLA Hospital.

My jaw will not stop its rattle; my lungs won't give me enough air to shout back to him. Still, I try. "Flying sure beats the hell out of rush hour on the PCH," I manage. The tradition in my family is The more fear, the more swagger.

The paramedic nods, pats my good shoulder. He has no idea what I just said.

There doesn't seem to be any warning when we land. The helicopter is not like a plane where the sense of deceleration is obvious, or perhaps it is obvious, but my body is too busy registering other feelings and can't be bothered with one more. I know we are on the ground because the doors open. The paramedic says, "Good luck," and then people in white coats, in blue smocks, fill the space above me, transfer me to a gurney. Talk, talk, talk. I can't get a grip on the information they're trading until one says, "Samantha? I'm Dr. Etminan. How are you?"

"I'm fine, thanks, and you?" Always be polite, my eyes searching until they find the face the voice belongs to. He has glasses, a square jaw, a few chest hairs curl out of the neck on his smock.

"I bet people call you Sam."

"I bet people just call you Doctor."

"Not my mother," says Dr. Etminan. He tells me I have

been seriously injured, that I will need to go to surgery as soon as they "assess the extent of my injuries."

"It's just my leg; everything else is fine," I insist, not mentioning the shoulder—it doesn't count; it's still under my skin. It's always best to split the difference in these circumstances, I have learned. Don't give anybody too much to worry about. People are easily overwhelmed.

He continues as if I never spoke, explaining that an orthopedic surgeon will take care of my bone, and then there will be a vascular surgeon to deal with the problem of the arteries and veins. There might be others; I lose track.

"All the king's horses and all the king's men," I say.

He asks me about pain, do I have any, and when I say yes he seems glad, as if I could have answered otherwise. Everyone seems to be walking very fast but he keeps asking me questions in a calm, measured voice. Do I know what day it is? Monday. Do I know what month it is? September. Year? 1997. Who's the president? Clinton, and I voted for him twice because he plays sax and likes McDonald's.

I know the reason he's quizzing me; inappropriate answers can indicate brain injury, trauma to the skull otherwise not seen. One of my first magazine jobs was at *Emergency Medical Services* magazine. I got fired; I was a worthless copy editor. Still, you learn a few things. But my real source of authority on medicine was my mother, a nurse with a specialty in ER and operating room. I grew up with the smell of antiseptic; at home we used a surgical steel hip prosthesis as a paperweight. At dinner she once passed me the plate of boiled cauliflower and said, That's what your brains look like. When I responded with a "yuck" in my eight-year-old way, she was bewildered. She'd been on call for the past fourteen hours. *What's the matter with you? It's just brains, for chrissake.*

I am telling Dr. Etminan this story. He has gone out of my sphere of vision, but I keep talking. By now the gurney has stopped; we appear to be in a waiting room. "Plus I've had a few concussions over the years," I add.

"Horses?" he asks, popping into view.

"Horses," I say, and he shakes his head.

Above me the space is filled with white ceiling tiles, the seventies kind with a pattern of holes. Some of the tiles bear amoebaelike, brown stains. Did something drip down or spray up? What would be spraying up, I wonder? Some of the tiles are torn at the corners, one is missing, there are marks on the walls, the hospital seems used, slightly bombed out, a Beirut quality. I start to panic—what are they going to do to me here? I'll ask to be taken somewhere else—and then it hits me. This isn't a restaurant, I don't have a choice.

"What do you do, Sam?" Dr. Etminan asks, his tone like he's making conversation at a cocktail party, then in the next breath he yells at someone to get such-and-such ready, Tell them I need it NOW! We're going on hour three! His face turns back to me.

"I'm a writer," I tell him, and my teeth start to chatter again. I am thinking what "hour three" could mean; what are the factors that go into telling time in a hospital?

"Great! TV? Screenwriter?"

"Books and articles. The kind that doesn't make any money." I have used this line many times in Los Angeles. It comes out with no effort, even through the clacking of my teeth.

"Well maybe you can write about this and it can be your first script," he says encouragingly.

"My big break," I say.

" 'Break,' very good. You're a professional, I can tell."

"Don't try this at home."

I can hear my own voice falter. Pain arrives in a series of bolts; the moment one subsides, another arrives. "I don't mean to complain, but can I get something for pain?"

I know he's going to say no, which he does, because painkillers can mask symptoms of other problems not yet detected. He says we're waiting for the X-ray department. He keeps looking at his watch. "Let me go check," he says. "I'll be back."

A parade of smocks follow; some introduce themselves, some don't, each has some medical function and each seems to need to lift up the blanket to view the leg. They are not shy with their comments.

"Wow!"

"Ouch."

I joke that I'm going to start charging admission if one more person looks at the leg. I feel like a roadside attraction.

A doctor with a long ponytail the color of sand leans over the gurney. She is telling me something in a loud, slow voice, and I want to say, My horse broke my leg, not my eardrums.

She asks if I have any questions, although I haven't any idea what she just said.

"Will I be able to walk again?" I quickly change the question when I see the look on her face. "At least ride?"

"Don't count on it." She turns on her heel without saying anything else, ponytail swinging out. She reminds me of the third-grade teacher who threw erasers at me when I kept repeating the same incorrect answers to my multiplication tables. Sandy Ponytail becomes the enemy, and I feel a flush of energy. Clearly it is more pleasant to hate than to fear.

"Nice meeting you, Miss Congeni-fucking-ality," I call after her, but my voice is not loud.

No one comes for several minutes. There is no way to be comfortable, no possibility of movement. My entire body now throbs with an ache that is much like the ache of biting into something cold. But it doesn't go away.

Another woman who doesn't introduce herself fills the space. She has a clipboard; she wants to know if I remember my insurance number, if I could sign this release form please, and this form, too, and just this one more, right there, yes, and on the back.

I want to be helpful, but it is difficult to hold a pen. I tell her I'm left-handed and that arm is numb from having the shoulder popped out and then in again, and I'm shaking because it's so cold. She seems not to mind that my signature isn't too well formed. "And we are calling this person you have listed, is he a friend or a relative?" she asks.

"Husband," I tell her, "that's my husband."

My chest tightens. There is more I want to explain about him, but none of it will fit on her clipboard. His name is Matt. I have known him since I was eighteen, since he was sixteen. He's the younger brother of one of my best friends from college.

Now Matt will be sitting in front of the recording console at his new job, and he will answer the phone. It will be a hospital clerk telling him I have been in an accident, and he will say she's been in accidents before, I'll pick her up after work, and the clerk will say, No, she's going to need to stay in the hospital for a bit, and then—

And then I don't know what he'll do.

Will he slam the phone down, angry that he has to leave work when he is trying to make a good impression on his new employer? Or will he feel anxious, imagine the worst possible thing that could happen, grab his keys and run to the parking lot? What for him would be the worst possible thing? Death or paralysis, a forever dependent wife? Maybe he will rush to the hospital and gun the accelerator through stoplights. Maybe he will need a cigarette and pull out the ashtray in the truck, and a joint from before will fall out, he'd forgotten he'd stashed it there in the back. Maybe he'll look at it and think, What the hell, perfect timing, and maybe he'll light it and then decide he needs another one. Then instead of going straight to the hospital maybe he'll think he should just swing by that guy's house, the guy from before, you know the one. Maybe he'll think to himself, It won't take very long and damned if I can face this shit this straight.

I feel suddenly as if my gurney has one wheel tilting off the edge of a cliff, clumps of soil crumbling underneath the way the ground does in California. I want to tell the woman with the clipboard to make sure he understands that I'm OK, insurance will cover this, I'll come home and everything will be fine; the only thing is, for a while he'll probably need to take the dogs out in the morning. Otherwise everything will be fine. I'll just need a few days to rest.

But the woman with the clipboard has already left.

A group of people surround me, among them a doctor whose name I don't catch. I am going into surgery shortly, they say. I am so cold, but I try not to shiver. I start talking, trying to be funny; I think it's the Monty Python "Holy Grail" routine where the black knight, upon having his limbs whacked off, keeps repeating, "It's only a flesh wound! It's only a flesh wound!" I honestly don't know what I am saying, but I do see the whites of their teeth, see them surprised by their own laughter.

From among the heads peering in at the space above me there is suddenly a hairline I recognize. He arrived so quickly. His hazel eyes are clear, focused; he's wearing a shirt I bought him, green with a collar and stripes down the front, I thought it was cool. I think he hates it but wears it anyway. Tears sting behind my eyes and for the first time since Harley pushed me to the dirt I think I will cry.

"Hey babe," Matt says, bending down to kiss me. There is no panic in his voice, just calm. "Are you OK?" He moves a hand to my cheek and rubs away what must have been a streak of mud. I become aware of the grains of dirt crusting my scalp.

"I did it this time." I feel the tips of his fingers trace the back of my hand. He must say something but I don't know what; I am only conscious of the fact that he is standing next to the gurney.

I hear Dr. Etminan's voice in the room, he's talking fast again, there are many things he needs to have other people do for him Right Now. His hands move quickly, gripping the gurney, and his voice is edgy, says we are going to X ray. Matt can't come, he has to stay in the waiting room, so just as quickly as I saw him I am without him again, traveling down a hall with greenish light.

The gurney stops at X ray; the room is dark and colder still. Dr. Etminan tells the lab tech he wants film on—what? My neck? I can't hear him. The break? I don't know why; you can see the cross section of bone by just lifting the cover off the splint. "I'll be back in a couple minutes," he tells me.

These couple minutes hang like something wet. The lab tech moves slowly compared to the paramedics, nurses, and doctors. His English is thickly accented; I don't know which Asian country he is from. Maybe it's Vietnam, maybe Cambodia. He's thinking to himself, Americans complain so much because they can't believe anything bad can happen to them. Lady, you should have seen the people who had their legs blown off in my country. They didn't snivel. They didn't even have a hospital to go to. They went back to work the next day. Fed their kids.

The lab tech wants to know if I can move at all, if I can hold a plate here, over the leg. I would like to, but I am so cold, I say. And I hurt. I really, truly hurt. There is the buzz and click of the radiation burning an image onto film. Perhaps there is another one; I don't know. My brain can't handle any message but pain, pain like I-want-to-die pain, and I recall reading about soldiers during the Civil War. When their legs were amputated all they had to comfort them was a stiff belt of rye whiskey, and now it makes sense, a mangled limb for a drink of booze. A fair trade.

Dr. Etminan comes in again. He should have wings, be named Michael, the avenger, because he always seems mad at somebody, and this time it is the lab tech. We don't have TIME. We have to get her in here. NOW. I mean it. No, that's it. Period. I don't care. We have to risk it.

The gurney is moving. A series of turns, some halls. Someone puts a cap on me. I say there's dirt in my hair. No one listens. Something must be going through my IV now because I feel a little warmer, lights appear brighter. There is a calm. I have to be moved onto a surgical table; I cannot tell how this is accomplished. A ring of faces in blue masks form a halo above me. All of them are men; all of them have kind eyes.

"If I had known I'd meet so many good-looking men, I would have mortally injured myself sooner," I say, probably sounding drunk. A little Mae West in the face of surgery can't hurt. There is definitely something coming through my IV.

The anesthesiologist prepares his potions. A stiff belt of rye whiskey in trade. Dr. Lui introduces himself as the orthopedic surgeon. "We are going to do everything we can to save your leg." Maybe he doesn't say that; maybe I want him to say that.

I wake up in a hospital bed to find my leg swathed mummy-like in soft bandages, elevated above the level of my head, a series of tubes and needles lodged in the veins of both hands, a catheter tube taped awkwardly up my urethra. Dirt still crusts my scalp.

I am not thinking about pain because it is just there, everywhere, the world and the filter on the world. Next to my hand is a small device like a TV remote, but with only one button. When I click it, a dose of morphine is administered directly into my bloodstream through one of the tubes running into the veins of my hands. A nurse must have explained this at some point; I don't think I knew it before. I quickly figure out that after a certain number of clicks the machine won't administer any more doses, even if the pain hasn't been beaten back. Click, click, click. And still it hurts.

I close my eyes. I open my eyes. I cannot say if an hour or second is spent in between.

I become aware that Dr. Etminan is in the blue-walled

patient room. He has some information that is very important and detailed to tell me, and I believe he repeats this
information many times, because I come to understand it.

"I need to explain some things to you: You have a barnyard open compound fracture of the tibia and fibula. This is a
serious injury, Sam," he says. He's talking to me in a Zeus
tone, as if throwing down thunder from Olympus. He
doesn't look any older than I am. Younger, in fact. "Fractures
are graded I through III, with III being the worst in terms of
infection risk, soft tissue damage, and loss of blood supply to
the area. You have a Grade III."

"Top of the class," I say, although the words said out loud
don't contain the confidence of the voice in my head. My lips
feel numb.

Dr. Etminan refuses my banter. "Within the class there are
groupings A, B, and C. Technically a Class C, a crushed limb,
is worse than what you have because the bone is pulverized
and veins exploded, but the severity of this injury increases
exponentially simply because it was done by a hoof. That's
why it's called a barnyard injury."

Barnyard, as in *bucolic*, as in *Rebecca of Sunnybrook Farm*.
What am I thinking. I know better. My uncle was a rancher.
My husband's grandfather, a sharecropper. I know about
barnyards and all they represent, wading through the soup of
mud and animal shit on rainy days, the sting of urine, the yellow bot eggs sticking to the hide on livestock, worms and
other parasites. You don't even need a microscope. The barnyard has entered my body.

Dr. Etminan is telling me the barnyard aspect is significant because it means the high risk of infection in this fracture has shot up even higher, further complicated by the fact that I lay in dirt and mud for more than an hour before the helicopter could reach me. He's explaining that this injury is messy, complicated. If I had been a soldier catching shrapnel, it would have been better, because the heat from a bomb would have cauterized the metal. If I had been a biker in a wreck with concrete and steel, my bones in a spiral fracture like a green twig being twisted, even that would have been better because it would be cleaner. "That's why we have you on this IV containing a very aggressive combination of antibiotics," he adds.

The needles burn and ache because they are loaded with chemicals to blast infection. Heavy artillery. "At least there's that."

"The danger," he continues, stretching the word out, *day-n-ger*, "is that such a high dose over a week could cause the kidneys to shut down and permanently damage them." He keeps looking at a clipboard, which is another weird detail that makes this seem like I am dreaming, because doctors from *Marcus Welby, MD* to *ER* have always looked down at clipboards in the exact same way. There are no emotions that haven't already been mined for thirty-minute segments on primetime. To see this familiar gesture from someone who has just said my leg could gangrene and kidneys collapse confirms I have watched too much television.

Dr. Etminan tells me that in the morning I will have another surgery he calls a "debridement," during which the doctors, using powerful microscopes, will attempt to completely scour the injury for all dirt and sludge and fragments of bone, any particle of which will, if left behind, cause an infection that will take my leg.

"And possibly kill me in the process?" It is easy to talk about this because I feel as if this is a story I have seen played out before. It's an obvious plot twist, a way of revealing character.

"We are doing everything we can to make sure that doesn't happen," he says evenly.

"I'm sorry, doctor. You missed your cue." Morphine makes me feel as if I have been encased in cotton. "You were supposed to say 'of course not' or 'that is out of the question.' "

"You lost a considerable amount of blood. The tissue damage is as serious as the bone damage in this injury," he replies. A plastic surgeon might be needed, because it could be necessary to take a graft from the latissimus dorsi, what in the gym they would call the lat muscle of my back, and use it to patch the calf. "But we will have to wait and see," he says. "I just want you to be prepared."

The good news just keeps coming.

My throat is raw from anesthesia tubes; it feels as if I have had a tonsillectomy, and I start to wonder if the surgeons didn't make a mistake and take those out. But those are already out. Age ten. I had surgery in the morning, and Mom brought me home at night when she got off her shift. She brought pistachio ice cream because it was her favorite and I liked it, too.

"I know this is difficult, Sam, but you have to know what's going on," he says. "The injury hit below the knee at about midshin, which means that circulation to the area is not ideal; it's a long way from the heart," he says, still looking down. "Because the anterior tibial artery was severed and so many veins cut, more than half of the blood supply to the area has been permanently destroyed."

"Irreparably."

"Sorry?" He pushes his glasses up higher on his nose.

"Irreparable. That sounds better than permanent. It's a question of word choice." I just want to sleep. "I worked at *Emergency Medical Services* magazine. My mom was an operating room nurse for half my life. I know the drill."

I hit the button for morphine. The truth about a narcotic is that it doesn't take away pain or make anything easier, but it does extract from one the ability to care, to be concerned, to give a good goddamn.

The doctor is still talking. Because Harley's hoof was a dull, imprecise tool, the largest artery in the leg, which runs in the rear of the tibia, was damaged but not severed. The vascular surgeon was able to save it.

"If not . . ." Dr. Etminan says, his voice trailing off into a kind of verbal shrug.

"If not, what?" I ask, wanting him to say the words, perversely wanting everything to be as explicit as possible.

"If not, there would be no chance to save your leg. We would definitely have to amputate."

To amputate.

Click, click.

Samantha Dunn, thirty-two, health and fitness editor, journalist, wife, book reader, equestrian, dog owner, recreational hiker, boxing-lesson taker, rock 'n' roll aficionado, blue-jeans wearer, amputee.

"As it is," he says, "there is some chance you may keep the leg."

I look at him. He says this as if it were a known fact, but this information changes the entire underpinning of the situation. I thought we were talking about the chance of losing the leg, not a chance of keeping the leg. "The leg," already not my leg. Something *other than, in addition to.* Now is the part where I would normally just turn and walk away from whoever or whatever presents anxiety, but I am weighed down by this *other than.* I have been hurt before but never like this. I realize I am hobbled.

And when I am formulated, sprawling on a pin
When I am pinned and wriggling on the wall.

I was seventeen when I memorized those lines, an exchange student in Sydney, Australia. I thought I had discovered T. S. Eliot. *Have you read him? He's really good!* What did I know. In the tiny New Mexico towns where I grew up, we had no bookstores, only a ragged library and racks of paperbacks at the supermarket.

Click, click, click. I close my eyes.

There appears to be a priest at my bedside, and this frightens me. Priests mean there is a death, or exorcism, imminent. My mother called the priest, just like when she called the priest the morning my stepfather died in the hospital. Frank got converted and had last rites in a sort of one-stop shop. No, the emergency room must have called the priest. The woman in the ER who wanted to know about insurance also had asked me at some point, "Religion?" "Catholic," I told her, but that was purely theoretical. If one were to have a religion, one would base it upon the mother and father's religious affiliation, and the sociopolitical context in which one was reared, factoring in, of course, the genetic predisposition toward papistry inherent in the Celts and the Italians, which largely constitute both sides of one's genetic history. It does not mean that since I had my leg ripped off I was expecting to see a priest. I don't even know how to say the rosary.

"Good afternoon, Samantha," he says. "God has given us a beautiful day."

Everyone in the hospital immediately calls me Samantha for some reason. Samantha is whom the phone solicitors and bill collectors ask for when they call, affording me the opportunity to reply No habla inglés. If people know me they call me Sam, or in the case of some very close friends and extended family—an interesting paradox there, why the most intimate friends and the most distant blood relations choose the same appellation—it is Sammy.

His name is Father Fitz-something-something. Irish.

Butter on those boiled potatoes, Father?

Don't mind if I do, my child. God is great; let us thank him for the bounty he has given us.

The priest presses a blue and white plastic rosary into my grasp, and I am put strangely at ease by this act. The beads are round, smooth. The priest is also round, smooth. He is so very fat. Unbelievably so. His fingers cannot bend inward to touch his own palm. There would be no way he could move such girth without thoughtful consideration about where it will land. He has literally become the church, the embodiment of it, mammoth, with many folds.

"How are you doing, my dear?" he says.

I must not be doing that well if they sent you, I say, but then again I probably don't say that. My pillows keep sliding off the bed. Maybe I ask him for assistance with them. Assistance. Roadside. Things found along the way. Hitchhiking once, and a NAPA Auto Parts guy picked me up. Actually, my car had run out of gas on a strip of highway outside of Carlsbad that no one ever traveled. Snakeweed literally grew out of cracks in the asphalt. The fuel gauge on my Datsun never worked. The wipers didn't work on that car either, unless you pushed in the cigarette lighter. The heater made the headlights come on. The lesson is never buy a car from a man who wanted to take a crack at rewiring.

"I learned some serious voodoo driving that car."

"Excuse me, dear?" says the priest.

The NAPA Auto Parts guy was quite a stand-up man. Couldn't believe there was a nineteen-year-old girl by herself on that highway on the way to nowhere. Pentecostal, I recall. Part-time preacher. I love to hear those Pentecostals talk. Sexier by leagues than the boring born-again Baptists. Pentecostals are scary, because they see everything in life containing an element of danger. The subtext is always annihilation. Everything is forever about to end. There are signs everywhere. I always thought it made sense on an emotional level, but, practically, in terms of everyday life, they are all just nuttier than fruitcakes. *Nutty as a fruitcake*. Gram always said that too.

"Samantha?" The priest pulls the curtain that is supposed

to act like a wall in this hospital room. He wants to offer me a blessing and this time I really do say, "Just give me the works, Father."

He places his hand lightly on my arm. The feather weight of his touch doesn't seem possible. Like something in a tutu. *Fantasia*. Elephants pirouette and poor little Mickey, how's he going to mop up all that water? I saw that movie with friends from elementary school at a matinee in an old theater on the Santa Fe Plaza. We went to Swenson's for ice cream afterward. Mom gave me money from her purse, which was a big tooled leather extravaganza containing lipsticks and used Kleenex and change, so much change it sounded like she was wearing sleighbells when she walked.

"Our Father," the priest begins, and I don't know the words so I just keep silent, as I did at the funeral mass for my stepfather. I sat next to Mom, on her knees on that wooden bench in front of the pew, her hands clasped together, her head bowed, her tears falling on the wood and I thought they would probably leave stains. They had only been married for four years. Tears: the steam that rises as the happily-ever-after evaporates.

The priest at the funeral gave the call and the rest of us the response. I read mine out of the paper pamphlet provided, but my mother kept her eyes shut and answered in a strange language. I tilted my head closer to her, watching her mouth form the words. She was answering in Latin. Holy shit, I thought. My mother hasn't prayed in church since Vatican II changed the mass to English. The act of her praying felt so private I turned my head away. How much is not known about her. I cannot even guess.

"... in your mercy, dear Lord," the priest is saying now, and it all seems so very beautiful that I start to cry. When I was a teenager, I would ride my horse Gabe up to the top of Porkchop Hill—it was a mesa, really, steep sides and a level plateau—and once I was up there I would just sit and let him graze. The tiny tufts of buffalo grass, when you look close enough, are perfectly formed arrangements. A Japanese design, the way the green and bluish tone and pale yellow weave into each other. That made me cry too. And the delicate bones of my horse's leg, the slender cannon bone, the ball of the joint. All the strength and muscle come down to such fine sculpture. That also made me cry. I rode Gabe so much I came to believe my heartbeat was the sound of his hooves. I rode him until he was so tired his head hung like a dog's, and then I would get off and walk beside him. I swam with him in lakes. I would put my nose to his muzzle to breathe in the narcotic scent of alfalfa.

The priest is done with his official duty. That was fast. Nothing like mass. "Well, Samantha, you're in God's hands now. I'll be praying for you."

I move to touch his chubby hand and he lets me, his skin smooth and rubbery as a boiled egg. "Thank you, Father," I tell him.

After he leaves I finger the plastic rosary, and then I sleep, and in my sleep I know the words.

"Sammy? Sammy?" Matt's voice soft but insistent.

Immediately I think something is wrong. Something more wrong. He's sitting right near my bed and reaches to touch my fingers with his large, square hands. How is it possible that these large hands can weave sound out of six thin metal guitar strings? He would have been a natural blacksmith.

"Sammy?" he says again. Why does everyone keep saying my name? "I saw Harley. I went to the barn because I was so mad at him. I was going to kill him, but I couldn't."

I open my eyes. "What?"

He pets me in a calming motion, as if I might bolt. "I wanted to do something about you being hurt. I guess I wanted to take something out on him." His voice is reedy, as if it might crack. "But when I went there, he was just standing in his pen with his head down. He looks so sad. It really seems like he knows he hurt you."

"I should never have gotten off," I say, wanting to clarify just who did what and why I am hurt. "I know better than that." This feeling is so awful. I can do nothing about anything. My world constricted to the size of a twin mattress. I start to cry again. More than I have ever cried in my life. I cannot wipe the tears away because the IV needles poke more deeply into my hands when I try to move.

People who don't ride always blame the horse, as if the horse is the one with the kind of brain that can build pyramids in the desert and create rockets that land on the moon. Matt used to ride with me when we were first dating. He hasn't done that in almost a decade. I haven't invited him, either. Did he not feel welcome at the stable, is that where our relationship started to go wrong? Now he'll be the one to have to feed the horse, and he'll figure out how much money I spend on Harley and he won't believe it and he'll blame me, I'll be called a saboteur, he'll say, "We could buy a house with what you waste on this animal!" "We could afford a kid with what you spend here" or, "I could buy five new guitars for what you waste on this animal, this murderous animal that could very well make you a peg leg, and who wants a wife like that?"

I wonder if I have been talking out loud because Matt says, "Shh. Everything will be OK. Harley's fine. Drew and Janice are going to take good care of him."

I nod my head and turn the corners of my mouth up encouragingly, but I am not convinced. Maybe the stable owners, Drew and Janice, will not want to take care of Harley. Maybe they too will blame him. Maybe everyone will decide that I shouldn't have a horse and will take him away from me, and I will be able to do exactly nothing about it. In the span of forty-eight hours I have become a child once more.

We sit with silence between us, focus our attention on the television perched above the bed.

"Your mom's on the phone. She's wigged out." Matt holds the phone up toward the summit of pillows where I lay my head.

"Please, can I talk to her in a little while? I just have to rest," I tell him. "Just let me close my eyes for a little bit."

Click.

It's likely Mom will call me a klutz, say, "Jesus H. Christ, Sam, what were you thinking?" or she'll laugh in that throaty, cigarette way of hers and tell a story about one of my other accidents opening with the line, "That reminds me of the time you . . ." She has many amusing tales in her repertoire. I am computing a mental list of all possible selections she could choose from, starting chronologically and limiting the list to only those that resulted in bona fide physical injury requiring some level of medical attention, not just the bruises, or the scrapes and stumbles, or the near misses. So far:

1. A split lip from falling on a wooden toy that had something to do with rabbits who ate carrots if you pulled them by a string.
2. A finger squashed by a car door when I was four and her friend Natalie felt terrible about not checking to see that my fingers were out of the way.
3. An open wound on my thigh—I think it was my thigh, or was it my back?—from a bite when Smoky, a neighbor's guard dog, chased me down the street.
4. A broken wrist from riding a bike with a Barbie case attached to the handlebars, which Mom insisted was a sprain until it turned purple and my grandmother said, Oh Good God, take her to the hospital, will you? So we went in the back way and mom's doctor friend gave me a fiberglass cast, which was great because I could go swimming with it.
5. A cracked rib and sternum separated from my rib cage when a player head-butted my chest during a playground soccer game, in which the player in question turned out to be the son of a neurosurgeon my mother worked with, and I always thought she had a thing going with him because the doctors she knew, well, they were always unhappy with their wives.
6. A concussion, my first, caused when the saddle slipped underneath my galloping horse during a gymkhana for the Santa Fe Junior Horsemen's Association where we had been

in the lead until the cinch, which I had neglected in my haste to tie the knot on, came loose.

That's the list up to age eleven, I think.

"What, honey?" says a voice that sounds very much like my mother's, and I think, How can this be? Then I realize it indeed is my mother's. Evidently at some point Matt wedged the receiver between my shoulder and ear.

"My accidents," I croak into the receiver. "I was trying to remember the ones from when I was a kid."

"Uh-huh. My poor baby. You better get some rest," which is what I say to her when she calls at two o'clock in the afternoon and has been drinking Scoresby's Scotch out of iced tea tumblers.

"Do you know what a Grade III, Class B tib/fib fracture is? Is *barnyard* a medical term?"

"Shit," she replies. She is quiet for a long time, or it could be that I fall sleep again.

"The doctor made it sound bad," I say.

"Shit." She makes that puffing sound which means she is lighting a cigarette. "You know the first thing I thought of when Matt called, don't you?" she says. She always asks questions as if she's setting up a punch line.

"Christopher Reeve?"

"Yep."

"I'm tired, Mom." My mouth is dry, and it feels like ants are marching all over my skin. The ants came all the way from that canyon in Malibu. How did the ants survive the helicopter ride? How did the ants survive the surgery? "There are ants, Mom."

"It just feels like that from the morphine. It's the way the drug plays on the nerves. There are no ants. Honey, listen to me, there are no ants."

I hear a sharp cry of pain that is not unlike the sound a dog makes if you should tromp on his paw. The room is now dark. The curtains, pulled. No one perches in the chair by my bedside and the phone is back in the cradle. There is another patient to the left of me in the bed by the door. We do not know each other's names, but we do know each other's ailments: she is a hip replacement and a cancer of some sort; the cancer drugs made a honeycomb of her bones, and her joint cracked from the pressure of her own weight as she lay in bed. She has three young children who cry when they come to see her, no husband; they will be orphaned on her death, but she tells them, Shh, babies, everything will be fine. She is experienced in true suffering; she bears it with a strength that seems to radiate across our shared room. Whatever she tells me, I accept as irrefutable.

"Pain pretty bad?" she asks.

The yelp was mine? "Sorry, I didn't mean to wake you."

"Couldn't sleep anyway. I need more drugs." She jams the call button for the nurse. "Morphine doesn't do anything after a while, for me at least. Ask them for Dilaudid. That'll fix you right up."

I would go to meetings with Matt while he was in drug rehab, and I recall the junkies pining longingly for Dilaudid. "Opiates," they would say with all the authority of a pharmacist, "are the fucking kings of all drugs," and they would return to sucking deeply on their cigarettes, nicotine the only drug allowed them in that expensive, Ambassador Suites–looking hospital. Experimental lab rats will happily hit the lever that feeds them the opiates until their lungs are paralyzed and they stop breathing. A rehab doctor said that during a lecture.

Click, click.

A wave of nausea. A side effect of opiates. The doctor had said that, too.

People are talking all around me, but with my eyes shut I feel above them, separate from their concerns. "She's on an HMO. Which one? Kaiser?" "Did we get that transfer order from Kaiser?" "Ms. Dunn, we are just going to move you a little to your side." "We're just going to proceed with the schedule until Kaiser takes her." The last voice is Dr. Etminan's. I open my eyes, which feels like exercise, a strenuous activity. "Sam," he says, slowly, "you're going into surgery."

He is bending over me. The tight furrows between his eyes turn the black arches of his brows into the shape of bat wings. "What does your mother call you?"

"Mohammed."

Name of the prophet. The Koran urges parents to teach children horseback riding, swimming, and good marksmanship. "Your family from Iran?"

"Good guess," he says.

"My mom and stepdad worked in the Middle East for a long time." I spent a summer in Saudi Arabia when I was seventeen and saw a prince's stable where horses with bodies like greyhounds stood on marble floors the color of snow.

He puts his hand briefly on my shoulder. "Mohammed?" I want to ask him if this is the surgery where they will take out my back muscle and put it on my leg, or if they could decide unilaterally just to prune, to hack, to cut off. But it takes too much effort.

Soon I am dreaming. I have the feeling of emerging from a cool, cavelike darkness into a bright, dry, California sun. I am on a trail that begins not far from my front door. I feel the impact of first one foot hitting the ground squarely, then the other. I can feel each part of my feet, the way my toes reflexively grab at the ground through the running shoes. My arms pump. My breath sounds loud to my ears. I keep running. I feel good.

A blanket covers me. "You're in the recovery room, Ms. Dunn. Everything's fine." Fine, fine, a new kind of fine. I am coming out of anesthesia. I know my leg has not been amputated because the pain pulses. I look up and see the ceiling tiles' holes; they grow bigger, the size of rabbit holes. And now I am Alice. And now I jump.

The great V of Harley's stomach. V an ornamental chevron. He is flying over me. He lands. I have to get that boot off. Damn. *And when I am pinned.*

A nurse stands facing a surgery scheduling board on the wall near me, the felt-tipped marker squealing across the white surface. The date written in black at the top: Thursday, 9/18/97. I went riding on Monday.

If this is Thursday, I had a lunch date with Valli O'Reilly, a makeup artist. Valli loves her dog, so mostly we talk about dogs, my pug and her Australian shepherd. Today she is going to show me a new lineup of lip glosses; famous women wear a shade of red she invented. At the same moment this IV drips down the tube thousands of women are looking in mirrors and considering the shape of their lips, rubbing a color not like flesh into the skin of their mouths. Yesterday or two days ago—it is useless to contemplate when, but at some point—I did the same considering of shape, the same rubbing of color.

So there Valli O'Reilly sits at a restaurant, alone, staring at a menu. She will be looking for the vegan option, checking messages on her cell phone, time she could be using to play with her dog or put her special red on beautiful stars to turn them yet more beautiful. But she is waiting for me. She wonders if I stood her up. She will consider this possibility because I am nearly always late for everything. Lunches, bill paying, assignments, appointments, taxes—anything that occupies a predetermined point of space and time.

I maintain this is due to the simple fact that I don't own a watch. I always either lose watches—forgetting them at the stable or the gym or in the car, or sometimes I just take them off at night and put them by the bed and they *simply disappear*—or the watches meet tragic ends: are stepped on, submerged in water, smashed against rocks, chewed by dogs. Others have suggested that my chronic tardiness is a product of resistance imbedded somewhere in the psyche, an explanation I like because it makes me sound mysterious and tortured, and because it is vastly preferable to what magazine editors, college professors, and my mother have called this habit: carelessness, laziness, arrogance, sloth.

Time must exist; I accept this. But I cannot get a handle on it. Each moment is infinitely expandable, pressing backward, then shooting outward. The present: merely the resting point between.

Matt sits in a chair beside my bed, his head resting on the vinyl. He looks tired. Dark circles have settled under the large, rounded, deep-set eyes.

When did they get there, where did they come from?

After all, it is 1983 and he is only sixteen. He has long straight hair that he dyes blond, exactly like other guitar-playing boys from Albuquerque, New Mexico, who consider Led Zeppelin, Hendrix, and Black Sabbath their Bach, Beethoven, and Brahms. He wakes up in the morning and drops acid, then falls back to sleep so he can wake up tripping. When the alarm clock buzzes, he puts a cassette of Jimi Hendrix's version of the "Star Spangled Banner" in his stereo, picks out chords on a Fender knockoff. He does this until he can play along with Jimi.

"Here, you should eat something," he says, holding up a quivering orange Jell-O square on a spoon. He puts the metal spoon against my lips, like feeding a baby. "I know you don't want to, but take a little. There."

Now his hair is black at the roots. He drives a red Volkswagen van his ex-girlfriend decorated with purple satin curtains. We attend New Mexico State University in Las Cruces but have to go to El Paso, Texas, forty-five miles away, to drink in bars because down by the border no one checks IDs. I am the college newspaper editor, a little square for him but he can get past it. Everyone thinks he's sweet and shy, but I stand close enough to him to know he's not so nice, keeping up a wicked running commentary under his breath. He makes me laugh, gasping-for-air, crying-it's-so-funny laughter.

"How come you never hear about gruntled employees?" he says. "If it's tourist season, why can't we shoot them? But what I really want to know is, Would the ocean be deeper if sponges didn't live there?"

He hates his computer science major, works in the concert hall as part of the stage crew, wants to go to a school in Florida to become a recording engineer.

He is completing his degree at the engineering school. I have returned to the country from a year overseas, and he wants me to go to L.A. with him. I have spent two weeks with my mother watching my stepfather die slowly in a hospital bed.

"It's like watching a car wreck on a tape loop, I bet." His voice on the phone.

"It's a horrible, horrible disease. Then there's Mom. I don't know what's going to happen when he dies."

"I was talking about your mom," he answers.

Matt also looks good without a shirt. "I'm thinking about

getting a tattoo of you right here on my arm." He points to the rounded cap of his shoulder.

I'm not sure of the appropriate response. "Matty, I am honored, but what if, you know, something happens with us—"

"Don't worry. I won't make it look too much like you."

Of course, I say yes to L.A.

I feel him brush a stray hair from my face. The tips of his fingers used to be callused by steel guitar strings. They are soft now. I don't remember when he stopped playing every day. "Think of it this way," he says. I see him looking at the IV stand. "I know smack heads who'd kill to score whatever you're on right now."

He is using one of his Emmys for television production as a doorstop to our bedroom. He walks into the bathroom where I am putting on mascara in front of the vanity mirror.

"I've been thinking," he says. "Forget this crap. Man, I hate working for TV. Dave and I are going to put a band together."

The band puts out a CD on a small label. It's great.

No one hears it.

The other guitar player quits and the bassist goes AWOL. Matt is dyeing his hair Manic Panic, a form of fuchsia. He washes his hair, and—there's no way to get around saying it—it fades to pink. He spends the day with the band's drummer, sitting in our living room, a bong attached to his mouth as if it is a ventilator. "We're working on songs," he says. I go to the barn.

He talks into the phone by the bed. "She's really out of it right now. No, she can't talk; she had another surgery today." I watch him through the narrow slits of my eyes. He winds a finger absently around the cord, one way then the other. "But I'll definitely tell her you called. Yeah, thanks. Bye."

"Who was that?" I ask.

"I'm not sure," he says.

It is Friday afternoon. It is no different than other days until Matt sees armies of spiders moving up and down the curtains. Matt tells me I am an assassin from the Colombian drug cartel. He figures out his boss is in a plot to steal all his money. Everything I say provides him further evidence.

"Everything's going to be OK." I approach him with arms outstretched, as if moving toward something feral.

"Don't lie to me! Don't . . . fucking . . . lie . . . to . . . me." He cries one minute; he stares blankly into space the next. Friday moves into Saturday moves into Sunday. I think he will kill me. Then I think, no, he will kill himself.

I call my friend, whisper into the receiver, crying, afraid he might hear and think I am contacting the cartel. See, see! I said you were lying. She says call the police. "Do you want me to call them? I'll call them—"

I say no; I say any moment he will snap out of his psychosis. But I'm more afraid that drugs are probably stashed somewhere in the house and that he will be put in prison. The truth: that I will be guilty.

Did you know about your husband's drug use, Ma'am?

Well, yes, Officer.

Why didn't you stop him, Ma'am? It was your job to stop him. You do not have the right to remain silent.

It is the Monday I hear him rummaging through his desk. I sit in the kitchen, trying not to make any noise. He finds me, shows me a pamphlet for a drug rehab center. "Take me there," his voice is small. "Just please take me there."

It is the first week in rehab. He calls to tell me he wants a divorce.

It is the second week in rehab. He tells me he loves me.

It is the first month in rehab. I leave our rental on the fringe of Hollywood; a friend tells me about a ratty A-frame for lease in a Malibu canyon that's not far from a stable. "It's a five-mile ride to the grocery store," I tell his parents. "Drug dealers can't find this place." They give me money to move. "We always hated where you lived," they say. "We want you to be safe."

The room is dark, lit only by the flashing colors of the television. Matt sees that my eyes have opened and puts his lips to my forehead. "Sam? Sometime tomorrow they're going to transfer you to Kaiser Hospital in Woodland Hills."

"I don't want to. Can't I just stay put?" Babies cry because that is their only defense against the world. "Can't things just be the way they are for a while?"

"Babe, you'll be home in a couple days. The night they told me about your accident I made a bed for you on the couch so you wouldn't have to climb the stairs to the bedroom.

I thought it was just a broken leg. Sam? Sammy? Go back to sleep."

Matt sober: He is sitting on our couch, his shoulders rounded over a root beer, which he holds as if it were a bottle of Bud. His large hazel eyes look as if the weight of those long eyelashes is too heavy for the lids to hold up. His hair is buzzed short, a natural, walnut-shell shade of brown. I ask him, "What do you want for dinner?"

He looks across the room at me like I am someone he is meeting for the first time. "Don't ask me for anything, because I can't give it. I'm just barely hanging on."

Our house is built of eggshell and blown glass. No sudden movements. No loud noises. Pressure of any kind can be disastrous.

The formula for bone: calcium, phosphorus, hydrogen and oxygen. It sounds like a simple assignment from tenth-grade chemistry, but it takes months and sometimes years for the body to concoct it once the integrity of a bone has been destroyed. In the case of a large bone like the tibia, part of the appendicular skeleton—as in appendage, as in arms and legs—there is a danger of "non union," to use the vernacular of the orthopedist, which is to say that what once was one now is in pieces, and those pieces, now separate, cannot get together again, no matter how much those pieces might want to, might know that it is better to be one than two.

For the treatment of serious fractures, it is common to use an external fixation device, what amounts to a steel cage around the broken area; spokes pointing inward drill through the skin and hold the bone in place. But in a Grade III fracture where the skin has been sliced, the muscles ripped apart, and the arteries cut, the problem is how to stabilize the bone while the soft tissue heals. To do this doctors use an internal device called an intermedullary nail. This device is not a nail at all but a kind of rod, about the length of a ruler, made of titanium, the same metal used to make warheads. It's the only metal that seems capable of bearing the tremendous concussive pressure involved in standing, walking, jumping, and running that is absorbed every day by the human skeleton. Nevertheless, it is not impossible for the titanium to snap. By opening the knee and cutting the ligaments to move the kneecap to the side, doctors are able to shove this titanium rod through the center of the tibia. Then the kneecap is replaced, and the rod is secured into place with devices that look not much different than Phillips screws, anchored below the knee and right above the ankle.

The problem with this technique is that infection rates are higher than with the external cages; some studies have reported amputation rates for Grade III fractures up to 40 percent. Doctors are not gamblers and do not like to enter into any procedure with that potential for failure. But when there are no better bets, even doctors will play the odds.

Kaiser Hospital is new, with puce blankets and nurses' aides who wear flower-print smocks. Whenever I open my eyes, someone is asking if she can get me anything. "Water?" "Bedpan?" "Jell-O?" The morphine drip has been removed and instead I am given Percodan, which takes longer to kick in but doesn't make my skin feel as if armies of insects are crawling over it.

The fluorescent night-lights along the base of the room's walls glow, some alien chartreuse sunset. The window shows a view of night with no stars and one parking-lot light. No one is in the visitor's chair; the bed next to me is empty. Voices in the hall break the silence, and then the door opens and a man walks in. He's wearing a lab coat, which makes me think of mice, experimentation, tested on animals; *if I were a mouse I'd bite*. He has corn-color hair, freckles, eyes the blue of Frosted Flakes cereal boxes.

"I'm Dr. Mesna." He is, mercifully, without a clipboard. "There are some things I need to go over with you."

Mesna. Transpose two letters and you have Mensa. Genius. I take this as a good sign.

"This is just a horrific injury," he begins, chronicling as Dr. Etminan had the difficulties of infection, of compromises to blood circulation, of tissue damage, a list so long it begs a ". . . and a partridge in a pear tree." He speaks in a midwestern pitch that sounds to my ear much like the Emergency Broadcast System's minute-long tone that breaks into radio programming. He has nothing good to say, objectively reporting on my injury as if he were talking to a colleague—Did you see the tib/fib in bed 2? What a mess!—and this makes me feel nostalgic. It reminds me of my mother's voice.

Mom, thank God. Mom, I . . . think I'm having a heart attack. I have chest pains and my left arm is numb.

Were you lifting weights or doing anything stupid like that?

I . . . (panting breath) . . . was . . . at . . . the . . . gym . . . today . . .

I'd make book it's costochondritis. Cardiac arrhythmia would be unusual in a twenty-five-year-old with no congenital heart irregularities.

What's coastal condri—

Costo. It means the cartilage in the chest wall is inflamed by overuse. It's a typical sports injury. You see it in football players all the time.

Mom, it . . . hur . . . it . . . hur—

It hurts. Sure it hurts, but it won't kill you. Go to the ER if you want. They'll give you a shot of adrenaline and an anti-inflammatory and tell you to lay off the exercise for a while.

Thanks Mom.

No problem. That will be three hundred dollars, please.

Dr. Mesna says that unlike the surgical steel used in past years, the titanium nail is an inert metal, meaning bone will grow around and actually into it.

"Then how will you get it out?"

"We won't." He sighs. "I've had patients who get the idea they should remove their intermedullary nail. I strongly advise against it, because what we then have to do is go in again through the kneecap and try to remove the nail. It is possible to shatter the knee and create hairline fractures in the bone in the process, so you are potentially asking for worse problems by removing it."

And to think how I worried about the tiny piece of mesh surgeons used a few years ago to repair the hernia I gave myself from trying to do a hanging sit-up at the gym. At what point do I become bionic? Is there a proportion, a ratio that has to be established? Who decides that?

"But we're getting ahead of ourselves." Dr. Mesna doesn't require any help in his conversation. "The nail may not last long enough to fuse with bone. A lack of callous growth can be a real problem in this situation. The nonunion rates are significant. Amputation could turn out to be the best option, eventually."

"For whom?" It feels like I am sitting beside my own voice, listening to it say things. "Best option for whom?"

His brow furrows and I believe I can hear him thinking: She's getting uppity. One of those righteous, illogical types. Incapable of dispassionately evaluating the evidence. Next thing you know she'll feel sorry for herself.

"A latent bone infection can arise even a year from now. I

had a patient once who had been injured in World War II, and forty years later he developed an infection," he says, moving down toward the foot of my bed. "The damage to the ligaments and the nerves and bones will likely prevent you from walking normally. Luckily your tibial nerve is intact; otherwise there would be no chance. Running will be an extremely unlikely probability. But the advances in prosthetics are astounding. Chronic pain won't be an issue. With one of those you could run, and you could even ride a horse, if you want to do that again."

"And do you ride a lot of horses, Doctor?" I hear the voice I sit beside say.

"I just want to make you aware of all your options," he replies.

I am watching him remove the blankets covering the leg, worried about his intention. I have developed a fear of being touched. Any movement triggers this image of the leg toppling off its mountain of pillows and shattering to the floor. *All the king's horses and all the king's men couldn't put Humpty together again.* Perhaps this fear sprouted out of the pain that results from any motion, even a deep inhale.

"Do you feel this?" he says, touching the toes.

I don't look at the leg. I don't want anyone else to look at it, either. "Kind of," I say. "I don't *not* feel anything, but it's more a sense of pressure."

"Uh-huh," he says, like the sound men make when they are watching television and you want to know if they liked the twice-baked potatoes you made with Parmesan. "And can you move your toes at all?"

He asks this casually, but it is a serious query. If the toes are frozen, if there is no sensation at the bottom of the foot, the leg from the shin down is a dead thing, driftwood.

I look down at the toes, putty colored, a Play-Doh sculpture. When I was little my grandmother would tuck me in bed so tight I felt as if I were tied down, and I would start to loosen the constraining sheets by wiggling my toes, then my feet, finally kicking the covers free. I try, harder than I have tried in my adult life to do anything, to be that child again.

"Very good," Dr. Mesna says. "That's more than I would have expected."

Pain rakes my body as if I have just grabbed an electric fence. Dr. Mesna tells me he'll see me again in the morning, and again in the next week, and again, and again.

"Good night," he says, checking his wristwatch. "Sleep well."

Three A.M. must be the official Hour of Self-pity.

For once, it looks as bad as it is.

A horse with a broken leg is no longer really a horse. Its horseness requires four legs, a walk, a trot, a canter, a flat-out gallop. Motion is not separate from being. A horse that breathes and sees and feels but cannot move fast enough has already become food for cougars and wolves, birds of carrion, a curious or starving squirrel, for dogs and tabby cats, has become fillets for the French and the Japanese. This is a constant in the natural equation. A shark that can't swim fast enough to move water through its gills is already a dead fish. A grizzly with a wounded paw is a bear about to be eviscerated by other bears.

No one but me seems to be thinking about these things. I was born in the right part of the right decade in the right century to the right species that holds the top order on the food chain. In fact, as an amputee I will have no quotidian concern; so many function with wheelchairs and walkers, access to almost everything has been made equal. Look at the success stories! *People* magazine. Quadriplegics. Paraplegics.

On *Oprah*, a double amputee who runs marathons—marathons, what most people with two good legs can't manage. A slight amputation from the knee down, on one leg? When you've got another leg? Who *cares*? The horse didn't step on your face, thank God. Carry a whip when you ride a horse and even the horse won't know you don't have a leg. In public wear a long skirt, always, and high boots. Pants with a wide cut can do the trick. Avoid swimsuits, and shorts, and no one need ever be made uncomfortable.

Men won't mind. Doesn't interfere with the ability to have sex. Think about it: during sex, what guy has ever had occasion to look at the part of the leg that will be missing? In fact it might be good to have it out of the way. Even that is theoretical because you're married, and he's in a forever contract with you, one leg or two, no matter.

But I know my horseness.

I was not more than four years old when, one weekend, it had to be in the Pennsylvania autumn, the leaves mustard and rust, I stepped out the back door to make my way all by myself to my cousins' house. They lived two miles away on Maple Place, which made me think of syrup and pancakes. I don't recall what prompted my expedition. Maybe there had been an argument between the adults in my house, maybe I said, *No Mommy, YOU shut up* and my mouth had been washed out with Safeguard soap, or maybe my mother was just exhausted from working and going to night school, my grandmother in the kitchen doing dishes or in the backyard filling the bird feeder. For whatever reason, no adult saw a child with strawberry blond pigtails and a blue sweater walking alone on the shoulder of a heavily trafficked two-lane road, or witnessed how she crossed it, or saw her travel four blocks down a sidewalk to the clapboard house where the white paint had worn to a shabby gray. All I recall is watching my own feet in tan moccasins skip over the lines in the sidewalk. Sometimes I would stop and hop over a line, pretending it was a snake that would bite me if I didn't jump high enough. I looked up at a tree, the leaves like yellow tassels waving down at me, and how when I stared up long enough it seemed as if the tree and all the leaves were moving down toward me, or that I was moving up into it, and beyond that into a sky puffy with clouds.

Finally I reached my cousins' porch and knocked on their front door, thinking something about cookies. There were always cookies for me at their house. And my Uncle Mutt had a mustache. He picked me up; he had a big, pillowy stomach, and I put my cheek next to his rough lips. My Aunt Marietta dialed the phone, which was black, and simply said, "She's here." Mutt told Marietta, "Tell them to leave her awhile. She must have wanted to come all this way. Tell them I'll have John drive her back."

My cousin Johnny had green eyes and a head full of dark brown hair and I loved him. He drove a convertible blue Mustang and when he sat me in the bucket seat he slid the seat belt over my legs and clicked it into place. He had been to Vietnam, whenever that was, and as we drove he sang, "Oh Suzy Q, oh Suzy Q, oh Suzy Q baby I love you, Suzy Q," changing the second chorus to, "Oh Sammy Q/Baby I love/Sammy Q."

When we pulled up to the house, my mother seemed to lunge for the car, sliding me right through the seat belt without unhooking the buckle and enfolding me in her arms so tight I struggled against her, certain I'd be smothered. Her face was wet. "Don't ever do that again, honey." She seemed mad and sad at the same time. She told Johnny she thought I was playing with my Palomino rocking horse in the dining room. But then she realized the house contained a quietness no house with children ever has.

When she called for me and there was no answer, she and my grandmother didn't even take the time to yell at each other, they only began tearing apart the house. I wasn't in the yard, or the closet, or the bedroom, or the other bedroom, or the bathroom where I usually climbed up on the sink to rummage through the cabinet looking for the grown-ups' makeup to play with. By the time Aunt Marietta called to say I was safe in their kitchen, Mom and the neighbors were wading in the creek in back of the house, certain I had drowned. My grandmother was in her bedroom, crying, thinking she was never going to see me become Miss America or even a Girl Scout.

Mom kept the back door locked after that. Soon I was old enough to open any door anytime I felt like it, but we had moved to New Mexico by then, and there was nothing to run to except open country. There are entire years of my life I do not remember being indoors except during school. I do remember the sand of the arroyo under my feet, in winter how the red mud caked into bricks around my boots. Staghorn cactus pierced my jeans but then there were times magenta flowers decked its crooked arms, the blossoms vivid but without scent, like papier-mâché piñatas. In the fall, when you shook a piñon tree, nuts fell from its cones in a brown hail. I'd bring them back to my grandmother to roast and salt in the oven. I remember the fish-scale color of early weekend mornings, getting up to ride my horse, finding an opening or making one in a fence to get onto the Bureau of Land Management's vast holdings. If worse came to worst and we couldn't get around a fence, Gabe would jump the cattle guard on the road; the danger of his hoof catching in the open metal grate made me hold my breath. Somehow we always found a way onto the blond waves of the llano, the burnt mesas and arroyos and pine-scented hills. We would travel for hours. I'd come home more deeply freckled, lips chapped, bruises running down the inside of my legs from the seam of my jeans.

When I was thirteen, we moved into a house far outside the limits of Las Vegas, New Mexico, which is nothing like Las Vegas, Nevada. It is a place of juncture, a northern New Mexico village wedged at the point where the Rocky Mountains meet the Great Plains, a point on the Santa Fe Trail later carved up by the railroad. It is the place people conjure when they imagine the Old West. Most of the 13,000 residents trace their roots to the Spanish settlers who came after the conquistadors, to the mestizos who slept with Apache and Commanche, or to the Yankees who came later, in the 1800s, with the railroad. And then there was my family, connected to nothing, three strangers hovering on the land. We were escaping Santa Fe, where we had lived in an apartment and then a beautiful adobe house where the walls turned orange with every sunset. But the rent was too high, finally impossible. Debts caught up with my mom.

The rent on the Las Vegas house was low enough for my mother to make, but the landlord left the yard filled with gutted Chevys, broken pickups, and tires from cars long wrecked. The kitchen was painted lime green, and my room had a rainbow mural covering all four walls but only one tiny window, more like a porthole. The carpet smelled of dog piss. Soon after we moved in, friends of my grandmother's from Back East called to say they were passing through in their RV and wanted to come for a visit.

"Oh, that's too bad, but we're going to be away this weekend." I can still hear my grandmother's voice on the phone. Gram had been in a sorority in high school. She had worked for thirty years as a buyer for a department store. She drew exact lines between white trash and respectable people. The cars put us clearly over more than one of her lines. "No, it's impossible to change our plans. I know you don't get out this way much. It's been eleven years, that's right. Too bad, really. I feel bad about it, I do, but it can't be helped."

She cried when she got off the phone. I tried to put my arm around her. She shrugged it off. *Jesus H. Christ almighty, I would rather drop dead than have them see this.*

I volunteered to clean up; I would start with my room. But the yard, that worried me. Maybe we could rig something up: we'd hitch Gabe to one of the old cars, and he'd pull it out and we could roll it off the property. Or at least move it so it wasn't in the front yard. She pretended I hadn't said anything.

My mother refused to feel sorry for her. "If you'd get a job, we could live somewhere else," she said, to which my grandmother replied, "I worked all my life, and you owe me," or "Someone has to take care of Sam," or "Go to hell." It was a litany I memorized.

The only good thing about that house was the pasture on the side, a half acre of grass and alfalfa. Mom and I moved a bathtub from the yard and used it as a watering trough for Gabe. We kept sweet feed and bran in metal garbage cans in the carport, safe from the rain. In the middle of the night I would slip out and find him in the pasture, sit on the ground and watch him graze. Sometimes I would lie down near him as he stood dozing; the breath he blew on me smelled of molasses and oats and corn. Pretty soon I wasn't sleeping at all, and I would obsessively walk around the house in the middle of the night, crying for I don't know what. I thought about Santa Fe; I fantasized I was in a Judith Krantz novel where the heroine goes to Paris and becomes beautiful and so rich everyone forgets how ugly and ignored she had been before. I would pretend to speak foreign languages, spending hours inventing syntax for tongues that did not exist. I memorized the names for all manner of horse, beginning with Andalusian, Appaloosa, Ardennais, Arabian, Barb, Brabant, Cleveland Bay, Cob, Connemara, and ending with Quarter Horse, Saddlebred, Thoroughbred, Trakehner, Yakut, zebra. I would wake up the dog and brush her with my mother's hairbrush. I would take a shower, and while I was still wet I would turn the water back on and take another one. I would do sit-ups until I felt a rug burn on my tailbone. I wrote really, really corny poems on blue-lined loose-leaf paper and stuck them in the spines of books. I would leave all the lights off. When not disturbed by a flashlight, the human eye has sensitive night vision; the secret is not to look directly at any one thing but to take it all in at once.

"She doesn't think anybody notices her Lady Macbeth routine. I think she's cracking up," I heard my grandmother tell my mom.

"It's just puberty," my mom said.

Gram told her she was wrong. "You've got to do something, I swear to Christ."

So they put me on a Greyhound bus to Washington State to spend three weeks on my Aunt Gay and Uncle Roy's ranch. I could spend all day down at the Stillaguamish River if I wanted to, ride with my uncle in his Jeep as he checked on the cattle in the evening. Aunt Gay made pancakes or French toast every morning and at night strawberry short-cake with whipped cream and Bisquick biscuits. I helped my aunt pick apples and pull weeds; sometimes we went to the grocery store in town. For my fourteenth birthday she bought a cake from the Blue Bird Bakery and my uncle had three pieces. Every night I fell asleep, exhausted.

What is needed in hospitals is a swivel-pedestal thing on which a phone can be located, doing away with the need to painfully reach over the rail to the bedside table, extract the phone from its cradle, and bring it to the ear, a process which spans the time of roughly ten rings.

"Hello?" I say.

"Were you sleeping?" It is a former editor and friend who

is always in so much of a hurry he has edited "hello" from his vocabulary as an unnecessary lead-in.

"No. I just sound like that now."

"Listen, you need to shoot that fucking horse."

"That's a cliché."

"I'm serious. How many times are you going to get hurt? This is redundant. Enough already."

"Are you trying to tell me you love me? That you're worried about me? I am so moved."

"Whatever. Call me if you need anything. And get rid of that stupid animal. You're too old to have a pony."

When he hangs up, I lay the receiver on the puce blanket. By the time the nurse comes in, a sharp series of beeps blares from the receiver. She kindly returns it to its cradle.

When I got back from Washington, a couple of the cars had been removed from the yard, and Gram had gotten the dog piss smell out of the carpet. The Encinias family, our nearest neighbors, had bought a new horse, a leggy gray mare named Linda which their eighteen-year-old son, Gene, came out from town to ride. He said hello to me while I was walking through the pasture with my saddle, a carrot in my pocket to bribe my horse into standing still for the cinch. I pretended I didn't hear him. He had just graduated from high school; he drove a car; he could not possibly have meant to talk to me.

A little while later as Gabe and I ambled down the dirt road toward Lake McAllister, the clacking of hooves on the hard ground made us both turn. Gene rode the mare bareback, his hands loose on the reins, his back straight as if the top of his head was pulled skyward on an invisible string.

"Hey, you don't talk to your neighbors or what?" he said. His teeth were white and a downlike fuzz springing from his upper lip suggested a mustache. "Odalé, you all stuck up or something?"

"Not even," I said, in the northern New Mexico Spanish cadence I had learned to mimic. I didn't know what else to say.

"So, you know my horse's name? It's Linda," he said, pronouncing it the Spanish way, Leen-da. "You know that means beautiful? Like you. Qué linda."

I felt broadsided, I didn't know how to respond. "Shut up" was the only thing I could think of. "Does that nag run?" I slapped Gabe's side and the horse bolted forward. His horse shied and I thought he would fall, but he recovered and galloped that mare to catch up to us. I remember the feeling of wind so strong it seemed to suck the air out of my lungs, the two of us laughing, crazy with speed. The horses were tired when we walked back from the lake. Gene reached over to put his hand on the cantle of my saddle.

From then on, every day after I got home from school Gene happened to be at his parents' house. He rode Linda bareback over so many miles he wore a hole in his jeans and a sore on her back where no hair grew. We would sit on a picnic bench at the lake, and in my head I would pretend we were pioneers with no house to go back to, just Apache land in front of us, and we would ride all the way to the ocean. The first time he kissed me his hands smelled like the eucalyptus of

Absorbine Jr., the liniment he'd massaged into Linda's legs when she came up lame that day.

When the snow arrived and we couldn't ride, we drove in his car, a Mercury Comet with blue vinyl seats. With the thaw, he taught me to drive on the dirt roads and in the Safeway parking lot. Now I was mobile. I could go all the way to Santa Fe if I needed to. I would never be stuck in that house again.

I talked Gene into joining the army with persuasive techniques I was learning as a Model United Nations team member in high school. My argument began with a plea to fulfill his potential as a onetime honor roll designate for West Las Vegas High, followed by the reasoning that he would be entitled to a free education, which would translate into a higher standard of living. When none of this moved him I switched to scare tactics, saying he'd never be able to earn a promotion from bag boy to produce manager at Safeway unless he took action. Still, he avoided the recruitment office. At that point I sent him one of my "theme poems" explaining that I had to get out, so if he wanted to be with me he'd have to find a way to escape, too. He said the poem made him sad, but that he thought I was exaggerating.

It was time to pull out the big gun. "My mother was in the air force for four years." I spit out the words. "Are you telling me you're afraid to do something *a woman has already done?*"

The army sent him to Mississippi for basic training, his first trip outside the state. He sent me letters and a wooden cross on which he carved Te Amo Sam. He told me he wanted to marry me when I got out of high school, that he could wait the three years. He was sure I would change my mind about wanting to see Europe, or, he suggested, we could see it together. After that, we could come back and live on the property out by the lake next to his father. He wrote that he would always be with me, and as I read I felt as if I were being pushed into a bag and feeling the air supply dwindle as the drawstring was pulled tight.

While Gene was away we moved into a newer, nicer house that only needed a fresh paint job and was closer to town. When he came back, he knocked on the front door, and although my grandmother invited him in warmly, I walked right past him with just a hello, and I ran down the steps to the school bus. After class, he waited outside in the parking lot.

"Qué pasa?" he wanted to know. "Mira, I still love you . . ."

"I can't, please," I told him, not breaking my stride. He had to get up and walk to continue the conversation, but I had nothing else to offer, no further explanation. I kept walking. My legs were longer than his, so with each step I moved a little farther ahead. He stopped. I walked faster.

All I want is to be able to wash my hair. I have grown accustomed to having to sleep on my back; I have grown accustomed to the physical therapists who come in twice a day and get me to stand up with a walker, and the way I feel like passing out as soon as I am able to balance on my one good leg. But it has been six days since my accident, and I cannot grow accustomed to the dirt from the canyon that still grates on my scalp, like the sharp dust off an emery board.

I am getting strong enough to travel the five feet from my bed to the bathroom. I am not supposed to go in there without help from an aide, because I might faint or slip on the tiles. Those dangers do scare me, I know they are real, but I make the trek by myself anyway. It's not that I am embarrassed about going to the bathroom in front of another person, although before the accident I would have been. I am not embarrassed now because they are not seeing me; they are seeing a leg, an arm, a shoulder, a haunch, parts of something totally organic and biological. I, meanwhile, reside in a small space located at my forehead that extends into my skull at an immeasurable depth. I, me, the person I am, cannot be seen, so these details concerning the body do not matter. I am bothered by the dirt in my scalp because it is closest to the place my actual self inhabits.

I stand in front of the bathroom sink leaning on my walker. Several obstacles to washing my hair become immediately evident. The angle between the bathroom sink and the faucet is too narrow for me to fit my head into so that I can let the water run over my scalp. Another is the problem of balancing on one leg to do this; I need my arms for support. Then there is the fact that all the blood in my body feels like it's draining out of me again and I think I'm going to pass out.

How did the victim break her neck, Detective?

Well, sir, it appears that the victim's head became lodged in the sink, she passed out, and when her one good foot slipped on the tiles, the porcelain crushed her windpipe.

Fine work, Detective.

The skin has taken on a translucent texture. It seems thinner, like fabric, to be sewn upon. The eyes feel like glass beads, the face carved down, the shape of an overbite more pronounced. The nurse finds me in the bathroom examining the face in the mirror.

"Samantha, why didn't you call me? You should not be in here by yourself," the nurse scolds.

"I didn't want to bother you," I tell her, which is part of the truth. The whole truth is that nothing is more pathetic than asking for help. My Uncle Roy, who taught me to fish and to throw alfalfa off the back of the Jeep to the cows in winter pasture, shot himself in the head when I was fifteen because he discovered he had cancer and didn't, in the words of my grandmother, want to die moaning like a dog. *Can you imagine being sick and burdening your family? God awful.* My great-aunt told me he was actually clinically depressed and ran out of lithium. I told my mother what really happened. She didn't see there was a difference. Either way, she said, cancer or depression, either way, what kind of a life is that? Probably for the better. I raised you all by myself and never needed a handout from the government or anybody else, she said. No welfare Velveeta in this house, I agreed.

"Let's get you back to bed," the nurse says, steadying my waist with her hands.

Her long black hair looks thick, coarse as peppercorns. "Please, can I wash my hair?" I ask her.

She looks at me, then at the sink. Immediately she seems to understand. "Well, I don't know how we would—" she begins. "Besides, you can't get any water near your dressing—"

"Please," I ask once again, "I just can't take this dirt anymore." By this time I am feeling so faint I realize it's a losing proposition. She just barely reaches my shoulder even though I am hunched over a walker. She wears that bright flower print smock. I am afraid if I fall on her I will crush her like a pansy underfoot.

My IV jiggles as I get into bed. The veins burn and ache. "Can we ever, ever take this out?" I ask the nurse.

"One more day of antibiotics and the doctor says you're done," she replies. There is so much she has to do for me, prop the leg up on all these pillows, cover me with blankets, adjust the bed just so. I thank her. I tell her I think she must be a good mom, and she smiles.

"It's time for your pain medication," she says.

"Super magic bus," I say. "Don't want to miss that."

She is reminding me about the medication because yesterday I tried taking one instead of two Percodans to wean myself off opiates, nip addiction before it could possibly bud. I was feeling noble. I once heard a story about a former junkie who was so committed to his sobriety that as he was dying of cancer he refused morphine and all other pain-killers. About two hours after I took just one Percodan I began to appreciate what that junkie had accomplished. I now ask for three instead of two as a matter of personal policy. She just gives me two.

She wakes me. "Samantha, you have a call from a gentleman," she says as she wedges the receiver between my shoulder and ear.

"I thought I'd lost you. I called UCLA, and they didn't know where you'd been moved." It's Edward Albert. His voice sounds as if he is next to me, leaning near, moving my hair with his hand so he can talk directly into my ear. "I'm glad you mentioned you'd be moving to Kaiser. I only had to figure out which one."

He was looking for me. Were my grandmother alive, she would write in my scrapbook, *Edward Albert, star of* Butterflies Are Free, *wanted to talk to Sammy so he found the hospital where she was convalescing from surgery.* "Thank you for looking for me," I tell him, and I realize it is not the first time he has found me, and I want to think of clever words that will tell him how that makes me feel while appearing amusingly ironic and disengaged, but I cannot. What I can give the man who saved my life is my sincerity. I reach down for it, raw, fragile, and still a bit unformed. "I owe you everything. Thank you. I can't express that deeply enough."

"You don't need to. I was honored to be of service. It was profound." Maybe that is dialogue I heard in a movie once, or maybe this is dialogue he said in a movie once, or maybe he says it or says something else and this is what I hear. But whatever the order of the actual words, I believe he means what he says.

"You know there is a belief that when you save a person's life you are forever responsible for them," he tells me.

"You sure you want to sign up for that?" For lack of something better to add, I change the subject. "How was Harley after the accident?"

"He stayed at our barn overnight and we made sure he ate well. Drew came with the trailer to pick him up in the morning," he tells me patiently. "You don't remember, but we had this conversation the other two times I called. You were pretty far gone."

"I'm sorry," I reply, ashamed because I want to be present for the man who could have easily said, *No, it's just a hawk crying in the canyon; I don't have time to look.*

"You sound better now," he says. "You'll be dancing before you know it. Don't believe anything doctors tell you. You're in my thoughts and prayers."

The afternoon is warm; I can see the ripened September blue of the San Fernando Valley through the vertical window in my room. Friends drop in for visiting hours with the synchronicity of a parade. Mary Ellen brings six pairs of Jockey underwear in every color, and a cotton nightie designed so that I can get it on over the IV. "Now this is more festive," she says cheerily, too cheerily perhaps. "I bought myself some too. Where's Matt?"

"Working," I say. "It's hard for him with the dogs, the commute. A new job."

"Still . . ." She lets the word trail off. Mary Ellen is tall and long-limbed, her salt-and-pepper hair cut in a wedge with thick bangs that fall to her eyebrows. She is the mother I would have had if I could have chosen to be born to a family of Talmudic scholars and lawyers.

"He really is at work," I insist.

"Of course," she says, brightly again. She wants to know what drugs they are giving me, what plan of action is being taken. She doesn't trust an HMO. "I'm not convinced this orthopedist knows what he's talking about," she says, referring to Dr. Mesna. Her son is getting his M.D. at Harvard. "I'm going to talk to Jared about this."

Mike, my former intern now turned editor at *Men's Fitness*, brings my best-known vice: Filet-o-Fish, a Diet Coke, and fries from McDonald's. "Nothing like a nutritious meal," he says, putting the paper bag on the nightstand. I can't eat more than a few bites because the drugs and antibiotics have killed any appetite, but the act of unwrapping the blue paper makes me feel normal.

"Whoa, you're looking good," Mike says. He doesn't know if he should put his hands in his pockets or near the bed rail, so he nods at me encouragingly, "Really." Twenty pounds have seeped from me. My hair separates into blocks of grease. Tubes drip chemicals into my body. My wide hipbones stick out sharply like a milk cow's. I feel maggoty. I love him.

"You're the worst liar," I tell him.

His pale skin flushes to a shade of plum. He shrugs his shoulders and smiles. "Depends what I'm lying about."

Ann Marie and her daughter, Kayla, arrive after Mike leaves, bringing a body spray and powder that smells of lavender. Kayla stays in the chair farthest from the bed.

"What's the matter with *you?*" She says it like an accusation. She is six.

"Broke my leg pretty bad," I tell her. "Can I have a kiss?"

"Uhm, no, I don't think so," she replies, squirming deeply into the chair, as if she's hoping the vinyl upholstery will provide camouflage. Her mother looks mortified.

"All this stuff's pretty scary," I agree. "It scares me too. But you can't catch it."

This must be the reassurance she's looking for. She navigates the bed rail with her mother's help, diving into the tide of pillows to kiss me. "Get well, Auntie Sam. You're all bony. You look weird."

"Thanks, monkey butt," I tell her, bracing against the touch as if her small hands will push me shattering to the floor like some porcelain figurine. "You always say the nicest things."

I must have fallen asleep because suddenly I am waking. In the chair beside the bed sits my friend Renée, a light shining on her sleek brunette head as she leans toward the pages of a magazine, reading. She wears red lipstick and is dressed in black. She is always dressed in black, a dream in Donna Karan. Renée has large brown eyes and full lips, is the kind of beauty that belongs on a canvas. I call her the Angel of Darkness, a black-appareled seraphim who always appears in my worst moments. It was Renée who found the house in Malibu when Matt went to rehab, and who has twice in the last year alone taken me to the local emergency clinic. Once for the slight concussion and broken coccyx from falling off Harley over a jump, once for the ankle sprain when I fell down the flight of stairs at the house. There are numerous examples. She and I sat at the bedside of our friend Donald as he lay disfigured and delirious in the final stages of AIDS. She sat longer than I. Much longer. She is the kind of person who can hold misery.

"We have got to stop meeting like this."

She looks up from the page. "Hey, girl. I was just thinking the same thing. How are you feeling?"

"Like shit. You?"

She arranges the blankets on the bed, wants to know the details of the accident, the course of treatment, the drugs prescribed. "Are you in pain? The minute you feel pain, you tell them and make them give you something, right away."

I tell her about my new friends: morphine, Dilaudid, Percodan, Vicodin. "Probably serves me right, this whole thing,"

I tell her. "I should have just stayed on and not gotten off him to cross that water."

"What?" she looks at me, annoyed. "Don't tell me you think this was your fault. This was just an accident."

"Yeah, but there's a rule. Never leave the saddle. You're always safer on a horse than on the ground."

"That's absurd," she waves me off. "If you had stayed on maybe something worse would have happened. Face it, you're just accident-prone. Some people are. There's always one person who's going to bump their head or trip on the step."

"How attractive."

"It's part of your charm, my dear," she says, busy cleaning the bedside table of trash, arranging a bouquet she brought. "I also brought some cookies. Do you want a cookie?"

The nurse returns to my room. Her shift has just ended, she says. "I've been thinking," she begins tentatively. "Maybe if you can stand up long enough I can wash your hair over the sink with a cup."

This must be how people feel when they open their front door and the van from the Publishers Clearing House Sweepstakes is parked outside; not sure whether to laugh or cry or just get busy cashing the check.

"If you will do that for me, I can stand as long as you need me to stand, I promise," I tell her, talking fast, as if my words can plug any crack where a change of heart could get in.

We make an awkward path to the bathroom, the nurse on one side of me. She sees how I manage the walker and IV stand by first moving the walker, then bracing my weight with one hand as I use the other to push the stand on its wheels a few inches ahead. "You shouldn't do this by yourself," she warns again.

"You're right, I know. I won't anymore," I tell her, because I am grateful and because I would not want her to get into trouble if I fell on her shift. Of course I will have to do exactly this when I get home, but without the IV. I need practice.

Finally, we arrive at the sink. I lean over and immediately feel weak, but I grip the walker as tightly as I am able. Sweat begins to gather on my brow, but, beautifully, wonderfully, it is rinsed away by warm water as the nurse pours it over my head. She applies shampoo and rubs it in with her small fingers. My hair is so dirty the shampoo won't lather, it seems. The sting of soapy water reaches my eyes, but I don't tell her. It doesn't matter, and it might make her stop.

"Is the water too hot? How are you doing?" she asks, reaching one arm around my waist as the other raises a cup of water over my head.

"It's great, it's perfect," I tell her, although white spots have started flickering in front of my eyes. I reach a hand off my walker to touch her waist. "What's your name?"

"Sophia." She wrings the water from my hair and puts a towel over my head. "There, that's as good as it gets. Now you have to get back to bed and stay there."

"Sophia." I love the sound of it, the Greek word for wisdom, divinely inspired, the name of a Muse, of a goddess, of a movie star I wanted to look like once. "Sophia. Thank you."

"You're welcome."

"I really mean thank you. Thank you isn't big enough to tell you what I mean. What can I give you? I am going to name a cat after you. No, a child," I vow.

She smiles as she helps me back into bed. "I am glad you're happy. I just wanted to help." She produces a comb for my hair.

"Sophia, Sophia, Sophia," I say. "Sophia." I have no children, but she makes me want to have a daughter so I can tell the story of how she got her name, and how that name means complete kindness.

The hospital sheets feel cool against my skin. Sophia spreads a towel under my head to absorb the moisture from my damp hair. I have a happy sense of fullness, and it hits me that this is what lingers after the asking and the grateful receiving of help.

[II]

ACCIDENTS ARE LIKE A FEVER.

A horse is a huge expense for any single mother but especially for my mother, who had been left bankrupt by a man she married when I was seven. She cosigned a loan he needed to start a flower shop; I still believed in Santa, but even I wasn't surprised when he left with another man, taking with him the small amount of money she had inherited from a Pennsylvania relative. A daughter with a horse is like having a daughter plus the responsibility of an extra child who will never grow up and get a job. But selling the animal was not an option. That was never even discussed. It was always till-death-do-us-part.

As a consequence, I grew up understanding there was not a cycle of life but rather a seesaw of life, rich and poor. When we were rich, my mom dug through the frozen food section at the grocery store to find lobster tails, shellfish like old snowballs, which my grandmother would then grill in the oven with bread crumbs and butter. When we were rich, we went shopping at the T, G & Y. Mom bought me new jeans and sweater sets. When we were rich, everything was possible. I went to horse shows at the rodeo grounds, ran for student body president, and tried out for the track team. Mom bought Scotch with brand-name labels and remembered to turn up the volume on her auburn hair with a dye from Clairol called "Mediterranean Passion." Gram filed her fingernails into sharpened ovals and painted them pink.

When we were poor we ate potatoes and beans just like the neighbors. "One day away from being homeless, without any possibility of a future," my grandmother would say, and I believed her. I would stay home sick from school and reread Harlequin Romance novels she kept in a stack beside her La-Z-Boy. When we were poor and the propane tanks ran out of gas, sometimes Gram heated water on the electric stove and filled a bath for me before school.

When we were really poor the dogs were fed stale bread and milk, and my horse was turned out to pasture on a friend's ranch. I never prayed except when we were really poor, that there would be enough grass to keep my horse from going hungry. Sometimes the prayers didn't work. Once Gabe lost so much weight the hollows above his eyes deepened into pits, his ribs stuck out like the wooden seams of a shipwreck. My mother cried when she saw him, borrowed money from I don't know where to rent a pasture for fifty-eight dollars a month next to the Enchanted Hills Trailer Park, the final stop in our dismal series of Las Vegas homes. Our farrier felt sorry for us three gringas with no man and built a shed where we kept hay and which sheltered Gabe from Rocky Mountain sleet and those murderous July thunderstorms.

This is how I measured Mom's commitment to the idea of me having a horse: She wore the same pair of black cowboy boots from the time I entered elementary school until I started college. She never bought herself anything on our spending sprees at the T, G & Y but instead waited until Aunt Gay cleaned out her closet and shipped the castoffs in cardboard boxes down to her and Gram. Our '67 station wagon doubled as a truck, hauling hay bales and grain sacks; she kept it running until 1982, when it literally cracked in half as she hit a pothole going twenty-five miles an hour, the frame rusted through, dissolving into flakes and red dust on impact. Still, I had riding lessons from the time I was old enough to sit on a horse, a fact she proudly held up to my grandmother.

"Your kid doesn't have a father, and what the hell kind of life is this?" Gram said. She had many variations on the theme, but this was one of her favorites.

" 'What the hell kind of life is this?' She has a purebred half-Arabian horse! How many kids can say that?" My mother's voice would tremble, and she'd try to cover by overenunciating her words. My mother stopped riding when she was twelve, scared by a nasty throw from a Tennessee Walker named Becky. But nothing was going to deter her daughter from riding, not if she had anything to do with it. "In case you are not aware, she belongs to the Junior Horsemen's Association. That is pretty god-damn-good, if you ask me. But, of course, you won't ask me."

Even Gram seemed to think the problem wasn't so much the horse as the lack of a man in our lives. She had all her life been a great horsewoman, or at least that's what she said. I never actually saw her on a horse, although I saw many pictures of her riding when she was young. She would point out her posture. *See, straight as a ramrod.* I do know she was good with horses, because she always knew exactly how to touch one. There was a gentleness in the lay of her fingers along their bony foreheads, along the half-moon crescents of their jaws. She made bran mashes in the winter for Gabe, an elaborate offering, chopping carrots and pouring molasses into it as if it were a gourmet oatmeal.

To Gram, how something looked was in fact what something was; appearances were never deceiving to her. Everything revealed its exact nature, meaning that whatever didn't look good, wasn't. She put butter on peanut butter and jelly sandwiches; she quartered the bread and always served the sandwich on a plate. Once when it was snowing my mother couldn't manage the drive home from work because the road was closed. There was next to nothing in the house to eat— we were poor that week—but Gram figured out a way to make a bowl of soup from an onion, some old spaghetti, and a chicken leg she found in the back of the freezer. She put a lace tablecloth on the dining room table, served the soup in a rose-patterned Franciscanwear bowl, and lit candles. I ate and she smoked a pack of Kools. " 'Act as good as you look and you'll have no trouble,' that's what my own grandmother used to tell Gay, Mutt and me when we were kids." She told me this often.

Her law of aesthetics strictly applied to my horse as well. Even when we were rich we couldn't afford fancy halters, so Gabe's was a standard rope job. But then Gram got ahold of it and elaborately braided over it in blue yarn she bought at K-Mart for forty-nine cents a skein. She crocheted a forest green border on my saddle blanket, put tassels on the ends that bounced when I asked him to trot. She taught me that blue rinse would always get the yellow out of a white mane and used her own Alberto VO-5 conditioner to smooth the tangles out of his tail. "Act as good as you look." She told this to my horse too, kissing the rubbery part of his nose between the two nostrils, staining his gray muzzle with her lipstick.

Mom was interested in what things actually did. She would sit by the rail at my horse shows, mirrored sunglasses obscuring her green eyes and most of her upturned nose. "Keep your heels down," she'd yell as I passed, in a throaty bass tone she must have believed fell below the frequency the judges' hearing could register. "He's on the wrong lead!" The picture Mom carried of me in her wallet was of my first riding lesson on old Big Red, my short legs barely able to straddle the sorrel gelding's back, the size of his huge head nearly as long as the length of my entire body. In the picture I have on a red shirt tied at the waist; Big Red has one ear turned to the camera.

I'm not driving you there. No way, José," says my mother. She has taken two weeks off from her job as a nursing director in New Mexico to stay with me; she says "visit" but really it's to act as my chauffeur for the twice-weekly appointments with Dr. Mesna since Matt has to be at work. We are returning to Malibu from the hospital and I have asked her if we can drop by the stable on the way home. I want to feel something organic in my fingers, feel wind press against my face and replace the smell of Betadine solution. Forget the orange stain of it on the skin when Dr. Mesna opened the bandage and I saw what is beneath, the bloated and purple flesh like a mammal drowned then beached, the crude cross stitch with thick black thread running the circumference of the thing.

"I just want him to see that I'm OK," I am pleading. I cannot believe she, of all people, cannot see the logic of this. "Please. It's been five weeks, I think. The last time he saw me I was bleeding."

"As if he cares. You can hardly sit up in the car. Don't be an idiot."

"Yes he cares," I say. "I can sleep when I get home." My life now: sleeping, getting ready to sleep, and waking up so that I can go back to sleep.

"Do you hear anything Dr. Mesna keeps telling you about infection? Do you think he's making that up? That he just wants to hear himself talk? Well I've got news for you."

"I'm not going to roll around in the dirt. I'm just going to pet my horse."

"I think we should shoot the son of a bitch." Her voice is harsh.

"What is with you people!" It's as if someone I have never met is sitting next to me in the truck.

"Well I do. I never trusted him." She purses her lips into a bow; the red of her lipstick feathers into the lines around her mouth. "There's a reason he was a freebie from the slaughter yard."

"Oh, right." I want to make her take it back so I resort to guilt, my only defense. "Aren't you the mother who bought me a green-broke Arabian when I was eleven, the mother who put me bawling and shaking back on that other gelding when he ran away with me when I was, what, eight?"

She sucks in her breath. "I didn't want you to lose your nerve."

"I never have."

Mom puts both hands on the wheel, drives in the slow lane because even the vibrations from the road are tortuous for me. We are only a mile or so from the stable now, driving up the Pacific Coast Highway, the burnt and stubby scrub oaks of the humpbacked canyons on the right, the ocean side rough and stone colored, something resembling gravel more than water. A row of mailboxes appears, the familiar uphill turn.

"It's coming up."

She sighs in an exaggerated way that means shut up. "Gangrene. Airborne contagions."

"Like from this car, you mean?" We are in Matt's truck, a ten-year-old Toyota, a large dent on the driver's side, another in the flat bed, and the rear differential out of whack from the time it was struck by a passing trailer. My wheelchair props just so in the flat bed, Coke cans and empty potato chip bags littered around it. Cigarette burns pockmark the worn upholstery, cellophane wrappers and french fries from visits to a drive-through wedge into the folds of the seat. Were a hand to lay across the dashboard it would disturb the mantle of dust that has turned the blue interior to tan. The leg nests in newspapers and other debris on the floor of the passenger's side.

"For fuck's sake, Sam. If your leg rots off I am not . . . feeling . . . sorry . . . for . . . you!" Mom often yells in the way she is doing right now, spacing the words out so that each is stressed equally. The antidote is to reply in a deadpan tone, nothing for her words to refract against.

"I sure won't come running to you," I tell her.

She stares straight at the road.

" 'Run,' get it?" I am talking at her profile. "*I* won't come *running*, ha-ha?"

I feel a deceleration; Mom turns the steering wheel into

the driveway for the stable. She pulls up to the gated entrance, still not looking at me. "Fine. Be that way."

The iron gate creaks open slowly on its electric hinge. My eyes scan the grounds; there are a number of bays at the stable but I am looking for the distinct inky points of Harley's ears, unlike any other.

I love my horse. I don't mean I love my horse like I love Ben & Jerry's Chocolate Chip Cookie Dough Ice Cream. I mean that my relationship to Harley, a living, breathing, sentient being, is as important to me as any human friendship in my life. More than some.

From the first week we arrived in Los Angeles, Matt was in the studio, or working on a show, or playing his own music. When we did manage to spend time together it was brief, intense, a perpetual romance. I would literally catch my breath when I saw him. For a couple years after we were married I still called him my boyfriend; we were not subject to the boredom, or the familiarity, quotidian routines instill. With his erratic comings and goings, I too tried to work, to fill every minute. I took classes. I volunteered to work with troubled kids. I freelanced for a music magazine that paid me five dollars to write reviews of local rock bands, but at least it kept me out of the house most weekends. White space on the calendar was my enemy.

Even so, for years I had felt adrift. Then one Saturday, on a lark, I went with friends to a rental stable in Griffith Park so we could waste a summer afternoon. The smell of leather, the juxtaposing scents of sweet oats and acrid muck, the wet sound of a horse rolling the bit in his mouth. It was as if a switch inside me had been flipped on. Riding again was like having amnesia and finally remembering my own name. I couldn't wait to do it again; I immediately started hanging out at the stable, leasing horses, riding any four-legged excuse for a mount I could find a way onto.

Finally I had a way to engage my body and senses at the same time, to get my hands dirty, to spend hours communicating without saying a word. I started to become part of the physical world again; I woke up before sunrise just to squeeze in a ride before driving to the magazine office where I worked. I knew winter was coming because the horses' coats grew longer, that the Santa Anas were about to blow because they became restless and spooked by the wheelbarrow, as if it had suddenly grown fangs. Each horse that passed under my care I treated as if he were a Triple Crown winner, brushing every inch of coat, down to the hairs around the coronet band of his hooves which I smoothed using a toothbrush.

A woman I knew from the stables brought me a poorly Xeroxed flyer she had found at the feed store. To a good home, it said. Just take over this gelding's care, period. "There's got to be something wrong with him," I thought as I stared at the picture, as if by closely examining the Xerox I would pick up the hidden message written in invisible ink. The evidence in black and white said plainly enough: large head, skinny neck, one section of mane that seemed to grow from the wrong side. A broomstick pony. But I liked his name, Harley. It sounded rock 'n' roll, all-American, tough but not unattractive. Sure, you might have to tinker with him all the time, but that was part of the experience.

The horse was stabled a half hour east of L.A. in Sun Valley, where it's always hot, land is cheap and residents achieve the dream of owning a suburban ranchette. People drive pickups and leave their dogs in the flat bed, put aluminum screens on their front doors, don't seem bothered by the dust off the dirt roads that filters in. I drove up to a house with pipe corrals in the back. Champion Mules, the sign by the mailbox said.

The gate to the rear of the property was open. To the side of the barn there was a huge arena, where sand was flying up as if a small tornado were passing through. At the center of it was a bay horse bucking and running. He was huge, dwarfing the mules that stood in their stalls, their long ears like antennae aimed at the ruckus.

A woman in dark blue jeans walked up, introducing herself as the owner of the champion mules. "He just loves to run," she said, eyeing the horse, keeping a wide smile on her face as she said it. "Yeah, he sure loves to run."

I couldn't believe this was the broomstick pony. He looked like a "mighty steed" from one of the illustrations in the horse books I devoured as a child. The exact bittersweet chocolate shade of his coat, and the way it darkened to a crow's black on the legs. The straight profile and large eyes, as if the mount of Alexander the Great depicted in Greek statues had shaken off centuries. The round shoulders and forceful haunch, two explosive circles of power. I put my hand on the rail and he stopped dead, snaking that neck around to better view what dared to disturb his enjoyment. He snorted, shook his head, the mane flopping to the wrong side, and then gave out a long sigh. He dropped his head and swung around, walking toward me with a loose, confident gait.

And, strangely, there was something about the horse's movement that reminded me of meeting my husband. How years ago he came walking into that college party with a case of beer under his arm, his shirt half open, his hair long, biceps pumped, bearing a more than passing resemblance to David Lee Roth of Van Halen fame. My best friend Tina had noticed my head tilt with interest and grabbed my arm. "No way," she had said. Steer clear of him; he was the younger brother of our friend John, the one who "had been in trouble." Rumors about drugs, a run-in with the cops; he was a guitar player, had a girlfriend who drove a Chevy Nova and carved his initials in her arm. "Plus," she reminded me, "you already have a boyfriend." Matt was also three years younger than us. Matt was all wrong for me. Matt was irresistible.

I expected Harley to mooch the carrots, but instead he slung his head over the rail. A deep scar cut across the bridge of his nose, the proud flesh where a gash had healed black and shiny. He stuck his tongue out about four inches, folding the slimy, bubble gum–colored thing in his teeth like a taco. Then he began to bob his head, tongue flapping against his nose.

Nothing I knew about equine behavior quite explained this. "What the hell is he doing?"

"Oh, he just likes you to pull on his tongue," said the mule owner, smile still fixed. "He's figured out he gets attention that way."

"Can I ride him?" The mule owner didn't care, he was not

her horse, just a boarder at the ranchette. The woman who actually owned Harley showed up minutes later. She had rescued him from a slaughter yard; he had been a depressed heap of bones held together by a thin hide, just days away from being killed. From the tattoo on his upper lip—the mark of a purebred who has raced—she'd been able to trace his registry and racing record. He'd been on the track for two seasons, won one $10,000 purse, then never saw the winner's circle again. She'd fed him, groomed him, and had him vetted. Only when he was strong enough had she started riding. "I just love him; he's a sweetie. But with kids and a husband, time only goes so far. You know how it is . . ."

"Yes," I agreed, although I didn't know how it was. For me marriage meant time stretched out in long, solitary periods. My life was more like a sandpit I was always trying to fill.

I mounted Harley. It was like being on top of an armored tank, something massive, unyielding. His trot was a malformed shuffle; he held his head straight up in the air in true broomstick fashion. When we cantered it felt like I was playing giddyup, his gait tense and unyielding, not the rolling motion a relaxed animal naturally provides. All of this was evidence of physical pain. Here was a creature ground down by hard riding and abused by relentless demands. His owner's recent care couldn't erase it. He had the quality of something that had been removed from ashes, smoke damaged, edges singed and crumbled, but otherwise intact.

"Now, there are a lot of little things wrong with him," his owner told me after I dismounted, ticking off a list of cracked bones, bad joints, pulled tendons, scars and muscle injuries.

"Maybe I can put some time into fixing him," I tried to say

lightly, but my voice must have cracked a little. I felt a sense of outrage and sadness for this animal. He who has no desire other than to avoid pain and just get along. He who is judged and condemned for what he cannot help but be. I stood close to his head and looked into the dark center of one large eye, trying to see if those feelings were expressed in it or if there was only the reflection of what I was putting there. It didn't matter either way. I blinked quickly because suddenly something burned in my eyes like ammonia.

"You can always give him back," the woman told me.

Even then I knew I had no intention of ever giving him back.

The sight of Harley pricking up his ears when he hears my car pull into the stable has marked my days for years now. When he hears the sound of my voice he screams for me as if I am another horse. As I groom and tack him up, I talk to him; he nickers back. It's a running conversation. If I stand brushing his forelock he'll lift his head and put his muzzle on my shoulder and rub his nose along my neck and into my hair, in imitation of the way horses groom each other. You'll see them standing in pastures sometimes like this, their large bodies facing each other, necks intertwined, using their horse lips and their horse teeth to gently scratch each other's back.

"It's amazing how much that horse adores you," Janice always says, who along with her husband, Drew, owns the stable. "Too bad he can't die and be reincarnated as a man. He'd be your true love."

Ours isn't a perfect match, however. Under saddle he is a difficult horse. He requires an extremely gentle hand; precise, consistent pressure with the leg. I am not naturally gentle, and I am inconsistent by his standards. He is prone to tantrums when things don't go his way. He has been known to rear, and bolt, his whole front end tucking out from underneath me in a catlike leap to the side. He bucks but not very high, more like a cow kick, off to one angle. I always carry sugar, which is a problem, because sometimes, without warning, he will simply slam on the brakes and crank his neck around to look up at me in the saddle, imploring. Such begging is never rewarded; he does it anyway.

But, sometimes, there is a moment when everything works. When I forget I have legs and arms, and the motion of his back becomes not separate from my very being. When it works I think something—turn, canter, change leads—and I blink, and in the space of time it takes to blink I am rewarded with a tremendous power that builds from underneath me, and we are launched forward. And then there is a space where no thinking occurs. It is just being and movement and a lightness I cannot describe. There is no word for it. The Greeks tried, I am convinced, and could not, and had to invent the image of Pegasus.

I hear the slam of a screen door. Drew and Janice come to the driveway to greet us, acting as if it is completely normal to help me into a wheelchair. The clarifying effects of time + distance ÷ loss of self-propulsion: "Stable" is a romantic label for what is actually a sprawling series of prefabricated metal structures and pipe fencing struck at sharp right angles, built upon an uphill slant of sandy soil and decomposed horseshit, becoming again the grass it once was. Hoses to watering troughs and animal piss cut rivulets in the dirt, and when baked by sun become as impossible to cut as concrete. Drew breathes hard as he wheels my chair up the slope toward Harley's corral and my mother steadies the cotton blanket she has put over me. I have to suck in my lip because even after three Vicodin this motion is something to be endured.

Janet talks quickly, smiles. Her large eyes, the shape of globes, dart here and there, her gaze landing anywhere but on my ridiculously oversized gray sweatsuit, the material on one leg cut to accommodate the bulky, shrouded column. They are so glad to see me, the weather's been nice, uh? Everyone is happy I'm feeling better, and oh look, here's Harley. He's been fine, really. He'll be happy to see me too. Harley? Come here, Harley.

Harley stands at the back of his corral, his haunch cocked toward us. He doesn't turn around.

"Harley, hey," I say encouragingly and try to whistle but my lips cannot form the shape.

Not even his ear flickers toward me.

The moment turns awkward. Drew, Janice, and my mother stand around my chair, silent. Hands curl in my lap, two useless things.

Drew yells across the grounds to the stable's groom, Juan, asks him to put Harley in the small ring por favor; la señora es muy triste. Janice goes to find a carrot, tells me not to worry. "It must be the chair," she says, and I agree, yes, the chair must scare him.

"Of course," she says, "he doesn't recognize you in it."

My mother remains silent as Drew wheels me to the side of the ring where Juan has released Harley. He ambles to the far side of the area away from me, head down, nose tracking the scent of other horses who've used the ring that day. Looking at the sway of his large sides, the shake of muscle as he walks, I am all at once aware of how small I am, and an image of a chipped teacup flashes over and over in my mind. The dust kicked up by his every step. Dr. Mesna's voice pours as through a megaphone in my head: *Risk of infection.*

Janice puts carrots in my hand and this Harley registers, turns his huge body toward me to cross the ring. I hold up a carrot and he swings his head over the fence, his eye only on the treat, grabbing at the carrot, attacking it with the intensity of a cat biting down on a mouse. As he jerks it from my weak grip I pull back, afraid, hating that I am afraid, embarrassed now, acutely aware of my sunken frame.

Harley turns away, distracted by the sound of another horse, and I realize that something else was broken on that trail, a spell, a trust, something I can identify now only by its absence.

Mom says, "Honey, this is a lot for you today. Let's go."

Drew and Janice agree, yes, long day, go home and get rest. I nod because I don't know what else to say.

On the way back down the hill Drew says that he'll have Harley leased out to someone so I don't have to worry about the horse being ridden and exercised. "Just while you get well," he adds. "If you want." His voice is so casual it is too casual, and I know he must have been practicing how to say this to me. He helps my mother lift me into the truck, situating me among the litter.

Mom and I ride the remaining five miles from the stable to the house in silence. You know you're pathetic when even your own mother won't offer a sarcastic, I-told-you-so comment. Even when I start to cry she doesn't say anything, just reaches a hand over and rubs my arm.

Pain is not a physiological fact, in the view of medicine. Bleeding is an example of a physiologic fact: cut a vein, blood appears, and that blood will occupy space; it can be seen. Pain, however, is something the brain creates as a response to stimuli, such as a wound or a cancer, or dreams or longings, anger, fear. The cut/bleed response is as certain as gravity, but the pain response changes depending on the circumstances. The same stimulus that in one circumstance would cause a person to scream might go unnoticed in another. A report made during World War II observed that soldiers who were severely wounded in battle didn't need morphine, so elated were they that their injuries ensured they would be sent home and away from the front lines.

For pain to develop, the brain has to regulate the traffic of competing messages. Only a limited number of "gates" exist through which pain messages can enter the thalamus, the traffic cop of the brain. Pain messages travel along the nerves at around ninety miles an hour, or less. The more horrific the pain, the more slowly it moves on the path toward the brain. However, the nerves that carry the sensation of touch are like a high-speed rail, shooting messages into the brain at about two hundred miles an hour. This is why the natural impulse is to rub a toe that's stubbed—the touch signals beat the pain signals to the gates, so there is not as much room for the pain signals to squeeze through. The result is that a stubbed toe that is rubbed doesn't hurt as much as a stubbed toe that's not.

Inevitably, however, a certain number of pain messages will crash through the gates. When they reach the thalamus, the thalamus directs the messages over to the reasoning part of the brain called the cortex, and to the limbic system, which handles emotions. What takes place next is an evalua-tion of experience: If the pain signals are weak and the brain recognizes the situation—as in, Oh, we're on a bike, we've been on a bike before, and this is a bruise, we know what bruises are—the brain will then release the chemical sero-tonin, which relaxes the muscles around the injury. If, how-ever, blood is flowing, if flesh is exposed, if bone is at all visible, the brain responds to the attack with its heavy artillery—norepinephrine, a form of adrenaline. Muscles tighten, blood flow constricts; the nerves become like tightly tuned strings waiting to sound the alarm should other attacks arise.

The brain begins to closely monitor the injured area. This hypervigilance means increased sensitivity, so that sensations as light as a caress translate as pain. Eventually, pain signals are cemented into the nervous system, becoming a physical part of it, just as ruts in a road become part of a road. Even years after a severe wound heals, pain can prevail. It doesn't need the injury anymore. It has a life of its own.

Who am I? An invalid. What am I? An invalid. All previous definitions no longer hold.

Identity is merely events in life taken in the aggregate; I never understood this before. I know I am an invalid because I lie on a couch instead of the bed where Matt sleeps. The bedroom is up a flight on a switchback staircase, and I cannot transport myself without the aid of a walker or crutches. Even then I cannot walk more than a dozen or so feet before needing to stop and catch my breath, my arms turned jelly, overcome by the pounding of blood in the leg. I am in constant pain. More difficult to explain is the phenomenon of feeling that I am broken into pieces, my body a collection of odds and ends, so that it is impossible for me to have sensations travel through my body, as if it were one thing.

My biggest effort to date occurred the day I returned from the hospital, made it into the bathroom with Matt's help, then positioned my walker over the scale. It took me several tries to balance just so and push off with the right foot, but finally I managed to arrange myself on the scale long enough to see it register: 126 pounds! A twenty-four-pound loss in just under ten days! At five-foot-eight, I finally satisfied the weight charts in *Glamour*. The one article I haven't written for a woman's magazine: "The Ultimate Near-Loss-of-Limb Diet: Do You *Really* Need That Leg?"

I know I am an invalid because Mary Ellen comes over and clears my closet of all clothing that is worn by a woman with two good legs: pants with narrow legs, riding breeches, skirts and dresses that fall anywhere above the ankle, platform heels, running shoes. If I were convalescing perhaps I would keep everything for that day when I will be well again, but being that I am an invalid, In Valid, the condition essentially permanent, all became donations to a women's shelter. "Give them to someone who can wear them," I tell Mary Ellen.

From the back of the closet Mary Ellen pulls never-worn hunt boots my mother bought me for my birthday, just a month before the trail accident. The leather smells just-off-the-cow new, the obsidian sheen not dulled by dust.

"You'll want to keep these," she says.

"Why would I?" Can't she accept the facts? That I no longer have a leg that fits into the left boot? Even if the leg grows—I think of it now like a salamander tail, either it will regenerate or it won't—it will never be the same leg that fit into that boot. *Keep your heels down Sam*. Like I'll ever need to worry about that again.

She sighs aggressively, which is her way of not saying, "I think you're making a mistake." I turn my head into my pillow and tell her I'm worn out.

"I'll just put these back in the closet. Just in case," she says. "You can always give them away later."

I feel tragic, like a character in a Victorian novel.

Let us be shed of those dreadful reminders of happier times. Yes, let us remove these Objects of Pain.

My physical condition has altered our shared environment. Matt finds us a one-level apartment, no stairs, the basement half of a duplex far up in the hills of West Malibu. The ceilings are low, the rent, high. Both contribute to the cavernous mood. The floors are tile. We don't put down rugs. "You could slip," Matt explains. Books are left in boxes, no pictures are hung on the plaster walls.

I seem to remember that not so long ago the pattern of my days was formed by caring for things: meals to cook, dogs to walk, horse to ride, plants to water. Now I don't even worry about taking the dogs out. This new place is a farther commute from Matt's new job, so he is gone for at least twelve hours of every day, sometimes more. He has had to strip animal care to its skeleton, leaving the door to the house open so that Nika and Ming come and go as they please. Turns out that when dogs are allowed to wander around in a somewhat rural area like this, they for the most part just stay at home. A huge bowl of dry food and a trough of water keep them from going hungry.

I have a sense that I used to be very concerned about these matters—the appropriateness of care, the specific dietary needs of each animal. I cannot remember the details now because everything except the essential tools of existence has become superfluous. All that is really needed for living is a bed. This bed must be big enough to accommodate: pillows to elevate the leg; a small cooler containing prepackaged meals and drinks, although drinking very much at all can cause the need for a trip to the bathroom, a laborious process best accomplished once a day when someone else is in the house to hear if a fall has occurred; a phone; and two prescription bottles, one for stopping pain and one for inducing sleep when the pain prescription has done all it can. A window is also helpful to determine whether it is day or night, although this doesn't matter as much as I used to believe.

The dogs and I live the same. Mostly we sleep. Like them I lift my head when I hear the rattle of a truck up the driveway. They hear the sound of Matt's feet in the living room before I do, and are able to pick their bodies up to greet him. Then I hear him coming down the hall, then I see him by the bed. He kisses me, the cool scent of the world on him.

Then, one day, instead of coming from the front door directly to the hall, I hear him stop first in the kitchen. After some minutes I finally hear him in the hall, and at last see him beside the bed. He paints scenes from his day for me, mimicking dialogue of his coworkers, the people I don't know but who now know him well. I feel jealous. I want descriptions of what everyone looks like. "What about this Kim? Is Kim pretty?"

Another day in another week. Instead of making his way from the front door to the kitchen to the hall to my bedside, I hear him in the kitchen, then in the hall, then in the extra bedroom. The house grows quiet again. "Matt?" I call. "Matt? Are you home?"

Silence. "Matt?" I sound shrill, I know I do. "Will you answer me, damn it?"

Silence again.

"Matt?"

I hear the squeak of his sneakers' rubber soles hitting the tile. He opens the door to the bedroom. "What?" Matt never raises his voice, the more angry or emotional he is, the quieter he becomes, until there is nothing left of his voice at all.

"I was afraid," I say, feeling so ashamed, knowing that this is exactly what every man hates, a wife who needs. Gram always said that. *The minute you need anything they'll be on the road with the nearest blonde they can find. Trust me.* "I thought maybe somebody else was in the house."

"I'm tired, Sam. I just need to chill a little. OK?" He keeps a hand on the doorknob, one foot in the hall.

I am the invalid wife he needs to steel himself against, I am the added pressure, the extra work, I am the challenge to his sobriety, white bottles of prescription narcotics within reach. I notice his gaze shift to the bottles. "Have you counted them yet?" he asks.

"Yes. They're all here," I lie. When I came home from the hospital he asked me to count my pills every day, so that if any were missing I would know he took them, and he would be held accountable. It was a strategy he learned in rehab. I don't have the power to stand, let alone the force to stop him from using. A small rebellion, lying to him about counting these little white pills, but it is my way to make him wrong every day.

"How was your day?" I extend the question like an offering.

He shrugs. "I'll be back in a little while," he says, closing the door.

There is no view from the window, pitch-black, not the moon or even a star to brighten it. All that is reflected in the glass is the room's interior: a bed, a mound of white bandages propped on a stack of goosedown, a stick figure covered in a green blanket.

After the drop-in visits stop and the casseroles quit coming, after the helpful articles about people who cure themselves with echinacea and green tea are read, only the phone remains. Yet there are only so many times friends can be called during any given day. I develop a grading system to determine who to call more than once a day and who not to.

Grade 1s can be called frequently, will relive with me all parts of the accident and want to know more, as in, What color was your blood? Is Edward Albert cute? How did they get that rod down your leg? Wait, what happened to your horse? Editors' and journalists' inherent inquisitiveness predisposes them to Grade 1 status.

Grade 2s can be called frequently but only want to cheer me up, will tolerate no self-absorption or graphic details. Matt and other family members are often Grade 2s, as are poets, fiction writers and equestrians, and editors and journalists who aren't Grade 1s.

Grade 3s are best left to once-a-week calls and pretty

much cover all the other people I know. They become squeamish and even over the phone I can hear them wince at any description of pain, physical or otherwise. Grade 1s can quickly morph into Grade 3s.

The length of time a friend can sustain a call usually works in inverse proportion to how close the friend was before the accident. The reason for this is that more distant acquaintances need to be caught up on the details of life leading up to the accident, the where do you live now, are you still married, what are you writing. Then, in the spirit of reciprocity, I listen to the same from them. The whole exchange can consume an entire waking period before I can rightfully go back to sleep. Close friends don't need to be caught up, so the conversation goes too quickly, as in the case of Tina, my closest friend since I was fifteen, college room-mate, professional colleague, a no-bullshit Grade 2:

"How are you?"

"Waiting for my leg to fall off."

"No, really, how are you?"

"The same."

"Any news from your doctor? Do you have any more sur-geries scheduled?"

"Not yet."

"Can I do anything for you?"

"No, thanks."

"OK."

"OK."

"Well, I've got to run [the phone is ringing, the baby's cry-ing, my editor's on the other line, someone is at the door]. I'll talk to you later."

As the weeks extend the population of Grade 1s dwindles to the point of extinction. I increasingly find myself with waking time that cannot be filled with phone conversation, or with reading, or by talking to the dogs and inventing their replies. The distance thoughts roam when freed of attachment to the body cannot be measured. Words and phrases fade in and out. The static, endless. My mind has become a car radio on an AM/FM frequency, searching for a signal along one long yawn of highway in the desert. *I know it's only rock 'n roll* once upon a midnight dreary **48 month financing!** *keep his head bent, shoulder in on the rail* Manhattan straight up no bitters *like it like yes I do* Admitted to God, to ourselves and to another human being the exact nature of our wrongs You are a fucking accident looking for place to happen missy **if you had stayed on maybe something worse would have happened Face it, you're just** accident-prone.

Accident-prone. How often that label has been attached firmly to my back, a cosmic kick-me sign. Not Acts of God or natural disaster. My incidents are all about bad timing, miscalculation.

I call Angel of Darkness Renée, Grade 2, to ask the meaning. She says the phrase means just what it says.

"Is it a condition? Does the AMA have a position?"

"Doubtful," Renée says. "Why don't you look it up?"

"Everybody has accidents," I hear myself talking myself out of the possibility. "Everybody has broken a bone or something."

She considers this for a moment. "No," she says finally. "I never have. A bruise is about the worst."

This is inconceivable to me. "That's not normal," I tell her.

"Compared to you," she says. "It's more normal than you think."

I decide she is a statistical freak and hang up. I begin polling everyone on my phone list; I find sprains, a few minor breaks, one bout with thyroid cancer but I tell her that doesn't count because that falls into the disease category. Even among my equestrian friends there aren't as many maiming encounters as I would have anticipated. No one besides me ever gave themselves an inguinal hernia from working out at the gym. Or suffered two broken toes and a severe foot sprain as a result of being smashed against a fence by a Thoroughbred just off the track. Or had a tooth cracked and nose bloodied by a rank old trail horse with a head-tossing habit. Or sustained a third-degree burn on a right ankle when a pant leg caught on the tailpipe of a boyfriend's motorcycle. Or sliced knuckles across the sharp stucco walls of a bar in Juarez, Mexico. That particular event produced gashes so deep I still see the scars when I type.

When I hear Matt's truck pull into the driveway I'm strong enough now to slowly make my way to the one big room that serves as living and dining room and kitchen. I ask him to set up my laptop computer so I can use the Internet for research.

"Did you get an assignment?" The anticipation in his voice underlines the worry over money he feels as our sole supporter.

The phone bill still has to be paid, the rent is due, the board still owed for the horse no longer ridden.

"Not yet," I say.

"Can you pay anything on the rent this time?" he asks casually. He's standing by the dining table, which is really the mail collection table; stacks of magazines, bills, catalogs unread cover its surface.

My chest grows tight and all at once it feels as if my heart is beating in my throat. I don't understand where this rush of panic is coming from. It's a legitimate question; he doesn't know what money I do or don't have. Our accounts have always been separate, he pays one bill and I another, our arrangement for years now. Yet I imagine Matt standing over me with a flat look in his eyes, his unblinking expression boring straight through me. I have seen this exact stare directed at other people—band members, a producer who owed him $20,000, a man who cut him off on the freeway—but never before at me. It scares me. His voice is a monotone. He tells me I have to leave because I can't make my half of the rent, I tell him I'm crippled, he says that's my problem. I wonder if I am going crazy, if I am the one with a psychotic break now, if this is how it felt to him during the hallucinations when I transformed into a Colombian cartel leader.

I do not have any money to offer, I haven't been able to work, I tell him. "But I will," I say. "I will soon."

"That's cool," he replies. Has he always talked to me like one of his band members, like a friend and not a wife? I can't remember exactly, but in the back of my head there is a sense of a time before drug rehab and everything that led to it, when we looked at each other when we spoke.

I turn to make my way back to the bedroom, feeling weepy, feeling angry, feeling I don't know what, emotions like sludge dredged up from the bottom of a pond, decompositions of other things, now unnamable.

In bed I cover my eyes with my hands and think about two young college kids who slept in a cold bedroom one December, it must be seven years ago now. The cinderblock walls of the cheap rental like bricks of an igloo, she holding him tight, wishing that she could just crawl into his skin as they lay on the twin mattress on the linoleum floor, coats and clothes piled on top of the too-thin blankets. His breath like apple cider, the touch of his lips over her neck, he let her wear his sweatshirt because she was catching a cold. David Bowie's song "Heroes" played on the cheap cassette player, it was the German version, the title was the only word they understood, he hummed along. She considered them high-wire acrobats, turning somersaults midair. They could even miss and fall, it would be all right, his net extended end to end. His father drove a Mercedes, his mother was a stockbroker. Churchgoing folk, roots that burrowed deep, branched out wide. She grew up in a world where people seemed always to be jumping out of airplanes and forgetting the parachutes. She clutched him more tightly and eventually they fell asleep with the music on.

There comes a time when that which excited now irritates. Like one too many rides on a roller coaster, the dips and heights no longer thrill. You just wait for the slowing, and, finally, the chance to get off.

But I don't say this out loud. Our covenant is not to speak of difficult things.

Gram always said, Start with the dictionary. For her, a concept or thing did not really exist if there wasn't a word to freeze its meaning.

I've made a makeshift table on my lap for the computer out of books and women's magazines, angled to avoid any pressure near my left side. The phone line and power cord Matt hooked up for me trail over the green bedspread. My new IV. I check the on-line *Webster's*:

> **ac•ci•dent-prone** *adj* 1: having a greater than average number of accidents 2: having personality traits that predispose to accidents <importance of identifying *accident-prone* persons—*Jour. Amer. Med. Assoc.*>.

I am blue-eyed because of genetics; I am math-phobic because of bad teaching; I am redheaded because my hairdresser stands behind my refusal to accept brown hair. But I cannot pinpoint the reason for this particular trait.

I call my mother. "You were just born that way," she says. She is exhaling blue smoke from her menthol cigarette into the receiver; I know it by the hiss of air on the line. "What can I say. Some people are born rich. You were born a klutz."

"Is that your educated medical opinion?"

"I think it's because you're left-handed," she says on an inhale. "You look at the world cockeyed."

I consider evidence: My attempt in seventh grade to have a basketball career lasted approximately two days, when, during practice, I actually made a basket against my own team. I was turned around, I couldn't remember which side was which. The direction everyone was yelling at me to run in didn't feel right. The world is just not ordered the way it should be. Voilà, the reason: I am left-handed.

Here I was, convinced all this time it had to do with my mother drinking gin and tonics during the hot summer months of her pregnancy, to the point she was convinced I would be immune to malaria, such were the levels of quinine water in my bloodstream. But she was right. I have never suffered malaria.

My propensity for using the left hand over the right might explain something, although exactly what it explains is hard to determine. Only 13 percent of the general population uses their left hand to write or to throw a ball or flip a light switch, and of that group, more than 50 percent are men. So to be a left-handed woman is to be a statistical oddity, the joker in the deck. The Japanese once considered left-handedness in a wife sufficient grounds for divorce.

Not one researcher can definitively conclude what abnormality subtly alters the right hemisphere of the brain to create left-handedness: it could be a recessive gene, birth stress, trauma in utero; some research points to higher testosterone levels. Groups with an elevated prevalence of sinistrality include alcoholics, architects and autistics, baseball players, criminals, Down's syndrome children and dyslexics, lawyers, mathematicians, migraine sufferers and musicians, psychotics, smokers and vegetarians. If we were dogs we would be among the lupine types, huskies and malamutes—prone to stray, dig holes under the fence, not good at obedience.

Wired to be difficult; is this the reason nearly every culture has taboos or prejudices against lefties? Several centuries ago the Catholic Church decreed the left-handed servants of Satan. The Church has since eased off that one, but the sentiment will never be uprooted because it is coded in language. In English the very word "left" is derived from the Old English word meaning "weak" or "worthless." The Latin word for left is "sinister," and the Roman phrase describing masturbation, I've been told, translates as "left-handed whore." In Spanish, to call someone clever you say no ser zurdo, which literally means "not left-handed."

Maybe there is a reason for negative associations; some research indicates that bad things do happen around us. One study theorized we die an average of nine years earlier than right-handed people. Another, that we are twice as likely to have car crashes. Other morbid findings: nearly four times more likely to die of crash-related injuries, more likely to have arthritis and swollen joints, more likely to have limbs severed in mechanical accidents.

On the other hand, as it were, many studies refute these results—findings can't be replicated, methodologies are revealed to be shoddy, premises flimsy. Reading the results of all these studies feels like having my palm read: the secret to my life is there in my hand, but I can't decipher it myself, and help is at best unreliable and inconclusive.

But there could indeed be a very good physiological explanation for accidents, especially if they begin occurring suddenly: it could be a brain tumor. "There could be changes in vision, hearing problems, a possible tumor in the cerebellum, the part of the brain that controls coordination," explains Clyde Flanagan, a psychiatrist and director of psychoanalysis at the University of South Carolina School of Medicine I cold call from a list of sources I use for researching magazine articles. He listens to the story of my accident and says he's sorry to hear about my leg; for a doctor he makes a surprisingly good Grade 1.

Instantly I feel a little weaker, I sink deeper into the bed's pillows, mentally ticking off a list of symptoms. I imagine tests, the white of hospital sheets, the stream of friends who cluck in disbelief, *To think she survived the canyon only to find she has a brain tumor.* Dr. Flanagan tells me not to worry, it's unlikely I have a brain tumor. However, if I am researching for an article I might want to look into the recent studies around attention deficit and hyperactivity disorder (ADHD). It's known as a cause of accident proneness in children because it creates impulsiveness, but it might also factor into adult problems. "Generally, accident proneness is like a fever—it's a symptom of something else," Flanagan says. "It used to be thought that you outgrew ADHD, but now the research suggests a lot of adults still have it, it just manifests in different ways." In some cases, he explains patiently, Ritalin, usually prescribed to help ADHD kids focus their attention, can also help adults.

When I think of ADHD all I can picture is a twelve-year-old boy who can't sit still and is really good at video games. I do a self diagnosis: One thing I have always been able to do is sit still. I could never even get the hang of Pac Man, let alone Tomb Raider. I decide I don't have enough energy to be an ADHD candidate.

So what about dictionary definition number two? What kind of people are prone to accidents, and do I fit those characteristics?

"Temperament seems to be a big factor," David Schwebel, a researcher in the University of Iowa's Department of Psychology, tells me in reply to an e-mail I send him. He assists Jodie Plumert in her work on children, published in the *Journal of Experimental Child Psychology*, which tries to uncover why some continually overestimate their physical abilities and end up having accidents. They are not the kids who see the cereal box on the shelf and ask Mommy to get it down for them. They are the kids who say, If I climb on the counter I'll get it for sure. "Children who are active and think quickly, the ones that seek out new sensations, seem to have more accidents in their history. Extroversion goes along with that trait," he explains. Schwebel and Plumert see the question as one of "low inhibitory control"—the ones who get hurt don't pause to consider possible dangers associated with their actions. "It seems to be something that is fairly consistent throughout childhood and into adulthood," Schwebel tells me. Although he does add that accidents tend to decrease as a child ages.

I call a sports psychologist friend in Texas I often interview, Edd Wilbanks, to get his two cents. He says that while it is generally true that the older you get the fewer accidents you have, it's not always so. Edd believes the "go-getter" types have very high levels of self-esteem and as a result often view no accomplishment as being too great. "They may tend to put themselves in high-risk situations just because they think they can handle it," he explains. "Nine times out of ten, the 'accidents' we see in sports are somehow behaviorally induced. Now, that doesn't mean you're crazy. It just means the choices you've made have put you in a position where you can be injured."

I like temperament as an explanation. It makes me feel rakish and cool, kind of sexy and a little dangerous, like Errol Flynn, like Mick Jagger. Better to burn out than fade away, the song goes. I tilt my head a little, turn the corners of my mouth up in a knowing smirk. *Hemingway? What a wuss.*

"As they get older," Edd continues, "these personality types will probably be successful in whatever they do, which then makes them even more sure they can push the limits. But physiologically, they eventually run up against a wall."

Then I realize there's a fundamental problem with my fitting into the rakish and cool category: I have been running up against walls all my life.

The circumstantial evidence might suggest that I am athletic: when I was five, Uncle Roy bought me my first pony, Mickey Merry Legs. I spent a good part of my childhood hiking and fishing with my uncle. As a junior high school student, I competed with Gabe in barrel racing. In high school, I ran the 880 and threw discus, joined the ski club. At age sixteen I succeeded in escaping Las Vegas as an exchange student to Australia, where I learned to scuba dive, rappel and rock climb. In college I started competing in endurance riding with a friend who owned more horses than she could keep exercised. We regularly covered twenty-five miles in a single morning.

My pretensions to athleticism intensified when I found work as a special issues editor at *Shape* magazine. I started weight training, took boxing lessons, volunteered for assignments requiring white-water kayaking and skeet shooting. And then there are the thousands of dollars spent on riding lessons.

These details do not reflect the fact that I have absolutely no athletic talent or ability. None. Zip.

I am not being modest. Even as an equestrian I am adequate, at best, even though the investment of time and money in this pursuit over the course of my life should be enough to make me an Olympic hopeful with the U.S. Equestrian Team.

I tell Edd all this, expecting his usual deep insights into

the manifestations of psychological disorders, symptoms, cures.

"Well Sam"—Edd only says "Well Sam" in his thick East Texas drawl when he is preparing to rib me about something—"maybe you're just not built to be an athlete."

OK, this much is true. It has something to do with my basic anatomy. I have large breasts, not the gorgeous helium-filled Amazon goddess breasts on *Baywatch* or anywhere on the west side of Los Angeles, but the real, fleshy, udderlike kind that swing when I move. I am convinced this disturbs my center of gravity, dragging me toward the ground, as if I have two magnets attached to my chest. I also have large hips and thighs that have never won a race, a little pot belly and long arms, neither of which seem capable of developing muscle, no matter how much iron I pump.

I have sworn off any number of activities only to wake up and attack them again the next morning. I always thought that someday I would succeed at something, but, really, that is not what has put me back in the saddle or in my running shoes. I crave the feel of wood, of iron, of the oil on horsehair, the intake of air through my nose, the sting of sweat in my eyes. I am the person who grabs the hot coal in order to know the nature of a burn. Stephen W. Hawking can divine the order of the cosmos while unable to do much more than move an eyelid, but without the kinesthetic registration of sensation, can I even think? My ideas are the result of accumulated experience. I struggle forward by feeling things first, then unraveling what they mean.

I thank Edd for his time and say goodbye. All this talk about activity has left me exhausted.

In the room the dogs Nika and Ming snore gently, the funk off their bodies filling the air. I can hear the metal sound of the hands on the clock as they move. I am hungry. I need to go to the bathroom, but I am afraid of the pain leaving the bed brings, of the possibility Nika and Ming will bump against me, that the tiles will be slick and the crutches will slide out from under me. It has happened before, all of it. I move hands over the body lying underneath the green bedspread, finding the sharp new angles, flesh loose and hanging, imagining the microbes growing like mold in my blood, in my bones, until the parts of me disintegrate on their own. I feel a shrinking, a moving inward, not like Errol Flynn, nothing like Mick Jagger.

Outside the window wind bends the eucalyptus, its gray-backed dagger leaves shimmering. Beyond the tree more trees, then the great blue of the Pacific meeting the sky at the horizon line.

It is November, three months after my accident. Appointments with Dr. Mesna are down to once a week. I get ready for my first weekly trip to the medical center as if I'm preparing for an opening night appearance. The ritual takes hours. I wash my hair, now cut short to the nape, easier to wash in the bathroom sink. I manage a little blue eyeliner, brush my teeth twice, gargle. An elastic-waist broomstick skirt falls to my ankles and a black shirt that was bought form-fitting now hangs loose. One flat black shoe for the good foot. Silver stud earrings accent the steel of the crutches. My audience: the taxi driver for the half-hour ride over the hill to the valley, a roulette of hospital receptionists, nurse Carryl and orthopedic technician Bernie, Dr. Mesna and the X-ray staff. The office for *Men's Fitness* magazine isn't far from the hospital, so my friend Mike says he'll swing by to give me a lift home and save me the sixty-five-dollar cab fare. I promise him that one day I'll be able to drive Matt's truck—it's an automatic, no clutch—and I will quit asking for the favor. "No rush," he says. "That's just what L.A. needs. Another woman on painkillers behind the wheel."

I complain loudly about the doctor visits but, really, I have come to love it here. I am encouraged to go into detail describing my pain, how I am learning to move on crutches, to talk of swelling, any signs of fever. There is much analyzing, worried hemming and hawing over X rays, the doctor meticulously examining the wound for signs of infection and slow healing. Dr. Mesna sometimes brings in colleagues to evaluate my situation so they can confer on treatment. I feel strangely relieved by the concern; the evidence proves the stakes are high. It is not just my self-absorption.

The trip from the curb to the lobby feels epic, through the Strait of Messina, past the rock of Cyclops. The cumbersome arrangement of my crutches; lifting my body out of the cab seat; the matter of my purse, how to carry it; the curb that looks like a cliff; doors, God, doors; the ever-present possibility of slipping or being bumped and falling, anticipating what degree of pain that would cause. Five minutes and already inside the black shirt my skin is damp with sweat. But when I reach the reception desk, I know I'm safe, finally arrived at Ithaca. Carryl quickly emerges to fetch me from the waiting area.

"Sam! Get in here," she barks, waving me in. Affection coming from this woman warms my heart. Smoker's skin, the New York edge of her voice that resists being dulled by years of southern California living, Carryl has seven kids, at least one ex-husband, and she is surprised by exactly nothing.

I am not on the examination table more than two minutes before she attacks the dressing on the wound with scissors.

"Yuck," she says when the scissors have cut through all the bandages. The black cross-stitch has been gone for weeks now but the skin up and down the leg is still a kaleidoscope of purple and yellow, thick scabs at the break produce a dark ooze, and there's swelling all over. "You look like the bride of Frankenstein." This is a kind of honor, to be on the receiving end of the humor medical staff reserves only for those they think can hack it.

"I heard that line before. You got it from *Full Metal Jacket*." The key to playing along is to just pretend to be my mother. The two of them would be good friends.

Bernie has come to set the new dressing and hears our exchange. A gold chain dresses up the V neck of his blue smock, an earring in the shape of a lightning bolt shines on one lobe. "What do you expect?" he tells Carryl. "This is basically a reattached limb."

Bernie loosens the wraps of the splint, whistles. "Oh baby, you are so *hot*!" he points to the wiry hairs that spring from the skin, now a good inch long. They create the illusion of a burnt forest after a fire. "When are you going to shave? Please? For me?"

"How can I shave something I can't feel and can't get wet?" I am trying for a hip, ironic tone but my voice has developed a chronic flinch to it, a sort of yelping pitch.

"Never mind," he says. "I'm getting you a Norelco for Christmas."

Today for Show and Tell, Dr. Mesna brings with him another patient, a man in a walking cast up to his knee, leaning on a cane in an expert way that makes it clear he's walked like this for a while. Dr. Mesna introduces us, says we have something in common: legs snapped by horses. More than a year past his accident, the man's bones haven't knitted together, although the injury is only a Grade II, Class B fracture, meaning the bones didn't even break the skin. No soft tissue damage. Not nearly as severe as my injury.

Amateur.

Dr. Mesna directs the man closer to the lighted wall where my X rays hang. "See," he says to the man, pointing to the picture of the metal rod filling the center of the damaged bone, the screws attaching just below the knee, other screws just above the ankle joint, their ends poking through the sides. "This is the type of internal fixation device I was telling you about. There are a number of benefits—"

"No way!" the man doesn't even let Dr. Mesna finish the sentence. "That thing looks so nasty. I would never want anything so ugly."

I look at him, mouth gaping. Does he not realize that the X rays belong to me, the person on the table next to him? That his astoundingly stupid and illogical comment will make me feel so worthless, damaged beyond repair? Forget external appearances, the messy core of me has been judged ugly. I think of Gram, who put on lipstick even to garden, even in a garden inside the chain-link fence that bound the trailer lot in Las Vegas. *Never know who you're going to meet.*

Dr. Mesna is, as usual, unflappable, his reaction positively Vulcan. "You understand, of course, that we're looking at an X ray. The fixator is internal, it can't be seen. The nonunion of your fracture suggests this might be an acceptable course of treatment."

"I've seen all I need to," the man says. As he turns to leave Carryl catches my eye and looks heavenward, mouths the word *jerk*. I once would have strode after him, ready to duke it out, yelling, "Did your horse step on your head too or have you always been an ignorant motherfucker?" But now anger dissipates as quickly as it gathers.

Dr. Mesna seems not to have noticed anything disagreeable has just occurred. If I said something to him—like, Why did you bring that moron in here?—he would be sincerely befuddled; he would never want to hurt my feelings, he's simply uncertain how all this subjective stuff operates. I can imagine that this particular quality of his, this earnest obliviousness, makes his wife want to throw things at him.

"Ms. Dunn." He turns his attention to me. The tissue healing on the wound is "acceptable," he says. "Not great, but that's what you would expect of this kind of injury." I feel embarrassed, as if this was a test I should have aced but instead squeaked by with only a C–. I'll be having a surgery next week because he needs to take out the screws that are located by my knee; the bone eventually will slide down the rod toward the break, which will help to spur some growth. A Popsicle melting along a stick. "And you've got to start walking for a little bit every day with your crutches, putting as much pressure on the leg as you can stand. Weight-bearing activity is the only hope of creating bone."

I look at him blankly. All I can picture is the sight of that leg cut open, flung out to the side of my body, flesh pulpy, unable to bear anything. I want to tell him: Listen, you don't understand. I'm an invalid. We invalids don't do things like

SAMANTHA DUNN

that. Invalids stay in bed. We sleep. We avoid touching our reattached limb. We avoid having anything or anybody else touch it, either.

"Oh. Joy." My smile is anemic.

I arrive home to a message from Drew on the answering machine. No luck leasing Harley. "One woman seemed interested but she backed out," he says. "Let me know and I'll keep trying."

The woman phoned me just last week; she'd given Harley a test ride and found him stiff, and tight on the left side. She wasn't impressed, still, she would like to start riding again. Why, exactly, was I laid up? "He jumped on me and whacked my leg half off," I explained, "but he didn't mean to." Her stumbling reply was the tip-off she wouldn't be calling back.

I know I sabotaged the deal. But it's as if by leasing Harley I will lose who I am. Who I really am. Or at least was.

But the first of the month isn't far off. I should make good on my half of the rent. Board must be paid, all the bills of horseshoeing and vetting must be met, and then there is the expense of having the trainer Calvin MacDonald, the man I took weekly lessons with before the accident, exercise Harley to keep him healthy. Harley has arthritis from old racing injuries, he needs work to keep his joints supple. Matt even found this basement apartment in Malibu just so we could remain near the stable; there are far cheaper places than this in Los Angeles. I should just give up on the idea of having a horse. Find Harley a good pasture somewhere in another county, maybe donate him to a riding program.

Yes. Pasture makes the most sense. The horse will be fine. Who am I kidding? I won't ride again. I know this.

But rather than look for the number of some riding program that accepts donated horses, I pick up the phone and call one of my former editors at *Shape* magazine. She's surprised to hear from me, wants to know how I'm doing. Feeling great. Yeah, much better. "Hey, guess what," I say, "I'm up for assignments."

She is quiet on the other end of the line, then, with all delicacy, asks what I feel I can do.

"How about a hiking trip in Costa Rica?"

There's no laughter on the other end.

"Seriously, I have an idea," I tell her. "I've been doing a little research on the idea of what makes people accident-prone."

At the turn of the twentieth century, industrial accidents were a common problem which cost plant owners time and money, so a number of studies were done investigating how to lower their incidence rates. What researchers found was, first, that people who had a history of accidents were more likely to have another than those who did not, and, second, that in any given plant a few people suffered the majority of the accidents. British researchers Farmer and Chambers were the first to use the label "accident-prone" in 1926. The seeds of why such a label might be important had been planted some seventy years earlier, when a Massachusetts Supreme Court judge introduced the idea of personal negligence into legal liability. Prior to that, victims of injury had been rewarded without consideration given to whether their actions had contributed in any way to the accident. But the rise of industrialization made it economically important to assign blame.

Studies tried to identify which factors might render

some people more accident-prone than others. Unequal exposure to hazards explained a few cases—the law of averages dictates that a guy who operates a slicing machine for a living is more likely to get cut than the boss who sits behind a desk. Differing levels of skill and training explained others. And, finally, it was determined that a person's state of mind was a more fleeting yet nevertheless significant factor. Simply put: Hotheads who are reckless and don't pay attention get hurt. So do people who are preoccupied, or under stress.

Sigmund Freud was particularly intrigued by what seemingly chance occurrences, gaffes and accidental injury expressed about the subconscious. In *The Psychopathology of Everyday Life*, published in 1899, Freud wrote that "certain shortcomings in our psychical functioning and certain seemingly unintentional performances" all have motives "unknown to consciousness." Accidents were to him expressions of unconscious intent, and the more severe the accident, the more clearly it expressed a desire for self-destruction.

Child psychology, sports medicine, emergency medicine, and psychiatry are just a few of the categories under which the subject of accident proneness has subsequently been examined, although on something of a hit-and-miss basis. The concept is "frequently discussed and rarely documented," researchers noted in the journal *Pediatrics*. Some reject the notion entirely, arguing that there's no statistical measure for accident proneness, that it serves as a convenient way to "blame the victim." Arguments against the label are commonly put forward in cases of industrial accidents—ironically, where the need to define the accident prone began—because it is used as a way to obscure the issue of companies putting people to work in potentially unsafe environments.

But among the available research conducted by a vast array of disciplines that have, at some point or other, tried to identify why some people suffer accident after accident, one phrase crops up repeatedly, the consistent common denominator: "psychological factors."

Many times studies begin with the premise that there's a baseline personality type that takes more risks than other types. Statistically speaking, these personalities will get hurt more often as a result of their behavior. But no matter the starting point, researchers inevitably hit upon the suggestion that some kind of psychological problem is lurking. An unconscious form of hurting yourself as a form of punishment for deep feelings of guilt. A misguided expression of grief. Even a self-defeating strategy to avoid dealing with success.

Or, in the language of research abstracts: "Victims of trauma, both unintentional and especially intentional, have a high incidence of psychopathology"—so noted the *Journal of Trauma*, enumerating depression among the factors. *Clinical Orthopedics* observed that "vulnerability [to accidents] involves both physical and psychological faculties. . . . The condition is referred to as 'accident proneness' especially when vulnerability is affected by psychologic predisposition." Psychologists coined the term "depressive equivalent" for depression in children that is expressed through activity. In adults the same idea is called "agitated depression."

Even when the researchers don't apply any term that begins with the prefix "psycho," they nonetheless refer to influences on mental health, as in a 1976 study published in the journal *Pediatrics*: "Children undergoing stressful changes in their lives were more susceptible to accidents."

Most studies appear to examine only male subjects or mixed groups, rather than exclusively female groups. A 1995 study that tried to define what types of behavior led to accidents in which physical impairment resulted, published in *Child Development*, noted that while heavy drinking, aggression and other "conduct problems" had clear ties to accidents experienced by adult men, for women those indicators were "less accurate." At one point a group within the American Psychiatric Association lobbied for a diagnosis called "masochistic character disorder," but others argued against it, protesting that the potential for the label to be applied more to women than men invited discrimination.

In 1994 psychologist Dusty Miller published a book titled *Women Who Hurt Themselves*. In it she proposed that women who hurt themselves—whether through cutting, burning, bulimia or anorexia, compulsive plastic surgery or through substance abuse—suffered from what she labeled "Trauma Reenactment Syndrome." Miller observed that, without exception, these women came from backgrounds that were either abusive or abnormally stressful in some other regard: "Her behavior is . . . a cry for help, a request for the protection she did not receive as a child." In essence, Miller argued, these women were using their bodies to reenact the harm done to them as children, because there was a strange comfort in it, and because it reinforced some deeply imbedded belief that they were incapable of protecting themselves as adults just as they could not protect themselves as children.

While she didn't identify accidents per se as a way of hurting yourself, her theories seem to echo larger themes in other studies that do.

I tell myself, In the last one hundred years most of the rest of Freud's theories have been dismissed as better literature than science. As for the rest, they might as well be potshots in the dark. Not one expert knows anything for sure.

So why then does it feel as if a wall is falling on my head, burying me in the rubble of things said and unsaid during thirty-two years. I turn off the computer. I shut my eyes.

My jigsaw memories.

Gram's face in front of me, *Sure, I'll take another highball*, holding out her glass, around the sides of which was etched a hunting tableau of pheasants being flushed out of the brush. *Whoopsie daisy!* she'd say if and when any Scotch was spilled. It would run down her arm onto the gold fabric of the La-Z-Boy. She always wore a short string of white plastic pearls around her neck, the plastic glowing with an unhealthy luminance, a certain larval quality. There Mom would be, leaning on the armrest of the davenport, her stocking feet tucked under her, a practice that eventually eroded the fabric off the cushion, leaving a permanent imprint worn into the foam. Rereading one of the paperbacks she bought at Safeway, her head bowed toward the pages while my grandmother recited the chronology of my mother's failures. Gram had a lovely voice if you didn't listen to what she was

actually saying. I knew Mom was memorizing the plot lines
and historical facts from James Michener, from Irving Stone,
as if they could replace the painful chronicles of her own life.
And if that didn't work, she would drink more. It never
worked.

I've heard of people who would pay big money to see
what happens when a wolverine and a bear are chained
together and thrown into a pit. I can say for sure that one will
die and one will come out scarred and limping.

To be the chain that links the two.

Gram's face turned from me. *I'll marry whoever I want.*
She had the rose clippers in her right hand. The seventy-year-
old flesh of her arms jiggled as she trimmed the branch.
Whomever. I am sure you will. Snap, snap. *Oh, fuck you.* She
stopped for a minute but still didn't turn to me. *Well fuck you
too, you little bitch.* But her voice wavered. Mine had not. I
had mastered her art and she knew it. I walked out the gate
to my car. She called to me. I didn't turn around.

Three weeks before the wedding. *Evelyn had a massive
stroke. She was dead before the ambulance got here, Sammy.*
Mom always called her mother by her first name. I had
not telephoned since the day of the roses. I went home to
New Mexico; Las Cruces, six hours south of where I was
reared. Mom and I cleaned out Gram's new mobile home—
"manufactured housing" is the current term—in an upscale
park with a guard at the gate, a swimming pool and club-
house, blue-collar bourgeoisie. Empty generic gin bottles
lined the backs of all the cupboards in the kitchen. The *Funk
and Wagnalls Dictionary* by the La-Z-Boy, its broken spine
splinted by duct tape, pages soft from use, the ink down

some columns smeared where she had run her index finger repeatedly. It seemed to me she had absorbed all the words. Her last crossword, done in ballpont. In the bedroom, the sewing box was opened. She had been making me a veil for the wedding. Mexican lace. I didn't wear it.

And why am I thinking of Gabe, the speckled pink-and-gray skin around his eyes, the dense white lashes? Boarded at a ranch when I went to Australia my senior year of high school. I fed him carrots in the pasture before I went to college. He was sold to pay for back board; by then Mom had taken a job in the Middle East and would be gone for nine years. Mom said it was Gram's fault and Gram said it was Mom's fault but I knew it was really my fault. A kid's camp bought him, the rancher said. Nice people, right up here off the highway, don't worry, he'll be happy. The rancher gave me the number. I kept it in my purse and never again saw the animal that lifted me through my childhood.

But only when I think of the past two years do the tears become sobs, my rib cage growing sore from the heaving. People will say, *After the time alone, the meals she never made, the times she was never there, the times he was never there, the band practices, the drugs, the horse, the money she spent, all that money, and the amplifiers in black boxes, and the guitar strings, and the guitar picks called Fender Mediums he leaves in his jeans and how they always end up clanking around in the washer. And then the rehab and the therapy and the group sharing for the families of addicts and the steps she refused to take, sitting in the back of those meeting halls, glaring at her fellow participants and thinking, "This is his problem, not mine" and "I*

will not come to believe you were powerless, just take responsibil-
ity for your complete fuckup" and *Losers, losers, whiners, losers.*

How long do I stay like this. Hours. The sun burns out over
the ocean, night seeps into the room. Matt arrives home, a
clatter in the kitchen. "I love you," he says when he comes
into the room. "Do you want something to eat?" No. He
leaves a minute later to watch TV in the living room, likely to
fall asleep on the couch again. The bedroom becoming my
exclusive kingdom, no way for him to get comfortable on
this bed with all the pillows and me who cries out in pain at
any unintentional nudge.

I flip the light switch by the bed and turn the computer
back on.

In 1945 the American psychoanalyst Helen Flanders Dunbar
put forth the description of the accident prone as those who
are drawn to adventure and excitement, in search of immediate pleasure. This type of person does not like to plan ahead
and detests discipline of any form, including the self-discipline
it takes to exercise caution. But Dunbar is most famous for
adding the term "psychosomatic" to the popular vernacular;
she argued that all illness must be examined within the context of a person's life, because psychology and biology fit
hand in glove. She saw the symptoms of any one illness as
"insight symbols," which could potentially reveal why at a
particular time in life a person is suffering a particular ailment

or—she noted this specifically—accident in the case of fracture patients.

Accident as allegory. For Flanders Dunbar, like Freud, there was always a mystery to unravel behind any accident. Sometimes a broken leg is a cigar.

For the next several days I sift through the research abstracts, books and essays I have accumulated, mentally constructing the story of my life, searching for the insight into what leads to the final climax in which I decide to get off my horse and cross the stream. What motivates the main character? This: Because she was born the illegitimate child of a single mother who was struggling through night school to earn a college degree, she felt she was the reason her mother had been forced to live with her grandmother in a miserable alliance to rear her. Later, she was the reason her stepfather died because she had failed to find the experimental drugs in Mexico her mother sent her money to buy. Finally, she was such a horrible wife that her husband became an addict to escape the reality of their hollow life together, and she didn't stop him. She keeps hurting herself in a subconscious effort to atone for it all, breaking her leg as a symbol of saying, I can't run from this anymore.

Or, to nab attention for herself away from the recovering husband.

The plot is complex, her motives are never pure.

It is just after Thanksgiving when I return home from the hospital after the surgery to remove the screws near the knee. I don't dare venture beyond the circuit of the bed to the couch to the bathroom. Dr. Mesna says I have to walk, but I reason that by limiting all motion I can cut to nil the odds of having an accident.

I explain that my lack of movement is owed to pain, but there is always some degree of pain, not a minute I've been without it since the instant Harley's hoof cut through the shin. The truth is I feel as if I have a bomb strapped to my chest, I could detonate at any time. Any misstep, a spilt glass, a book dropped to the floor, evidence of my psychopathology.

Edward listens for some minutes while I confess all this to him, the receiver made slick from the perspiration of my cheek. I never know when he is going to call, I just pick up the phone and there he is, voice calm, there is never any small talk, sometimes not even a hello. He is way beyond the grading system, my personal Obi-Wan Kenobi.

Finally he interrupts. "This is the problem with psychoanalyzing yourself," he says. Some of this may be true, sometimes. Some of it may not be. Some of it is crap you can completely discount. He says I am missing the point.

I feel as if he's deliberately ripped off my shell, the one that took me so long to find and fit myself into like a hermit crab. Edward has never talked to me like this.

"The question is, What are you going to do about your life now?" he asks. "I remember seeing you in the dirt, and the look in your eye. I said to myself, This has the reek of karma all over it. It was literally a breaking point. You could go one way or the other."

Karma, the accumulation of choices and action. Not like kismet, the Turkish concept of fate or fortune, beyond measure and calculation. I want directions, right or left? But he isn't offering, says I'm the only one who can figure it out. This is the old struggle, the big question: trying to construct meaning out of what we cannot know. To do otherwise would mean one of two things, either that existence is random, or that the design is more profound than we can fathom. "What we are really talking about is faith," he says. "Do you have it?"

Faith: a noun, meaning confident trust in a person, idea or thing. "Sometimes," I say. "It depends."

It occasionally crosses my mind that I am not having these conversations with him at all, that this relationship is a figment played out in my head. Each time we speak I make him tell me the story of my rescue in some shape or form, as if it's a bedtime story. With each telling he reveals a new detail. Today I begin with, "I remember you kept pushing my hair back. I could tell you didn't want me to look."

"I had to lean over you," he says. "The only way I could get the bleeding to stop was by pinching the artery shut with my fingers."

I'm hit with a slightly nauseous feeling, a jittery shake of muscle all at once, like the sensation of almost getting hit by a car but not quite. What did I think he was doing all that time kneeling over me? I look at my hand, I reach to touch my face, realizing this could be flesh dead and buried these months. I am too overwhelmed even to cry. The miracle of my life I owe to Edward and then to the paramedics, nurses, lab techs, doctors, all people who were willing to get their hands dirty. It occurs to me I have been operating my life on the fundamental lie that I am independent and making it on my own. I exist because other people have stepped outside of what is comfortable for them and made it so.

"I didn't have a belt," he continues. "I couldn't think of anything for a tourniquet."

How much blood can you lose before you bleed to death? It happens quickly, that much I know. I recall a line from an article in *Emergency Medical Services* magazine all those years ago: five liters in the average adult, about seventy cubic centimeters per kilogram of body weight.

I don't know what to say to him. I was not the only person experiencing stress and trauma the day of my accident. That canyon, next to his house, is a place he knows well. I wonder if the memory of literally holding a woman's life in his hands makes it a place he now wants to avoid. I ask, "Have you been back?"

"The next day," he says. The dried blood made a large brown circle where I lay, so he scraped the dirt until it was cleared. "You never know. I thought it might scare people. Or if someone else came riding through there and the horse smelled it . . . something could happen again."

I try to imagine a circle large enough to scare a horse, the dull color. How fast blood will oxidize when exposed to air, a smell like something left in the refrigerator too long.

"Listen," he says, "what we were talking about before— don't get caught there, in the reasons why."

But that is exactly what I do for the next few days, obsessively ferreting through computer link after link about accidents and the people who have them. I eat only peanut butter toast and black tea, my mind too busy to make choices about food. Matt has learned to live on cafeteria food at the office and bean burritos at home.

I find instructions for casting out demons—Pentecostals, God love them, have upgraded from tents to cyberministry. Accident proneness falls under a long list of "demon indicators," which include lying, wearing the color red, levitating, projectile vomiting, and using the Lord's name in vain. I think of the priest at my bedside in the hospital, the missed opportunity for exorcism. The *European Journal of Emergency Medicine* prints a study proposing that people who have repeated accidents have a higher rate of alcohol abuse and a "propensity toward violence." I report this to my mother. "They're just Irish," she says. I think of a black and white picture she keeps in her cedar chest of my Uncle Mutt. He's smiling, looking like a fat George Clooney, in each fist a can of Colt '45, hunting cap on, rifle next to him, ready for deer season.

I am looking for the one oyster that holds the pearl, that one magic kiss or glass slipper. Once I have it I'll know that I have broken the spell, that I am not meant for accidental ruin, or at least that I have the power to choose against it.

Accidents are not a constant in my life, they arrive like a bad rash. This pattern is supported by research. Some people are accident-prone for short periods, others suffer regular bouts over the course of their entire lives. People can be accident-prone for different reasons at different periods in life, writes psychologist G. J. S. Wilde, author of *Target Risk*, one of the most comprehensive looks at the subject of risk factors yet compiled. Potential triggers include problems in relationships, jobs and money matters, and loss of a loved one. *Rehab, freelancing, hospital bills, three out of four.* One study Wilde cites found that drivers suffering marital problems experienced accidents with greater frequency around the time they filed for divorce. That word again, divorce. Matt had said it on the phone in the first call from the his hospital. *No*, I said at first. Then: *If that's what you want.* I didn't repeat the word. Like *cancer*. Don't say it too much, or you bring it into being.

To accept accident proneness as the sum total of a person's nature is to commit what social psychologists call a "fundamental attribution error," meaning that a person's behavior is being held up as proof of his essential makeup or character, rather than as an indicator of his passing state of mind or environmental conditions. Get paid for it once and they'll always call you a whore, in other words.

The truth is that I am not prone to accidents. I am prone to jumping on the back of a horse and riding until the rush of wind in my ears erases the screaming and name-calling between the two women I love most in the world. I am prone to going to the stable rather than asking my husband if he can please take that fucking bong out of his mouth. I am prone to panic over when I'm going to get paid for my last freelance article and whether the check will arrive before the phone bill is due. I am prone to fly off the handle. I am prone to be sad for reasons I don't really understand. I am prone to want to see myself bleed rather than admit I'm scared. Accidents are just part of the deal.

I'm thinking you might want to see your horse." Calvin MacDonald on the phone. His voice booms from his barrel chest, he must stand six-foot-two and seems as big as some of the horses he rides, a self-titled Professional Irishman, bright blue eyes like gemstones out of place in a rough-hewn wood carving of a face.

"Is there something wrong?" The icy wash of guilt pours over me. For the past couple months I have literally turned my head as I pass the turn for the barn on the way to the medical center. I mail the board to Drew without even a note. Not willing to give Harley up but not willing to see him, either.

"No, no. I've been riding him." Calvin pauses for a moment. "But there's nothing like motherly love, now, is there? And it would do you good. Get some air in your lungs."

After we say goodbye I feel angry with Calvin. Doesn't he know how hard it is for me to get around? What does he expect? If I had my X rays I would wear them like a necklace so no one would ever be confused and expect too much.

But then I start to wonder about particulars I have not considered since a time before that day on the trail. Harley is a hard keeper, always on the skinny side. He's bound to catch any sickness circulating in the barn. Have Drew and Juan, the groom, remembered to put wraps on Harley's front legs? He develops sores from the hard ground of his paddock without them. Has his mane been pulled? It grows so thick and unruly, black hair stronger than twine. It won't hurt to see him, I tell myself. Just to check. Be a responsible owner.

I take a Vicodin preventatively. My strategy for local travel is to take a pill, get in the car and drive to my destination, which is never more than ten minutes from the house. That way, I can drive before that slow-motion, numb feeling sets in. Once I get where I am going, walking around with my crutches and putting pressure on the leg every step or so will produce enough pain to wake me up again, so that by the time I have to drive home I'm just enough on edge to be alert. It occurs to me that this is exactly the kind of behavior those studies on the factors in accident proneness are talking about; I see researchers in lab coats pointing to a large petri dish. *Exhibit A. Here we see the prototypical specimen.*

But what real choice do I have, to stay in the house for the next year, waiting for someone to take me out?

Well, yes.

All right already.

The familiar stillness of late afternoon at the barn. Calvin is gone, no one around except Juan. The horses stand quietly, all have their heads down, noses rustling through their after-noon feeding, searching for the sweetest stalks of hay. I sweat going up the incline to Harley's paddock, sit on the mounting block next to the gate to catch my breath. He turns his head for a moment, then returns to his hay. I watch the play of his jaw muscles under his thin bay coat as he grinds the food with his teeth. The lids hang heavy over his eyes; he looks content, half asleep. His black tail swishes at the occasional fly. It nearly reaches the ground. I used to keep it trimmed and level but now the ends are jagged, like a bad haircut grown out.

Juan comes out of the barn to sit beside me on the block. It is like him not to say hello, even after not having seen me for months. A baseball cap seems to be permanently attached to his head. He is not much more than a boy but has the pol-ished, jet-stone eyes of a very old man.

"Sam." He pronounces the "a" in my name in the soft way of Spanish, not in the flat, nasal way of American English. He gestures up and down the length of my body. "You muy flaca now."

"I know. Pero es bien por una chica to be skinny, no es ver-dad?" We speak a kind of pidgin to each other, his English and my Spanish about on par. He thinks I should speak bet-ter Spanish because of where I grew up, I tell him he has to learn English to make money in the U.S. I remember we had been trying to improve each other's fluency, but neither one of us ever seemed to improve much.

He looks down, pinching a stalk of hay in his fingers. "No, is no good. You have mucho dolor?"

"Sí. I have pain todos los días," I tell him.

"Es lástima," Juan says, shaking his head.

"You get used to it," I reply. We sit for a moment without saying anything, and I remember how I used to be more at home here than in my own house, but now am uncomfortable, feel I am a part that no longer fits.

"I put Harley in el corral ahora," he says, motioning to the round pen where horses are lunged, and I reply yes, OK gracias. I poke my way slowly through the dirt as Juan takes Harley away from the hay and leads him to the pen. Juan closes the gate behind us and there we stand, Harley with his head down and me leaning on my crutches, not looking at each other, awkward, kids at a junior high dance. Finally I remember the carrot in my sweatshirt pocket I brought as an offering. His ears prick with mild interest. He starts to wander toward me with that loose walk of his and I have to steel myself from recoiling in fear, he so big and me so easily knocked down. But he stops beside me and nickers softly, not reaching for the carrot. He too seems a little skinnier, a little meeker.

"C'mon boy," I tell him, reaching out to run my hand across his neck. The hair is longer, slightly rougher than I recall. "Hey, do you remember our trick?"

Harley knows one stupid pet trick, the so-called camel stretch, a bow in which he stretches his head between his front hooves. He would grudgingly perform it for visitors only if I plied him with enough treats to make it worth his while. With the end of the carrot I cue him for the trick by tapping him on the chest while holding on to my crutches. He blows air through his nostrils and bobs his head a couple of times, his oh-damn-she's-asking-me-to-do-that-thing response, unchanged after all these months. But then he surprises me by stretching down into a perfect bow.

"Guboy guboy guboy," I gush as I feed him the carrot, reverting to a cutesy voice I tend to use around dogs and horses, when no human is within earshot.

I am starting to feel light-headed from the sunshine, the Vicodin kicking in, and all the blood draining into the leg. "Juan," I say, my voice sounding feeble even to me, "necesito sit down. Can you open the gate por favor?"

I pat Harley then turn to make my way out of the pen; the dirt is deep and soft, makes for hard going. He follows behind me, puppylike, and as I reach the gate he starts pawing the ground. I slowly turn, bracing myself, expecting him to frisk my pocket with his muzzle for evidence of more bounty. Instead he steps away, and without any prompting performs another bow. This is an obvious ploy for another carrot, but it makes me smile, and I realize I can't remember the last time I have really smiled other than to put on a happy face for Matt when he comes home.

"Sorry." I balance my weight against the crutches as I pull my hands away from the handles to show him I'm not holding anything. "See? No more, mooch." A bad move putting my weight on the crutches; the pressure slows the circulation in the arteries under the arms, making me feel even woozier. But again Harley paws the ground, and again, he bows. More praise, then I turn, but each of my movements produces a new bow, another hopeful look upon its completion.

"Whoa, whoa," I tell him, and he finally does, standing beside me. I steady myself against him, my cheek on his warm coat, and when he doesn't move I lean in with all my weight, propping my crutches against him and throwing both arms around his neck.

"Hey, Sam," says Juan, "you OK?"

"Sí, sí," I tell him, pressing my face into the groove where Harley's neck moves into his shoulder, as if I can draw all the strength from there. And I talk quietly to my horse as his head curves toward me, telling him a hundred things as his coat grows wet where I have buried my face. He stands very still.

My first social excursion: meeting Renée for coffee at our local java bar in the overblown minimall that passes for Malibu's downtown. I drive the truck for the ten-mile trip, enjoying the speed at which the roadside flashes by, appreciating the control of being behind a wheel, like I am sixteen again, driving all the way to Santa Fe in Gene's Mercury Comet.

But that sense of power evaporates as soon as I maneuver to get myself out of the truck, crutches under both arms, my leg in a brace that encases the leg up to the knee and resembles the boots astronauts wore on the moon. My sweatshirt droops over my body, my shoulders like a wire hanger. In the parking lot cars drive past me, a truck whizzes so near I feel the rush of current on my face. I can easily see myself crushed under a wheel, I would make a popping sound not unlike an aluminum can. I try to hurry, I feel as if everyone is waiting for me to get the hell out of the way, and I think of the driving game Matt and I used to play, joking, Five points for the gimp! Ten if he's in a wheelchair, twenty for the blue hair shuffling with the walker. My punishment is not that I am the punch line of my own joke but that I keep hearing the aphorism *What comes around goes around* in my head to the tune of a song sung by Ratt. Retribution delivered by a heavy metal band; on which tier of Dante's seven-ring spiral do I reside, exactly?

In the window of the coffee shop I catch a glimpse of a woman plugging along on crutches, her sharp cheekbones, the trench lines around her mouth, her back hunched as she grips the handles. I have an image in my head of someone entirely different, a full-figured redhead with a stride designed to cover a lot of ground all at once. Not an urban, run-to-catch-a-cab walk, more of a steady rhythm developed tromping through pastures, on dirt roads. I cannot believe this is the face and body the world now sees. How puny I am. I can picture myself already an old woman, anxious of strangers, afraid of being hurt.

Renée has already staked out a table for us, she helps me situate my apparatus, arranges an extra chair for me to prop the leg on for elevation—too long down, and it starts to swell and throb. I tell her I have seen Harley and begin to launch into the story of going back to the barn—she'll love this, I know, she has two cats, and she knows how animals can be. She nods as I tell her, aw, that's sweet, really, but you weren't alone, were you?

"No," I reply, a little surprised. "Juan was there."

"Good." She looks relieved. "I think you should be careful." What she wants are the details of the appointments with Dr. Mesna, the most recent prognosis, descriptions of rehabilitation therapy. There are none to report. Dr. Mesna says there is nothing the hospital can do to grow bones that I can't do for myself, namely walk. And as for infection, beyond what has already been done in terms of aggressive antibiotic therapy, that's a throw of the dice. Either it will crop up later or it won't.

"I can't believe there's no rehab," she says. "Tell them you need better answers than that. Is it an HMO policy? I bet it is. I bet you it is."

I start to feel exhausted, and a little defensive. I trust my doctor. I need to trust my doctor. I don't have the energy to do anything but. I am an obedient patient. I tell her that's just the way it is with my injury. Best-case scenario, I will always have a limp and swelling that will worsen as I age.

I must say this in more of a grandiose, self-pitying tone than I realize, because she replies sharply, "That's not so bad. There are worse things than a limp." I look at her in a way that means, That's easy for you to say, gorgeous Audrey Hepburn-looking creature, you who stops traffic, you who can drink cappuccino and elegantly avoid getting a foam mustache.

"You know, I have a limp." She throws this out matter-of-factly, and I am stunned. She nods and says yes, one leg is slightly shorter than the other, she wears a small lift in one shoe. Have I never noticed?

Not in almost the decade I have known her have I noticed this. I blush. To say that I am contrite doesn't reach far enough. I look at my dear friend and try to imagine that it is for the first time, trying to see the person who actually sits in front of me rather than the mirage of ideas and preconceptions I have put in her place. What else have I neglected?

"I am so sorry for being an asshole," I tell her.

She takes a sip of her coffee. "You're never an asshole. Thoughtless maybe. OK, sometimes an asshole."

"And rude. Don't forget rude." I reach my hand out to touch her. Her wrist is so small. "I am really, truly sorry."

Renée leaves to run errands. Everyone lives within the lines determined, to one extent or other, by their physical abilities. Bodies change over time; everyone understands this is the process of age. How callow does it make me that it never occurred to me before? Up to this point I contrived a life of perpetual motion, creating the illusion that life stays the same. But when such constant movement isn't possible, now that I have watched the hands on a clock move forward from seconds to minutes to hours, I am beginning to appreciate the reality of change. I feel a profound sense of shame for the cocoon that I have built of my suffering, savoring what I silently believed to be its singularity.

"Skiing accident?" An older man in a pink polo shirt and tan slacks approaches me as I sit on a bench near a granite fountain at the minimall outside a flower shop.

"Horse," I say.

"I had a bad fall on skis once," he crosses his arms and stands beside me for a moment, commiserating on the ache of broken bones. "Well, get better" he finally says and with a wave he turns in the direction of the coffee shop.

When I could walk I never spoke to anyone in public places like this. No one ever said hello, I never said hello. But now I notice that if I shut up and listen, people talk to me in a way they never have. Because my injury is so obvious and my movement labored, I am easy to catch. Some people look away when they see me, as if made uncomfortable by my crutches and brace, but many more look directly at me, often stopping to offer encouragement or even to talk. And when they speak, it's no idle chatter. *I lost my bladder to cancer, I have a bag that attaches. I am so depressed. I was on crutches for a bad sprain; it still hurts. My daughter died horseback riding. My ankle had to be pinned in five places when a motorcycle ran over it.* They show me the missing parts of fingers lost in freak fishing mishaps, the lines of scars that pull at skin like ragged hems, the hearing aids behind the careful arrangement of hair. This was not part of my landscape before.

I run my hand over the rough stone of the bench and think about the people I have professed to love. How terrified Matt must have been that first night in the drug treatment center, unfamiliar bed and strange faces around him. My mom, how she had cried in pain and frustration those years ago when she cut her hand trying to jimmy loose a bad muffler on our old car with a piece of rusty bailing wire. A friend who works as a newspaper reporter, learning her lovely brown Cleopatra eyes are betraying her with macular degeneration. My grandmother, her hand to her forehead trying to ease the stab of a migraine, saying how much she hated rainy days, remembering being a child looking up at the stars to see if she could find the face of her dead mother, and how she would talk to the stars and wait for them to break their silence. How eventually she stopped looking up altogether.

The shotgun metal, the last taste my uncle knew as he decided how to die.

I make a vow to hold these pictures in my mind, fragile, some beautiful crystal image easily crushed. Then, instantly, I feel sad. It is my nature to forget.

It's been six months since my accident and for some reason the phone has started to ring off the hook with calls from my old stable of magazine editors who now want to know if I'm up for an assignment. Small assignments, mostly, brief blurbs of information I can easily track down by phone. I suspect something is going on but I don't want to ask too many questions, lest I jinx the current boon and the phone goes silent again. They never called this often when I had two good legs. Journalists are by nature inclined to collect and pass information among themselves, and that includes any gossip on one of their own. My story makes good copy: *Maimed by her horse! She and her husband had been on the rocks, are they together? How's she making it?* They have been trading worried clucks, flipping through the stacks of papers on their desks for items they can give me to pursue from my laptop desk in bed. I am grateful; it's given me a way to measure days, a reason to look at the calendar apart from the weekly visit to Dr. Mesna.

The most frequent caller is Stephanie, my editor at *InStyle* who has become a solid Grade 1, calling for regular updates, who never tires of hearing me retell the particulars of my accident in photographic detail. She knows about the thick scar that runs jagged and twisted around my shin and the dent in my calf muscle, the vertical mark from the bolt placement on the inside of my ankle, another on the outside of my calf, and still another that looks like a centipede running down my knee. "Sam-a-lama," she always says by way of hello, "want to make some money, honey?"

The assignment this week is simply to compile a list for a "fitness trends of the stars" piece on yoga and martial arts teachers who have celebrity clients. So far this has been easy for me to track down: after years writing about health and fitness I have a Rolodex full of names, and celebrities in Los Angeles are like ragweed in the rest of the country—you can't drive down the road without seeing some. In another sense, though, it has reminded me of all that I cannot do, and will likely never do again. I conduct all the interviews over the phone, keeping them brief, just the facts ma'am, politely declining the offers to come try out a class, come see the great gym.

A friend at *Shape* gives me a lead for a yogi named Gurmukh Kaur Khalsa. Grrr-MOO-k, I take the name down phonetically. A teacher of Kundalini yoga, as opposed to the regular kind of yoga I guess, the distinction lost on me. A list of famous names longer than my arm is said to attend the classes. I roll my eyes. *L.A., land of fruits and nuts*, Mom often tells me. She reads the magazines at the supermarket, she's far more current in the Hollywood scene than I am. *Just don't join a cult, for chrissakes.*

I call. A small voice answers on the other end, "Sat nam, hello?" stringing the sounds together so they become one word, satnamhellooo? I have the urge to say, Is your mommy home, Satnam?, but instead I ask for Grrr-MOO-k.

"This is she," replies the voice, and for a moment I don't know what to say. I was expecting an old Indian man with a thick accent. I tell her who I am and what I'm doing, can I get some information please on her classes.

"I would love to tell you all you need," she says. "Why don't you come down here?"

"I just have a few quick questions—"

"It's just that I hate to talk over the phone. It's so much better if I can show you," she replies. "I like to have a face to go with a name."

This woman clearly is not going to budge. Contact with celebrity is a kind of celebrity in itself; many in this town have figured that out, and have learned to leverage it for the optimal amount of publicity. This person is probably no exception. I consider ringing off with a "Sorry to have bothered you" but don't. There is something quaint about this woman who talks like Glinda, the good witch of the north. She asks if I can be at her house in an hour, and I want to tell her to expect someone damaged, that I have not been farther than the coffee shop in six months, that I walk with the aid of a leg brace and crutches, that despite the Vicodin I take every six hours I feel ground down by the aches that grate along my nerves, and that I am perpetually exhausted regardless of the fact I sleep fourteen hours a day. But I am just too tired to argue with Glinda.

I get dressed; my clothes hang on me like laundry on a line. I drive the forty minutes to her house, as directed. It is surprisingly easy to meld with the traffic on the freeway. Mike was right. Just another woman on painkillers.

The house is a Hollywood bungalow, tile roof, stucco walls, pampas grass overgrown and an uneven path leading from the yard to the door. I bite my lip as I plod along the path, certain I will fall, wondering what the hell I was thinking to say yes to a yoga teacher, Birkenstock-wearing-Volkswagen-driving-tofu-eating-noodle-neck who spoon-feeds New Age hoopla to TV actresses. I am so angry by the time I reach her patio entrance I have to catch my breath.

Each inhale is perfumed with the scent of the jasmine vines running along the walls, and nag champa wafts through the open windows into the courtyard. I know incense, how you burn it to get rid of the skunky residue of marijuana, but this scent doesn't seem to be hiding anything. A little plug-in fountain for good feng-shui gurgles by the carved wood door, purple geode crystals line the sides of the steps, a strategy to attract positive vibrations. You can't grow up around Santa Fe without being immersed in the culture of the New Age at some point—and, sure enough, a New Mexico flag, its bright yellow background and red Zia sun symbol, decorates a wall by the window. The collective impression is so goofy I find myself laughing out loud. A four-foot statue of a grinning elephant god only makes me laugh harder. Silly Ganesha, Hindu god of auspicious beginnings.

The door opens and a slight, barefoot woman dressed completely in white says hello, sizing me up with a quick look up and down my body. On her head is a white turban held at the center by a topaz the size of a baby's fist. Behind her others in white turbans and Indian dress pass, looking like some ward in a celestial version of the Red Cross. I relax. I know the deal here, they're American Sikhs, hippies who found a guru and got clean. They run a huge ashram in northern New Mexico, used to operate a cool little health food restaurant on the Santa Fe Plaza where as a junior high kid I'd scam cookies. I have a rush of nostalgia; it is a warm feeling.

"Oh, wow. What happened to you?" Gurmukh doesn't introduce herself. "Here, come in. Let's sit on my bed so you can put your feet up and have some tea." She leads me down a hall past beaded curtains to a room of rococo design and cozy opulence. Oriental carpets warm the wood floors, a double bed covered in pale shaded pillows fills a corner. By comparison I feel awkward, overly severe, my black turtle-neck and wide-leg pants stiff and uncomfortable.

We sit for nearly two hours on her bed. I am the one sup-posed to be doing the interviewing but she asks all the questions, my life strung out before her. As she listens she just nods, sometimes shutting her eyes, expressing no pity for me, not even a "that must have hurt." I feel glad about that. While I have come to expect attention because of my injury, the price of that attention is pity, its insidious effect a feeling of hopelessness, the sense that my very essence as a person has been reduced.

Then it is her turn to talk, and she becomes a Scheherazade, spinning story after story, about her previous life as a flower child in the Haight Ashbury, how she'd stumbled onto life as a yogini, tales about washing the floors in golden temples in India. She is the kind of person who says the word "God" with no question mark at the end. She tells me to return the next day to take her yoga class. I laugh because I think she's trying to be funny.

"You can return to wellness," she says. "You just need to decide you're going to."

My guard goes up; I have been lulled by this fairy-looking hippie who is now going to tell me that my pain is nothing a little wheatgrass won't cure. I look at her like she's crazy. If she tells me my broken leg is in my head, I'll snarl at her.

She sees my wary look and waves it off. "People in wheel-chairs can do Kundalini yoga," she says in a way that makes it sound practical, like taking out the trash or doing the dishes. "Even if you only sit there and breathe for three minutes, those three minutes will help you. We always say, Begin where you are."

I tell her I'll think about it and then make my way back to the truck. For several minutes after I put the key in the ignition, I sit staring out the windshield at the city street. It is January of the year I will be thirty-three years old. My hands grip the steering wheel, and for some reason I start to cry, really cry, the asphalt of the street and the row of stucco homes in front of me growing blurry, my sobs loud enough for an old woman wheeling a grocery cart on the sidewalk to turn and look at the truck. It's as if I have been wandering in the rain for a long time and have stumbled onto some shelter. I am afraid to go in, but also afraid to stay out in the rain.

I surprise myself by actually showing up at the yoga class. The problem had been what to wear; pawing through my few remaining clothes in the chest of drawers, I finally gave up and put on pajama bottoms. At Gurmukh's house I position myself at the back of the wood-floored living room she uses as a yoga studio, propping my crutches against the wall. A smiling woman with long blond hair helps ease me into a sitting position, the leg in its brace stretched out in front. This is the first time I have been on a floor since my accident, and it makes me think of the canyon dirt, how exposed I am, and suddenly I am scared. I feel like hell. I look like hell. What am I doing here?

Gurmukh comes in, the woman in her late fifties with the gait of a teenager. She waves at me, says she's glad I made it. The others in class turn to look at me and I put my head down, feeling like a child; if I don't look at them maybe they'll go away.

To begin the class she has us put our hands together, thumbs pressed to the center of the chest, and close our eyes. "We always begin with a chant," she explains. "These ancient and sacred sounds mean that we are bowing to the great infinite wisdom found inside ourselves."

I listen to the others as Gurmukh leads them in flat Sanskrit tones, *Ong Namo Guru Dev Namo*, and in my head are images of the Muslim call to prayer, the summer I spent in

Saudi Arabia with my mother while she worked there, every person on their knees, the plaintive pitch of such strange words as they echoed over the barren sky. It strikes me that I have not prayed with my hands together since I was a little girl, even in church those occasional times I was too proud or self-conscious to do more than bow my head. Now I push my thumbs tighter against my chest as if to pry loose something stuck there and feel, for the first time in my life, the desire to pray, speak in tongues, howl and let the sound fall on whatever is there, if anything is there.

We inhale the word *Sat*, exhale the word *Nam*, which, she explains, when said together mean "truth is my identity"; Sikhs use it as both hello and goodbye. I consider the implications of making this statement. If truth is in fact my identity, then my relationship to every other definition I have assumed for myself changes; they become clouds, or a morning fog, transient by nature. Accident-prone. Invalid. Wife. Even daughter.

When the class moves to standing postures Gurmukh directs me to sit and breathe, holding the positions in my mind. What we are doing, she says, is raising the Kundalini, the very energy of life. It sits coiled in the base of our spines, the movements like the flute of the snake charmer to the cobra, moving it up our spines to awaken us. I shut my eyes and listen to every word she says. The last posture is to lie flat on our backs, feet rolled out. She says it is called corpse pose, and once again I am returned to the dirt, Edward's fingers dyed crimson. I feel a touch and open my eyes to see Gurmukh standing over me, turning my palms up toward the ceiling. "If you keep your hands closed, how will you receive your blessings from God?" she says matter-of-factly.

In the class I experience a sensation that is not unlike falling in love.

That night I dream of snakes coiling around my spine, their eyes of topaz and moonstone, so many of them, until I myself become one. I see again the flying V of Harley's stomach, but this time I am quick and supple, no appendages to hit. I hear with my body the vibrations of his hooves as they land, then gallop away, fading as thunder does when a storm rolls out to the ocean.

I am at Gurmukh's classes three days a week, four if I don't sleep late on Saturdays. I would stay at her house if I could. I observe the way the yogis live, take any suggestion as an order; this is the way I learn foreign languages, mimicking every detail until I become fluent. As does my yoga teacher, so do I. Like her, I now take cold showers each morning, waking up as Matt leaves for the long commute to work.

The process begins in the bathroom by massaging almond oil into my skin, all of it, including the skin of the leg, where I can register the sensation of pressure but not touch. It is difficult for me to do the first time. I move my hand over my knee, the centipede scar, how white and shiny, then lower, to near the break where an indentation marks the point where the hoof penetrated. The sharp curve at the back tells where the muscles were sewn together. I have this fear that if I press too hard it will snap right off, like a dead branch on a tree.

At first it's like holding a steak before you put it on the grill—fleshy, heavy. But by the end of the week this part of my body starts to feel familiar again. There's a section of my calf that seems almost normal; my foot has feeling although my toes are stiff. My ribs I count like bars on a xylophone. I use my walker to enter the shower, to ensure that, oiled as I am, I won't slip on the tiles. Then under the cold needles of water I scrub until every inch of me is rosy, the chunk of metal in my leg humming, like striking a tuning fork. But, when I'm finished, my skin feels warm from all the blood brought to the surface.

After I dry off, I meditate in the bedroom for half an hour, rolling the still-foreign chants on my tongue. I thought meditating would be easy—I have spent months in bed, after all, how much more restful can you get—but at first I twitch, I'm anxious, five minutes pass slower than most hours I have lived. Then, I don't know when it happens or why, but one morning I shut my eyes, open them, and find that thirty minutes have already gone by.

I eat a vegetarian diet—vegetables, fruit and even tofu, which I have difficulty figuring out how to cook, because every concoction I prepare has a nontaste. The dogs aren't even motivated to beg for table scraps.

My days are increasingly filled with the business of healing, putting me on the road for a forty-mile round-trip in Matt's truck. I see a Sikh chiropractor who manipulates the toes of my bad leg and cracks my neck, a Korean acupuncturist who pokes stainless steel needles in me the size of hat pins and burns a strange moss on my skin like incense. The theory of the moss burning I don't really follow, but it's meant to send the body's immune system into a kind of overdrive, and I drink hot milk flavored with turmeric and honey because

the yogis swear it's good for bones—not because of the calcium in milk, but because turmeric is said to possess certain
healing powers. It tastes like chalk. I don't ask questions. I
willingly enter the Province of Suspension of Disbelief,
which no one in my life wants to follow me into.

"You're a *vegetarian* now?" Tina asks incredulously, the
way I imagine she would if I were to announce I was actually
a transsexual, or a Republican. "You can't be a vegetarian.
You're a real New Mexican, not a hippie New Mexican. How
do you suppose we make vegetarian carne asada? We don't,
pendeja."

"Oh Christ," is my mother's response. "Is this like the time
you joined Camp Fire Girls and I had to show up for those
goddamn hikes in the woods?"

I am afraid Matt will pull out his twin sabers, wit and sarcasm, and kill the pleasure I take from these new activities.
He surprises me by remaining more or less open-minded and
unbiased. It hits me that he is no longer the smart-ass guitar
player who strutted into that party years ago, but a man who
has had to rethink much of what he believed about himself,
more fragile around the edges, easily bruised. Well, not all
smart-ass guitar player, at least.

"So if your yoga teacher told you to stand on your head
and eat peanut butter sandwiches, you'd do it?" he wants to
know when I inform him I am forsaking sugar and artificial
sweeteners in all their forms and will hereafter drink green
tea instead of Coke.

"Of course." I answer without blinking.

"Well all righty then," he nods as he drinks his coffee, puts
one hand up as if to say "I surrender."

Dr. Mesna proves less accepting, in fact the term "freaked out" best applies. Unwrapping my brace he sees prick patterns left by acupuncture along the skin, the red dots where the moss has been burned. "What, exactly, is going on here?" It seems that all the color has drained from his face, making his freckles appear larger.

I explain my recent enlightenment, how the acupuncture is stimulating my chi, the yoga unleashing my Kundalini, the chiropractic care realigning my body. "I am a healing machine," I tell him. I suggest that he make yoga a requirement for all his patients.

"Ms. Dunn, Ms. Dunn, Ms. Dunn." He rubs his eyes, puffs his cheeks blowfishlike and exhales. "It's not the yoga I'm concerned about."

Nothing in the medical literature suggests these alternative therapies are viable courses of action for fracture treatment, he lectures me sternly. He enumerates in ghoulish detail the problems of letting someone poke needles in me when infection is the ever-present threat that could still have me wind up an amputee. I feel like a bad, bad little girl caught sticking bobby pins in electrical sockets. He is not wrong, nor is he small-minded. I have come to believe he is a good surgeon and a thorough doctor, who routinely takes a half hour or more discussing treatment with me. I never feel shut out of the process, but I have in effect shut him out by not discussing all of this alternative treatment with him before I did it. Still, the issue we are dealing with is my body and how I will be able to function in the world. In the kingdom of Me, he is high council, but I wear the crown.

While the soft tissue seems to be healing there is no new

bone growth, and the status of my current intermedullary nail is approaching the "failure rate," meaning the rod could break under the pressure of walking. If that were to happen, not only would the pain be excruciating, but I'd require a messy surgery to remove it, likely setting progress back another year. In any case I'll need another surgery soon to replace the rod with a thicker one. Dr. Mesna uses the term "dinky nail," which I find an unexpected and charming use of colloquialism; I think he might be loosening up. He hopes that surgery will actually stimulate bone production, but if there is no growth, I'll need a bone graft, where marrow is sucked from one hip and plastered over the break. "Infection on top of that could"—he hesitates, I think it's for effect—"be a serious problem."

I promise not to let the cute Korean acupuncturist who plays Sting CDs while he works stick those pins in me or burn any moss again. I am lying, because even Dr. Mesna cannot deny that the skin around the wound looks better, the color in the leg more fleshlike and healthy. I know there is some risk, but I am coming to understand that life is a process of calculating odds; given the options before me I do what makes the best sense for my survival at the moment. The acupuncturist is certified, he is recommended by people I have come to trust, and millions of people in Asia exist with this form of medicine as their primary means of health care.

The evidence points to my having made a good decision: I am beginning to bend my toes and flex my ankle back and forth, from side to side, and I can even bend my knee enough to sit in a semi-cross-legged position on the ground. I need my crutches less and less and can walk with just the moon boot, so much better is my balance. More than that, I have stopped taking Vicodin every six hours. Sometimes I skip it for two days in a row.

This progress could be a result of a regular yoga practice or simply the natural process of the body healing on its own, but I am afraid to tamper with the recipe. Maybe the acupuncture and chiropractor and breathing through my left nostril and milk with turmeric form some magical combination, a kind of alchemy. If I drop any one ingredient from the recipe, maybe all this progress will evaporate, maybe I will shrivel up and have to crawl back into bed and stay there, reduced, diminished.

What I cannot fully explain to anyone is what spurs this thirst for things mystic. I previously would have thought myself too hip, too cool, too smart to do anything but mock it all. But the truth is, when I put my hands together at the center of my chest, when I allow myself to bow deeply, pressing my forehead to the floor, I invariably picture a huge glacier suddenly cracking, falling into a blue mirror of ocean and floating away. It's more than a mental rerun of something I saw on the Discovery channel. I actually feel a chipping away, a melting, piece by piece. I think of my mother on her knees, praying in Latin, the translation of the words long forgotten to her, the prayer simply a current of sounds.

Even before Harley trampled me I believed myself to be broken, misshapen in some essential way, a condition I believed would never change. I have felt this way for as long as I can remember. I have worked out and dieted to become thinner, I have studied to become smarter, I have read Emily Post to pass, just to pass; I have predicated my entire life, it seems, on the belief that I am a problem which must be fixed. And since the day Matt stepped into the rehab hospital, the paradigm of drug recovery has permeated our lives and underscored my sense of being malformed in some deep sense. "My disease," "your disease," our prison of illness. I keep replaying the scenes from the rehab sessions for family members—I am "sicker than the addicts" in my life, I have been costarring in a warped play that will end as a tragedy for everyone concerned unless I too mend my ways.

Now I am having the experience of putting my hands together, breathing deep, and feeling that I am enough. My human self. I am all right. I have everything I need to live, broken leg and all. It's as if this is the knowledge my body has always possessed, but for the first time in my life I am registering it, sensing it, comprehending it.

The word "mystic" comes from a verb that simply means to close one's eyes and lips. I have taken from that an idea of what it is to pray. The way I do this is to shut my eyes and pretend I am a kid again, sitting on the rocky bank of the Stillaguamish River in the summer, watching the water flow by. Written on the surface are my thoughts, and I read them as they pass downriver. Edward's question is one that keeps running on the current. *What we are really talking about is faith. Do you have it?*

A certain ironic stance is the religion of my generation. Belief and faith are just another way to say ignorant and deluded, or so I have always thought. I have never had a concept of what God meant, but now I have an inkling that God must be something like the feeling of gratitude, the ability to wake up every day and be struck with the beauty of the strangest things, like the shape of a dog's paw, or the smell of orange juice.

I would like to say that my happily-ever-after comes now, that as a newly minted bodhisattva I am wise and caring. But this is not what happens.

[III]

A HORSE MAKES A WOMAN DIFFICULT.

When the Zen *roshi* Shunryu Suzuki was a young man he was playing the Chinese board game, go, with a group of friends at school. The group became hungry, the story goes, so Suzuki had the bright idea to requisition a melon from the kitchen's cold storage cellar.

So he went into the cellar and picked up a ripe melon, but then he heard footsteps on the stairs. He froze, not wanting to be caught red-handed with a stolen melon but having no place to hide. In a moment he heard a click, and then he was enveloped in darkness. He groped forward toward the stairs, the stolen melon in his arms.

All at once pain pierced his brow, a pain so nasty it took his breath away. Something warm and thick must have rolled down his eye, and his chin and neck and chest, and he must have realized it was blood. When he tried to pull away the pain, incredibly, got meaner. Reaching up he felt for its source; he discovered he was caught on a sharpened meat hook that dangled from the low ceiling. His face could have been a ham or a side of beef; it dangled just the same. He must have cried out. No one came. Tears probably spilled from his eyes, running down his face, thinning the blood already there, diluting it a lighter color, which he could not see.

Moving only forced the hook in deeper, as if he were a fish caught on a line. So he could only stand there in the cool darkness, in complete stillness, no different from those melons in front of him that he could not reach. There wasn't anything to do. He breathed, his blood flowed, his heart pumped, as it does in any living mammal.

When finally his friends realized that he had not returned with the melon, they came looking and found Suzuki on the hook. They must have been distraught, rushing around, unsure of how to extricate him without causing more pain. They feared he was blinded, but he was not, only sore and bleeding. Later in his life he would say one thing about being snared on that hook: he was awakened.

My days now include stopping at the barn. Juan puts Harley in the cross ties for me and then brings out a brush from my tack box. I stand near Harley, stroking his coat around his face and neck, not really grooming, that's an energetic process that requires some muscle, a sort of dance, the ability to move in close and smoothly work a brush and curry. I avoid getting too near his legs, am still leery, aware that I can't move fast enough and don't have enough balance to be truly safe around a horse. Should he spook or kick at a fly I could be hurt. But as he brings his head down for the treats I always carry, I move my face close enough to feel the thick hair that grows on the inside of his ears, soft like the edges of a powder puff. While I brush I talk into his ear, telling him everything I don't say to people.

I've heard it said that horses are substitutes for men. To me, horses are not men. For example, their emotional dependability can be charted. Harley, as was Goober before him, as was Gabe, as was Sunny, as was Breezy, as was Big

Red, all the way back to my first pony, Mickey Merry Legs, is clear about what makes him happy and unhappy and he never, ever, wavers from that. That is not to say that horses are at all alike in their personalities. Harley, for instance, loves to be brushed and fussed over, will even fall asleep as the whiskers on his muzzle are trimmed with an electric clipper. Breezy would not tolerate anything beyond knocking the dust off his hide. Harley hates the sound of AM radio. Gabe liked mariachi bands, would collect himself beneath me and prance in what felt like a jig.

Admitting this to anyone would just give more ammunition to the argument that horses hold a sexual appeal for women, that we equestrians get off by straddling a big brute between our thighs. I have ridden all my life and have yet to orgasm as a result—in fact sitting a horse correctly produces bruises and chafing, swelling and soreness. I am so tired of hearing about bestiality from men and from other women who either aren't self aware or are afraid to be honest.

In reality, the appeal of horses is so much more threatening than sex.

Little girls with their bouncing pigtails, grinning faces and lilliputian bodies look so cute as they ride ponies, but a serious metamorphosis is actually taking place. These girls are beginning to understand something that men historically have always known. They are tasting what it means to move freely with great power, and they are developing an appetite for mobility. They are learning not to take no for an answer, even when that no comes from a being who possesses one hundred times their strength. Riding is not the experience the girls will have when they get older and can drive a car, because their horses will nicker for them and will show affection and will favor them over others. A girl will work hard to earn her horse's loyalty, and this will be returned, and this is the dynamic she will come to expect of all others in her life. If a girl begins riding at an early age and continues until she is grown, all of this will be ingrained. In fact her bones themselves will be shaped by it.

There is no way around it: a horse makes a woman difficult. The French knew this and called equestriennes "amazones." Amazones were nothing less than a separate "race" of female. This race was composed of equal parts female, male, and animal: a spellbinding "centauress," the word invoking the myth of Centaur, the Greek image of a people that stood for drunkenness and violence. The myth has its roots in stories about the brutal Kassite tribes of Iran in the second millennium B.C., who rode into the Near East bringing horses and decadence. The French considered the amazone dangerous, a knife poised at the seam of the social fabric, because of her mobility. Mobility suggested sexual promiscuity, which in turn implied a certain brazen power, something to be feared.

This power is what as little girls we are ultimately falling in love with as we beg our mommies for pony rides at the state fair, lie in bed looking at our *Misty of Chincoteague* posters, hugging our Beyer horse figurines, in our heads constructing arguments for why we will positively die if we don't get to have riding lessons.

Gurmukh has taken it on as a personal mission to see that I am healed, and to prove wrong all predictions on the ultimate functionality of my leg. "Western doctors are not bad, don't ever think I'm saying that. I mean, how amazing was it that they could put you back together?" she says, her hand over mine, as she leans in as if to share a secret. "It's just that sometimes they're . . . limited . . . in what they believe to be possible."

With little more than two months left until the surgery to replace the "dinky nail" Gurmukh introduces me to John Hanrahan, an Olympic-wrestler-turned-personal-trainer who is intrigued by the challenge my injury presents. He develops special weight-training exercises to help strengthen my leg and restore some vigor to the rest of me. I like John immediately and our rapport is instant, him like the older brother I used to wish I had. At our first workout I am hesitant, imagine the rod in my leg cracking if I do much more than walk. But his competence instills in me a certain amount of security, and we move slowly through some gentle movements, using his hand or a wide elastic band for resistance. John starts calling a few times a week.

"Let's get you back in the gym, girl."

"John, I'm going to have to owe you."

"Pay me when we run the L.A. Marathon," he answers. "Just meet me after yoga, all right?"

Mike calls to offer me an assignment. "How would you like to interview Bruce Lee before he became famous?" I used to have a thing for Chinese action movies, took boxing classes, and was one of the few women he knew besides his girlfriend who would watch *Ultimate Fight Challenge* on cable with him. I point out there are a couple problems with this assignment. One being Bruce Lee is already famous, and, two, quite dead.

"Gee, thanks for the update. Do you want to hear what I have to say or not?" There's a former navy SEAL who has developed a supposedly revolutionary approach to the martial arts; he thinks the guy might make a good article.

Immediately I imagine a screaming boot camp drill sergeant in a judo gi. I could not be more disinterested if Mike were proposing that I write "Root Canals: Up Close and Personal." Still, I am working for my horse and to keep up my half of the bills, so I say yes.

It occurs to me when I meet Mack, the SEAL, that lately I have been consistently wrong about almost all my preconceptions of people. He is not a walking cliché. Mack is soft-spoken, well read, and his ideas do make an interesting topic for Mike's magazine. When he invites me to sit in on one of his classes, I accept, and that is how I find myself walking with him, about to across a street in Burbank to a park where several of his students wait, leaning on one crutch in a Tiny Tim way. I am talking, looking up at him, when suddenly I feel an excruciating jolt that seems as if my leg has been banged with a hammer; I didn't gauge the depth of the curb, and I have tripped. With a sickening sense of losing my balance, I drop my crutch and hurl face first toward the street.

Mack catches me before I hit, scooping me up in his arms so that I am cradled against his chest. I allow myself a fraction of a moment to relax before he releases me. There is a feeling of rescue, of intense relief. I savor it. Then I become profoundly self-conscious.

"Thanks. Did I mention that I'm a professional klutz?" I say, trying for casual, trying for unruffled.

He gives me a tight, polite smile, and we continue on for several steps making small talk about the class. When we reach the other side of the street, he turns to me.

"Listen," he says, his tone serious. "I don't know you very well, and forgive me if this is none of my business, but I don't think you're a klutz. It seems to me that you don't care enough about yourself to pay attention to what you're doing. That's why you keep getting hurt."

I could not feel more nonplussed if he had just reached out and slapped me across the face. I have a you-read-my-diary feeling, kind of queasy yet angry at the same time. I have an urge to smack him. *If I wanted your opinion, I'd beat it out of you*, a favorite saying in my family. My mother dated a string of these special forces types before she met my stepfather, and they all had the same air of being convinced of their absolute authority regarding literally everything on the planet.

"I'm sorry if I spoke out of turn," he finally says. "It's just that I am trained to be observant."

"Swell. They gave you Superman X-ray vision in SEAL team?" I snap at him as I continue forward with my head down, eyes focused on the ground.

"No. We just leap tall buildings," he says.

"The few, the proud, the opinionated."

"That's not us. 'Admit nothing, deny everything, and make counteraccusations,' that's us."

"Whatever."

I observe his class for a short time, then excuse myself, saying I have another appointment. On the drive home through Malibu Canyon, I pull the truck over and sit in the cab with the radio turned off. For a long time I watch the circle of two ravens as they spiral from the height of the canyon's jagged walls down to the crooked muddy line of creek below.

His comment digs at me like a sliver under the skin. Where exactly is it written on me that I have been careless with my life? Is it in the tilt of my head, the way I talk with my hands? The slump of my shoulders? I suppose I believed that two months of yoga postures, lentil stew, and cold showers would be enough to remedy a life history. This is addict logic, one fix and I'll be fine, when really it takes the rest of a life of constant tending to undo what has already been set in motion. There is a reason for the expressions "yoga practice," "spiritual practice."

All at once I feel overwhelmed by the task ahead of me, to sift through which feelings are mine, which really belong to my mother and grandmother. I put my head on the steering wheel and shut my eyes.

Gram was the kind of woman who was so beautiful when she was young that she hated the look of her own skin as she aged. Her eyes were a shade of dark brown that appeared black. *Black Irish*. She could count to one hundred in French and insult you, *Taisez-vous imbécile*. She wanted to go to business school after high school; when she told her father this, he was angry and shocked, and he hit her. Women didn't do things like that. She didn't leave the house for a whole weekend. In some of her versions of this story, her father only cried at hearing her desire to attend business school. Perhaps he did both.

Whatever the truth was, it is certain that soon after that incident she eloped with my grandfather, a young man whom she had known for three months. He was a flute player and a bus driver, and for a while they owned a diner where she overcooked the meat. They divorced in the fifties; he ran off with a plain-looking woman who already had two daughters. *Peggy had the biggest ass*. It was a detail she could never reconcile with the rules she thought she knew about what men find valuable in women. He left my grandmother with their one child, my mother, to raise. For the rest of her life her voice would shake when she said his name. She'd tell my mother, *Your dirty rotten son of a bitch father. You look just like him.*

Being a divorcée did get Gram into business, at least: she became a lingerie buyer for a department store and traveled from her tiny Allegheny town in western Pennsylvania to New York City regularly. *All by myself on the train.* She once stayed at the Waldorf-Astoria and shared an elevator with Ronald Reagan when he was still just that actor in *Bedtime for Bonzo*. He noticed what a great-looking dame she was, she said. First: he smiled at her. Then: he asked her out for a drink. And: she said no, she wasn't that kind of lady, the kind that would have a drink with a handsome, famous man she'd just met. Of course she was that kind of lady, so I have no idea what really happened. Maybe he did not notice what a great-looking dame she was. *You lying two-bit shyster,* she'd yell at the television when he was president. She would tune into State of the Union addresses just for the pleasure of getting mad. *How you got elected I'll never know.*

My mother spent her childhood trying to figure out what she had personally done to make her father leave and her mother so unhappy. Her hair had the sheen of new pennies and curled in ringlets around her face. She memorized poetry from Kipling; she took ballet and rode an old paint horse named Salty. By the time she got to high school, she declared herself a rebel and dyed her hair black. In the pictures of her yearbook she looks like the prototype for Stockard Channing's take on the Rizzo character in *Grease*. She too got sent on a Greyhound to spend the summer with Aunt Gay and Uncle Roy in Washington. After high school she joined the air force and distinguished herself by having the highest IQ score of any enlistee that year. She requested assignment in New Mexico because she'd read about it in Zane Grey novels. She felt comfortable in the openness of the high desert, liked the fact that you can see things coming.

After four years as a Waf, Mom returned home to work as a cocktail waitress and a nurse's aide so she could save money. That and the GI Bill would get her to college for sure. It was the sixties; things were possible. She wanted to be a doctor. An internist, or possibly an ER doctor, she couldn't decide. She was in her first semester of college when she went to a party and spied a tall, fair Italian man dancing with a blonde.

I knew some Italian thanks to the crowd I ran around with in high school.

What did you say?

I said "ciao," and he asked me if I spoke Italian. I told him, "Soltanto nel mio cuore," which I think means "Only in my heart." Might have been a Mario Lanza lyric; I forget.

Very cool.

I'm a classy broad, what can I tell you.

She had a black, three-quarter-length dress, with spaghetti straps that had the habit of falling off her shoulders. Mom also has this way of arching her right eyebrow. The blonde had no chance.

The Italian left after a few months. Then I arrived. She had to rethink her medical career. Nurse was the next best, most viable option, but it would require moving in with her mother. My mother ranks three events in her life by their order of severity: her parents' divorce; the death of her husband, my stepfather; and the day she found out she was pregnant with me. I could have been named Calamity.

I think about why it felt so good to be caught when I tripped. To not have to pick myself up again.

Two days later, I am driving down the Pacific Coast Highway to an evening yoga class when the whirl of red lights begins to flash behind me. Traffic cops on the Pacific Coast Highway are a constant plague, locusts in the wheat field. They're bad enough if you drive a Jaguar or a BMW, but if you happen to be in a dented Toyota truck with a tailgate covered in bumper stickers for punk bands with names like Johnny Cats and Man Will Surrender, you should expect to be swarmed. I pull to the berm and prepare myself for the interrogation. *License, insurance, please. Where are you headed? Please step out of the car.* They are always looking to catch someone with drugs; the truck fits a profile. I breathe deep and reassure myself those days are gone, there's nothing to fear. Still, I check the ashtray. It's empty.

I roll down the window as I hear the crunching sound of feet along gravel. The officer shines a flashlight in my face, he just a dark silhouette in back of the light. "Here you are, sir," I say as I hand over my license and insurance card. It is useless to ask the charge; cops have a hundred ways you can be guilty and not know it.

A hand takes the items. "Are you aware that your registration tag is not current?"

"No, sir," I say. "This is my husband's truck. I am just driving it because I can't use my own car." I tell him I have a busted leg in a brace, pointing down to it. "See?"

The officer lowers the flashlight and peers in the side window. He is about my age, blond mustache, side part. His eyes scan the littered interior, the dust on the dashboard, the single crutch next to me. He asks if I have the registration paper, so I search through the overstuffed glove compartment, pushing past cassette tapes, receipts for oil changes, ancient check stubs, until I find an expired registration with Matt's name on it.

The officer regards it for a moment, then passes it back to me. "I'm not going to cite you, ma'am," he says, and a wave of relief crashes over me. "But," he adds, "can I be blunt?"

I have never heard a police officer ask permission to be blunt, so I can't imagine what's coming. "Please," I tell him.

"Ma'am, if you were my wife with a broken leg, I sure wouldn't let you drive around in a car like this," he says. "Tell your husband he needs to take better care of you."

How to respond to a comment like this? *Thank you?* I nod and roll up the window, wait for him to get in the patrol car so I can pull back out to the highway. How dare he. He doesn't know us. He doesn't have one idea how we are with each other.

Only after I mentally call the cop every insult I know—an extensive list, it takes a while—do I start to cry. I see Matt's Raphaelite face, the smoothness of his skin, think how long it's been since I have seen him look happy. Dragging himself out of bed before dawn so he can make the forty-five-mile drive to work. No friends from before, and the people from rehab back in the orbit of their own worlds. Our life only a gray space between what used to be and what might come next. He is trying to make sense of his life. He is doing the very best that he knows. And although I want it to be, I want more than anything for it to be, it is not enough for me. But I can't demand more. It's just not fair. And I don't know how.

I have had this feeling since I was a little girl: I am standing on a plank, my heels off the edge. Behind me is a sheer drop, at the bottom sharp needles and broken bottles. A net? There is no net. I have to keep moving forward.

When I arrive home, I check my computer, find an e-mail from the navy SEAL. He says he noticed I have developed a walk where I turn my bad leg out at a slight angle and push off in a rolling motion.

> You'll get hip problems that way, I would like to suggest some techniques for walking normally. I would be happy to have you take a class.

I think he's joking. I tell him that's a good one, but that I feel lucky to walk as well as I do. No solid bone, tendons, nerves, muscles cut. I walk fine, considering.

He replies to my e-mail instantly:

> Considering what? Considering yourself handicapped? Your definitions of yourself and your limits on what you consider possible are the only handicaps you have.

I stare at the screen, debate whether I should just delete the message. Wonder why today is the day strange men want to offer their opinions.

To be caught. A net.

I start to add up all the people who have extended help to me in some form or other since that day in the canyon; I tick three dozen names off the top of my head. Perhaps I have confused a cocoon with a net. No one is guaranteed to be insulated from the work of surviving, but those extended hands form their own net; it's simply up to you to do the weaving.

I write:

Thanks for your offer to help. Can I come to your class next week and get some pointers?

It is the last week of May. A gray marine layer blankets the coast but the San Fernando Valley roasts under a clear sky. I am being wheeled into the operating room of Kaiser Hospital for the surgery where Dr. Mesna will replace the "dinky nail" with what I have termed the "macho nail." The macho nail is light green, not as attractive as the robin's egg blue of the current one; I note this to an orthopedic technician I know from my many weekly visits. "You can't have everything," he says. He takes my hand as we wheel into the room. I have asked him to, since the nurses made me leave my sandalwood mala in the preop center. Fingering the round wooden beads had been my own form of Valium.

"Nervous?" he asks.

"Nope. Just wanted to hold hands."

"Oh, I forget. You're a pro at this by now." He smiles. He's losing his hair, it gives his smile more face to cover.

In the operating room "Sweet Home Alabama" is blasting through a boom box, it's a party, come on in. I realize how comfortable I feel in the hospital; I know the lingo, joke with the staff. I have a flash of anxiety that has nothing to do with the fact that I am about to undergo a surgery during which my knee joint could crack from the trauma of the rod insertion, or hairline fractures could develop in the tibia from the violence of the placement. More disturbing at this moment is the realization that, someday, I will not need any more surgeries, and so will lose the part I play in this ongoing theater. I will have to leave my role as the injured person and again assume the identity of someone who can literally carry her own weight.

The music changes to Natalie Merchant, and I know Dr. Mesna is in the room; he has a thing for female singer-songwriters. Carly Simon is a favorite. "Ms. Dunn," he says brightly, just his blue-masked face in my view, his freckled forehead. He raises the electric screwdriver he'll use to remove the bolts at my ankle holding the rod in place. He revs it a few times. Vroom, vroom. "Ready to get started?"

"Is that a Black and Decker? Can you build me some bookshelves when you finish?"

His mask moves. I think he smiles. "Did I mention I worked as a carpenter during college?"

"Construction workers make the best orthopedists," I tell him. The anesthesiologist has arrived, and she is telling me something about my IV. The lights suddenly appear more brilliant, Dr. Mesna's voice like he is talking to me down a long tiled hall. He is giving a lecture about angles, carpentry.

In postop I come out of anesthesia slowly, aching. Feel as if I have been drugged and dragged behind a car. I get shivery, my teeth clack. Dr. Mesna is beside me. "Everything went smoothly," he says. "No complications." He continues to talk. Three days of recovery in the hospital. Back up on crutches by tomorrow.

Shut up David, I want to say. Instead, "Can I have some drugs?"

The pain is worse this time than any I can remember, a stabbing, twisting sensation with a tenacious grip. I wake up in the hospital room, bob in and out of sleep, somnolence like the tide. I keep fighting to break the surface. Gurmukh calls, says she prayed for me today. My mom calls, says I love you, baby-doll. Each time my eyes open there seem to be new visitors in the chairs beside the bed. I collect a series of still shots: Renée in her black long sleeves. My friend Lola discusses the basketball game showing on the room's television with the navy SEAL, who brought carnations. Bernie in his blue smock enters the room. Hey, Sunshine. Carryl says hi. John Hanrahan and Mike sit next to each other with backs straight, hands on the armrests. More flowers. How are you feeling? Not up for a workout, John. Ha ha. Next week? OK.

I always hope Matt will fill the frame, but Lola reminds me that he's at work. Yes, I knew that. He has to meet a friend from rehab. I knew that. He has a commitment to his sobriety group he cannot break. I knew that. Finally: "Sam, wake up, look, Matty's here," says Lola, her voice loud and cheerful, a pep squad of one. Thank God. His smooth skin, the brush of his goatee. I want to wake up but I am so tired, so achy. It is night; the lights of the room now yellowed and dim. He says, "Hey, I bought you a portable CD player." He holds the earphones to my head, the music faint.

Later, I feel a touch against my hair. I half open my eyes. He is leaning over me, trying to gently stroke the hair from my face with a small brush. His large hands tentative. There is something beautiful, mournful in his action. I shut my eyes and hope he continues. *Why didn't you come earlier?* I realize this is a touch I will recall for the rest of my life.

I cannot make sense of what comes next other than to say I start to experience that airless feeling from long ago with Gene and the Mercury Comet, the drawstring being pulled tight. *Qué pasa? Mira, I still love you.*

A few weeks after my last surgery, I am driving in Culver City, and I pull up to an intersection to make a left-hand turn. For a moment—or perhaps it is longer than a moment, perhaps minutes go by—I lose track of where I am. There are many factors involved: Vicodin taken several hours before for that biting pain, a cell phone, images from the archive of my life, like flipping pages in a photo album. Here is the first fish I caught. There is Matt in mirrored sunglasses. Tina and her spiky hairdo, reading a book in our college dorm. The white stripe in the dark tail of a buckskin gelding named Sunny. My mother pouring coffee, black, no cream. *Breakfast of champions.*

Anyway, I hit a car in front of me.

It's nothing serious, a fender bender they call it. Still, it's the first auto accident I have ever been involved in. Going only ten miles an hour, luckily. The other driver is surprised but not hurt. She had been stopped at the intersection in the turn lane. Didn't I see the light was red? No. Yes. I . . . I . . . have no way to justify myself.

But, wait, I tell myself. Hey, things happen. The environment we exist in is extremely forgiving; otherwise every stoplight missed or speed limit exceeded would result in something bad happening. But that is not the case. Maybe I have been dressing up with complicated rationales what is just the order of chance. You win some, you lose some. But even as I say this to myself, I see the reams of research abstracts I once pored over. People who attribute important events in life to chance, rather than make the association that something within their behavior had an influence, are more often involved in accidents. I consider the words I say each day: *Sat nam*, Truth is my identity.

Only after we trade information and I get back in my car do my hands start to shake so badly I consider for a moment this is some kind of seizure. *Petit mal* would be the term, but no, it is merely an excess of adrenaline. This is the cue that I am terrified. In the past my accidents have involved only me; I have been the one to get hurt. This is the first time my actions have directly jeopardized the life of another person. What if that had been a kid on a bike? A woman like me, unable to move fast while crossing the street?

I am recalling the study that found drivers with marital problems were more likely to have accidents around the time they filed for divorce. But more than anything, I'm feeling angry and ashamed. I have the experience and the reasoning capabilities to know that if you take a Vicodin, talk on the cell phone, and daydream, you're not just inviting risk. You're marrying it. My lack of attention is a willful act.

I cannot get around this: I have to say out loud the words that have been running silently through my mind, because if I don't, I am not only a danger to myself. Maybe, next time, I will kill someone else.

Almost every person I know has been in therapy at some time or other. When I ask for recommendations, I receive so many phone numbers for psychiatrists, psychologists, and family counselors, I finally just play ceny-meeny-miney-moe. I look at the number then change my mind, search through all the papers where I have numbers written and call the one for the therapist with experience in "family dynamics and addiction issues."

The therapist is a little man. His office a sleek design with modern furniture and a black couch. "Nice leather," I tell him, not sure of how to begin. A rendering of Buddha hangs on the wall. The therapist sits leaning forward with his hands on his knees; wrinkles like tributary streams surround his brown eyes.

"Welcome," he says.

"I don't want to use up much of your time," I say. "I only have a couple of questions."

And then I burst into tears. I empty a Kleenex box. He hands me another.

Each July I go to New York for business, my yearly trek to remind editors who assign articles of the fact that I exist. Bruises from the surgery have turned to yellow, and the fresh incision at my knee looks a healthy pink. I decide I'll go this year.

But New York has become a gauntlet, a nightmare of stairs and uneven sidewalks. I press myself crablike along walls as crowds pass by; I know what it feels like to be trampled, and these crowds have that energy. Mentally I bless the sprawl of L.A., the wide freeways, valet parking, and mini-malls with spaces in front.

My leg aches by the time I arrive at a meeting, my brow slick with perspiration. An editor friend winces when he sees me wobble slightly as I rise from a chair.

"It's hard for me to see you get around this way." He takes my arm, steadies me.

"I left my good legs at home," I joke, but he does not smile back. He looks worried, and this jolts a little. At home everyone tells me how much improved I am, how well I am doing, and I realize they are measuring against the stages of my healing since the initial impact. But this man only has the "before" picture of me to contrast with the woman he sees in front of him now. I have a panicked feeling, like I should think up something quick to prove I'm the same as always. *Original Formula! New Packaging!*

I think of the therapist sitting with his hands at his knees, my litany of questions.

What kind of a wife am I? What kind of a professional? What kind of a person am I? Well, what kind?

Perhaps you can try existing without a label for now.

Could it be that if I give up the ideas of who I should be, I can make room for who I am? What does this person look like? I don't know yet.

"Here," I say to my friend, "give me a hand. I need one."

When the end of Matt and me comes, there is little yelling, just the thud of finality, an aching strain of regret. *Not with a bang but a whimper*. It is the evening I return from New York.

"I was the sick one." He says this sitting on the couch, his hands in his lap. He is looking at me with those huge hazel eyes; how beautiful they are. "Now you're the sick one, and I just want you to get well. For yourself. Not for me. It's too late for that."

I am not sick, I think. Angry, but not sick. In pain, but not sick. Confused, but not sick. Still I cannot say these things to him; words choke in my throat, sentences painful as chewing ice. The doctors said I would not be able to run again, but this is exactly what I do. I run out on him rather than force the words from my mouth and stick around to see what happens. *If it seems like I'm free it's because I'm always running*. Jimi Hendrix said that.

Matt packs my Nissan sedan; it hurts, but I can push in

the clutch now. He fills the car to the roof with luggage, a few books, my laptop computer. There is room for just one dog, my pug Ming. The big dog, Nika, stays with her dad. It is a modern arrangement. He fills the ashtray with $150 in cash. Walking-around money, he says. No, he doesn't say that. I think that. Gram used to give me walking-around money, a quarter when I went out so I would always be able to call home.

I drive to Renée's house for the night. She doesn't ask questions. Her cats regard me coolly with their green eyes, as if they have seen it all already. I sleep for twelve hours in Renée's guest bed, Ming curled into my side, ensconced in the frothy comforter. In the morning, late, after coffee, I move to Mary Ellen's house at the top of a crest in the Santa Monica Mountains. Both her sons are gone; she has an extra bedroom. She's waiting at the door, puts an arm around my shoulders. Why did Matt stay? Why were you the one to leave? She wants to know. I always leave, I tell her. It always feels better, safer, to keep moving.

"This is home for as long as it takes you to figure it out," she says, then proceeds to the kitchen. "Eating will make you feel better."

I think nothing will make me feel better.

The room Mary Ellen has given me has a twin bed with a pine frame, and a window that looks out onto the roan-colored hills of Calabasas, all covered in a nubby spread of shrunken oaks and the occasional thrust of yucca. I spend days just lying in that twin bed, as I did in those first weeks

after the accident. This is the real break; my leg was just practice in seeing what I thought was inseparable from me
become a distinct and unattached entity.

Lying across the white bedspread with my cheek against
the thick cotton pillowcase, I think often about what Lucia
said. *God touches us with a feather, then if we don't listen, he
starts throwing bricks.* Ironic those words should come from
her, the most renowned professional female boxer on the
planet, who puts herself on the line physically every day of
her life. *Aren't you scared sometimes?* I asked her once. *No, not
anymore. I learned to listen.* As a teenage champion in Hol-
land, she was almost killed in a kickboxing match when she
was pitted against a man. Her managers and trainers wanted
her to fight him; it would make a great show, they said. She
listened to everyone but herself, and the man knocked her
cold. More than ten years later, she has not been knocked out
again. Nor has she lost a single match.

I think of Harley standing over me, the rush of my blood,
its fresh color, the impossible white of my bones exposed to
air. This was the brick. Finally, this was the brick.

Edward finds me at Mary Ellen's. We haven't talked for more
than a month; I did not leave a forwarding number. I am worried he will be disappointed in me and my pending divorce;
he's been married more than twenty years and believes in the
institution. He says no, there is never any room for judgment.
"What this means is that a space has opened in your life," he
says. "Resist the urge to fill it right back up again. See what
comes in naturally."

That evening I go to yoga. At the end of class we sit with our hands at the center of our chests, eyes shut. Slowly the voices around me build, singing the song that always comes at the end. The words form an odd lullaby. *May the longtime sun shine upon you, all love surround you, and the pure light within you guide your way on.* I hear it now as an incantation of release, words of letting go. At the finish I bow my head to the floor and leave it there a long time, listening to the others as their bare feet pad across the wood to the door, until I am the last one in the room. My face is wet. I taste the brine of something with my tongue. It could be tears; it could be sweat.

It is a slow process, assembling a life. I search for pieces that fit like putting together a puzzle. I begin again with the things I know: I wake up. I feed my dog. I work on magazine assignments from the little room at Mary Ellen's. "Keep breathing," Gurmukh says on the phone. "If you only do one thing, keep breathing."

It is perhaps a week after I move into Mary Ellen's. I am at the barn, grooming Harley. I lay my hand across his smooth back, rub the ridge of wither. He has an old scar at the top where the hair has grown in white. Much like the white lines of my own scars. Suddenly I have the intense urge to know again the view from up there; the world has always made sense to me from the vantage point of a horse's back. Perhaps, if I sit there for just for a moment, I will see everything clearly.

On the spot I devise a plan to tack Harley up and just sit

on him while he stands. To do this I need to enlist Juan's help. Because I still walk with a rolling motion to my gait, left foot slightly turned out because I don't have the power to push off in a normal stride, I can't manage the steep steps leading to the tack room. Even without the added weight of my saddle and bridle, I risk either losing my balance or stepping down hard on my bad leg. The pain of that would suck the breath out of me and cause spots to appear in front of my eyes. I know this because about a month ago I wanted to go inside to grab a curry comb, and couldn't make it past the first step.

Juan is at first wary but agrees when I promise not to do more than sit for five minutes on Harley's back. "Cross my heart," I tell him, making the motion. "No problema."

After Juan saddles Harley, he leads him to the mounting block. I put my riding helmet on; it seems to me like putting on a seat belt to sit in a parked car, but, still, I am not so arrogant to ignore that caution is a worthwhile investment. Then the problem is how to actually get high enough so that I can slide onto his back: Juan holds Harley's bridle with one hand as he steadies me with the other, and I crawl onto the mounting block on hands and knees. Reaching the saddle, I steady myself there, then lean my weight over Harley, finally swinging my moon boot across his back and righting myself in the saddle.

Surprisingly, there is no fear, only the high of feeling completely able-bodied. It is as if I am seven years old again and have been set astride Big Red, intoxicated for the first time with a sense of the possible.

Harley stands quietly, flicks his ears as if waiting for

directions. *What now, boss?* My leg immediately starts to throb from the pressure of hanging, but I ignore it for now. My hands run over his shoulders; I inhale the smell of him, the scent of oil and dried sweat, a single green stalk of alfalfa tangled in his mane. I grab a handful, the wiry black strands. How like suture thread; I never noticed that before.

I am happy, truly happy. Then Drew spots me.

"Sam!" His voice is strained, the tone chastising. "I can't be responsible for this." He walks quickly from the other side of the barn, talking the whole time about insurance liability, what if, what if. He looks pale, in disbelief, as if I am straddling a dragon and not a horse.

"Drew," I answer caustically, "I take responsibility for my own actions. I am not going to sue you. Get over it."

But it is too late. The magic fairy dust has evaporated, and I see what he sees: a woman who was nearly killed and who still is not fully healed on the back of the animal that injured her. I become aware of just how ridiculous I look, my floppy sweatshirt, leg brace, helmet matting down my hair, and of the tremendous size of my Thoroughbred, the distance from his back down to the hard topsoil. I am seized by an image of myself as an eggshell. *Humpty Dumpty sat on a wall.*

I apologize to Drew. "You meant well, I know," I tell him. "I wasn't trying to alarm you." Getting down scares me, even with Juan's help. Harley makes a small step to the side, and I clutch his neck, easing myself down with my left leg bent, reaching toward the ground with my right foot, landing all my weight there.

On the twenty-minute drive back to Mary Ellen's house, I think about my mom, how that fall from Becky frightened her so deeply she would never again venture onto the back of a horse. I never understood it before, but now I realize how that becomes possible. I feel a sense of sinking, being drawn down into a dark place, an undertow of mourning. Then, as if breaking the surface, I feel a rush of air in my lungs. No, I say out loud to myself. No no no no.

I will not lose this.

I will not.

My mother sends care packages: canned green chile, a refrigerator magnet etched with the saying, "Hang in there, Pussycat," lacy, peach-colored bras and underwear ordered from the Hanes discount catalog, "Kathy" and "Peanuts" comics she has cut out of the daily newspaper, a horoscope where it is confirmed that people born under the sign of Leo are, in fact, having a bad month. Everyone else, including the therapist I start to see once a week, gives me the same advice. "Exist in a state of not knowing." "Don't make any decisions." "Examine your feelings, see where they originate." This is all murderously difficult to do. At one point I stand alone on Mary Ellen's balcony, mesmerized by the rough hillside. I think I would rather throw myself down this incline than feel what I am feeling right now. Then it occurs to me: maybe throwing myself down hillsides is exactly what I have been doing my entire life.

A friend introduces me to an essayist named Mike Heher. He turns out to be Father Mike Heher, Catholic priest. Funny how things come around. Back with the Catholics where I started, or, more rightly said, didn't start. We begin a correspondence about writing, religion, updates on what celebrities I have interviewed and were they nice.

I ask him in one communication, What do I do with my life from this point forward? Just tell me, and I'll do it. I feel like he has already taken this test and knows the answers for the final.

He writes:

Someone once said that life must be lived forward but can only be understood looking backward. I think we have to endure much before we can see how God has guided our steps. To do it prematurely is to make as real only what you wish were real. I am of the providence-is-a-mystery school. By that I mean that human and divine life is so complex and inter-related that it is almost impossible to see how God acts or why. I don't see the suffering of innocents or the dreadful acts of the holocaust have any place in God's providence. But I believe that God is there, even there. I live providence as a belief and a question. Perhaps this will get you started.

D r. Mesna is not surprised when I tell him of my recent split from my husband. Slow-healing fractures have the effect of a tornado on a person's life, he tells me. Often jobs are lost, patients go bankrupt, and marriages fail.

"Thanks for the heads up on that one, Doctor."

"You're one of the lucky ones," he replies, instantly turning my self-pity around in the rational, let-me-explain-the-facts-to-you manner I have come to rely on. He says serious fractures like mine more often befall men who ride motor-cycles or work in manual labor. Frequently they are blue-collar guys whose livelihood demands an able body, meaning they lose their earning power, sometimes permanently. At least I am a writer who can work from bed. Think of that French writer, the one who ate the cookies.

"Proust," I say, glad for once to be on a subject with him in which I am the resident authority.

My appointments are down to once every six weeks. The soft tissue healing is "superior," I have more flexibility and less swelling than he anticipated, but my X rays show the bone is still not producing any significant signs of "union." We are nearing the one-year anniversary of my accident, and it looks as if the surgery replacing the rod didn't stimulate growth as hoped. He schedules a bone graft surgery for the month after next, a prospect I dread because even Dr. Mesna says the section of hip from which the marrow is drawn will be sore.

"You think the break was bad," Dr. Mesna tells me. "Most of my patients who've had a graft say it's worse."

Now I will have to heal from that, too. I think about being back in bed, giving up the mobility I have finally achieved, unable to move around my horse, practice yoga, work out with John, or improve my walking. I feel like a failure, that the effort I have put toward my healing hasn't been good enough. The furtive drinking of Diet Cokes, the mornings I have fallen asleep during my meditation. My effort at healing not unlike the effort I put toward marriage. Less than perfect. Next week in my fifty-minute session the therapist will ask why I question myself and not the alternative therapies, or my husband's role in our marital collapse. Maybe by next week I'll think of a good answer.

Upset and defeat must register on my face. "I remember my first divorce," Carryl says right away when Dr. Mesna leaves to see another patient. "You'll be fine." She shuts the examining-room door for a woman-to-woman, as is our habit when I come for my check-ups. "Here," she says, pulling something from the pocket of her smock. "I just went back for my son's wedding. You remember the one? Take a look at these pictures of my grandkids . . ."

After yoga class a few days later, Gurmukh pulls me aside to talk. "I've been thinking so much about your leg," she says. I had called her after the appointment with Dr. Mesna to report the bad news of the bone graft surgery. "Will you be my tiny pet?"

"Excuse me?"

She laughs and explains that as her "tiny pet" I would be the subject she works with when she attends a daylong teacher-training workshop led by GuruDev Singh, renowned in the Sikh community internationally as a master of Sat Nam Rasayan. Sat Nam Rasayan is a healing meditation practiced among the Sikhs, which, very roughly explained, means meditating on your problem with a practitioner. GuruDev, Mexican by birth and marginally fluent in English, once joked that his students should use their loved ones like "tiny pets" to experiment on. The word he had been looking for was "mice," but the phrase stuck.

This meditation is not a laying on of hands or faith healing; in fact the practitioner doesn't even touch you, doesn't even have to see you. I think the idea is more akin to the common practice of saying a prayer for someone in the hope that prayer resonates in the cosmos and produces a result. Sat Nam Rasayan is supposed to work for broken hearts, bad backs, cancer, troubled minds, any and all manner of ills.

I had experimented with this months ago with a friend of Gurmukh's, whom the American Sikhs recognize as one of the country's few expert practitioners of this esoteric practice. I remember she told me to "release an intention into the universe." I lay flat out on my back in corpse pose—the easiest yoga posture to master—and sank into a relaxed twilight that was not quite sleep and not quite meditation. I tried to think of some really great intention—world peace, an end to nuclear proliferation, another Bruce Springsteen–E Street Band reunion tour—something many people, not just myself, would benefit from. But, for some reason, what flashed repeatedly through my mind was the image of Michelangelo's painting in the Sistine Chapel, where the knotty finger of Adam and the hand of God touch tip to tip, the spark of creation where they meet.

When we were finished, I had felt deeply relaxed, but the sensation was no different than waking from a good night's sleep. I made a note to save money and just sleep. Still, who am I to say there was nothing to it? More things between heaven and earth, indeed. "Of course," I tell her. "Always happy to be a tiny pet."

Fifty people dressed all in white are sitting with legs folded in lotus position or are lying prone, quiet as stones. Blankets, mats and downy sheepskins form a dreamy patchwork over the floor in a space the size of a high school classroom. GuruDev, a large man with a long black beard and glasses, sits atop a mound of cushions surrounded by flowers and a bowl of fruit, at which he seems to occasionally nibble. I am snuggled among sheepskin and a thick cotton blanket. I doze lightly, but each time I shut my eyes I see the Michelangelo image again. I try to think why this is. I have never been to

Italy, but perhaps it is some genetic memory passed from my unknown Italian father, my only inheritance. GuruDev lives in Rome and has flown in to give this workshop, so perhaps my brain is making an association. That, however, doesn't account for the first time I experienced this mental picture those months ago, long before I knew anything about this teacher.

I figure that the meditation is exerting some powerful form of placebo effect, because for the last few hours I really have experienced less pain. In fact, no pain. One theory for why placebos can work is that they lower anxiety levels and therefore diminish the expectation of pain. The thinking in Western medicine is that a placebo effect becomes profound when a person's belief in the treatment is combined with the confidence and enthusiasm displayed by those administering the treatment. On the other hand, perhaps GuruDev is actually subtly rearranging divine energy in the cosmos to lessen my suffering. Who knows? Does it matter? He seems like a nice man, with large, soulful brown eyes and the tendency to let out a belly-shaking laugh. I am sure if he could personally lessen the suffering of each of us, he would. Perhaps that intention is enough.

At a break Gurmukh takes me up to the cushioned platform to introduce me to GuruDev. I have prepared the usual story about my leg injury, expecting he will ask. He doesn't.

"Your shoulder," he points to my left side. "What is the problem?" This catches me off guard, and I stammer for a moment, collecting my thoughts. Yes, this is the shoulder that was dislocated and popped back in. It gives me the occasional twinge and ache and is weaker than the other shoulder, but I had almost forgotten about it, so much has healing my leg been the focus of attention.

"Tell me about your horse. I rode the horses when I was a boy. In Mexico. Oh, I loved it," he says, his accent decorated by his native Spanish, further complicated by years of speaking Italian. I tell him how Harley had been bound for slaughter when he was rescued by a woman, who then gave him to me. I try to make myself sound like a rescuer too, telling him about the money and time I invested in the broken-down racehorse.

GuruDev stops me, waves a finger in my direction as if he's admonishing a naughty child. "No," he says, his voice so soft I have to lean in to hear him. "You did not save him. He saved you. He is your guru. You know what means *guru*? *Guru* means 'that which brings you from darkness into the light.' "

When the workshop ends, I drive directly to the stable. By the time I reach Harley's paddock, the honeyed light of dusk is already blending into one of those blue Pacific nights. I watch silently while he chomps at his hay, a hind foot cocked lazily to the side. "OK guru," I tell him finally, leaning on the cold metal of the pipe corral gate. "Don't get any ideas about me putting fresh flowers and incense in your manger."

As if in reply Harley looks over at me, sticks his tongue out, and flaps it against his muzzle before swinging his head over the gate. Then with that rubber nose he rifles through

my jacket pockets to take his usual booty of peppermint can-
dies. I run my fingers along the ridge of his long nose. In a few
moments my hand looks beaded with horsehair. The blunt
shapes connect, black ends to brown tips, tiny letters of
another alphabet.

It would make sense for me to be terrified the first time I ride my horse again. But I am not. That comes later.

When Calvin calls to say he thinks it's about time I got back in the saddle, start back with my dressage lessons, it sounds like the most reasonable proposal in the world. I have been thinking about it too, going to the stable each day, watching the girls at the barn as they take their jumping lessons on their perfectly groomed hunters, watching Vicki take her gray mare Gigi around the ring in the familiar patterns of dressage. I have been trying to occupy myself by teaching Harley more stupid pet tricks, namely, how to count by stamping his hoof on cue, but we have both become bored with the process and given up. And, more and more, when I watch Calvin as he exercises Harley, I imagine myself back up there, floating in a leg yield across the diagonal of the ring, rolling with the motion of his delicate canter.

To others, my resuming riding does not appear to be, in any way, a reasonable proposal.

Mary Ellen remains silent for some minutes when I tell her of my plan: I will not attempt to ride on my own; I will always wear my helmet; I will only take lessons with Calvin in the ring, and then only for fifteen-minute intervals, but will stop at any point if the pain in my leg becomes unbearable. We are in her kitchen, my favorite part of her house. "Well," she finally says, rising to clear the dishes, "all I'm going to ask you is, really think about this."

My mother's feelings are more transparent. "If you get hurt again," she warns over the phone, "I'm going to come out there and shoot that horse, then I'm going to shoot you."

"I love you too, Mom," I reply.

I schedule an extra appointment with Dr. Mesna to discuss this, knowing I won't receive a blessing but still wanting him to approve my course of action. I list the evidence: I don't need a crutch anymore, only the aid of a cane. I regularly make do without my moon boot now. He listens, seemingly not surprised by what I am telling him. "But I won't ride if that could harm my leg," I offer.

He appears for a moment to mull over my plans, then tells me, no, since there is a new rod in place there is little chance of it snapping. Once the bone is healed it will be much stronger than my right leg. I might experience some pain while riding because of the angle of the stirrups, but the only real concern is that blood circulation will be disturbed from the pressure and increase swelling. "But, otherwise, since you are probably going to do it anyway," he says, "just don't fall off."

SAMANTHA DUNN

Do you know the feeling of a carousel, the wave of fancy carved horses gently moving up and down, round and around? Why should such a simple motion evoke any pleasure? But it does, and that is exactly what I feel, back up on Harley, riding for the first time in a year. Calvin has to give me a leg up to mount from the right side; I accomplish it awkwardly, doing the motions in the complete reverse of the traditional left-side mount. But I don't have any choice; the pressure on my left leg makes mounting the usual way excruciating. Calvin lengthens my stirrups so there is almost no bend in my knee, my feet barely hitting the metal of the stirrups.

The movement of Harley's first steps exhilarates me, the rocking, the height, the distance from the ground. Calvin leads him by the bridle, and I am a little girl on a pony ride again. But then, as if of their own accord, my hands close around the reins, my shoulders draw back to form a straight line through my hips to my heels. The body remembers.

Which is why I am shocked by the delayed reaction, about two weeks later, when I feel real terror for the first time on horseback. It hits me like a series of slaps to the face, each stronger and more stinging than the next.

We are trotting a slow circle in the arena. Harley is moving slow over the deep, even dirt and stumbles slightly, just one step, from the sheer laziness of not picking up his front hoof. For a second my left leg presses against the stirrup. Pain racks

228

through my body and causes me to hunch in the saddle, chest caved inward, gasping. Then come the snapshots of the past year: All that blood, the morphine drip, sponge baths and the grains of canyon dirt that stubbornly clung to my scalp, X rays of the chunk of bone missing from my leg. The days I passed alone, the clink-clink of Vicodin coming out of a bottle. And I know one thing: I never, ever want to go through that again.

"Pick up a canter along the rail," Calvin calls to me from the center of the ring.

I nod, gulping. *I'm safe, nothing will happen.* I chant a yogi mantra, I try to remember the words to the rosary; surely syncretism is pardonable under the circumstances. I try to visualize a perfect ride, but I experience a physical rebellion. I literally can't grip the reins. A tremor runs through my body; I see it in my hands. I can't describe this feeling other than to say it seems as if I am in front of a firing squad and have heard the clicks of the hammers on the rifles being pulled back.

Worse still, Harley senses all this. Horses take their confidence under saddle from their rider, so when the rider is terrified, the horse figures there's probably a good reason, and becomes likewise. I feel the sudden tension and the stiffening in his back; his head flies up, his steps become mincing and tentative.

"I can't," I finally yell, near hysterical. "I'm scared; I'm so scared. Calvin!"

I don't think I have ever admitted to being scared before. I brace myself for him to shout back, Get over it, just do it! This is a man who jumps horses through six-foot obstacles with a cigarette in his mouth, he is tough and rough around the edges, saving most of the gentleness within himself for horses and the barn cat.

But, instead, he slowly walks over from the center of the ring. "Whoa, laddie, whoa," he murmurs to Harley as he takes ahold of the bridle. He reaches to put an arm around my waist and carefully guides me down. "There. That'll be enough for today." He pretends not to see the tears running from beneath my sunglasses and launches into a story of the time he was sixteen. A championship show in Belfast. He'd broken his leg months before but painted the cast black like a boot and rode anyway. "I can tell you, when we came down after each jump"—he whistles through his teeth—"that was something."

I nod as I listen, not knowing if this is a true story or one of his tall tales but not caring, grateful for either. The two of us walk from the ring, me hobbling and him trying not to seem as if he is shortening his long stride for me.

After Harley is put away and I have fed him his carrots, I feel better. Perhaps I was pressing too hard, Calvin and I agree. The sensible thing to do is go back to basics, ride in the round pen used for training young horses. Practice the kind of exercises used to teach people to ride. You know, Calvin says, the Spanish Riding School trains its riders for years like that; it's a fine tradition. Yes, I say, that'll build confidence. Yes, we agree, that's exactly what I need to do.

My preop appointment comes a few days before the bone graft surgery. It is just a routine check; the hospital requires that I fill out papers saying I won't eat twenty-four hours before the surgery, have read the policies about wearing no rings, necklaces, or other jewelry, and will arrive at the hospital free of makeup—the one rule I always break. Really, what can a little Maybelline Great Lash hurt? I had X rays last month, so am not scheduled for more on this visit. Dr. Mesna, however, is the kind of careful record keeper who would rather spend the HMO's money than miss anything. He sends me to X ray.

When the film comes back, he stands for several minutes looking at the pictures against the lighted screen in the examining room. I am lounging on the examining table, finishing the same *National Geographic* article I started last visit. "You guys need some new magazines," I tell him.

"Huh," he says, still looking at the film. "Huh."

"Well, David?" I ask when I can stand the suspense no longer. "Anything you want to share with the class?"

I get up and stand beside him. He points to the film, making a circling motion around the area of the bone break. There, in the gap that has remained vacant all this time, is a fuzzy, milky image. A cloudy white form grows from each end of the break, stretching out to points that touch at the tip. Michelangelo.

"Whoo-hoo!" I pat him on the arm; we are on friendly terms but hugging would be pushing it. "Houston, we have bone growth."

"Pretty good," he agrees with his usual reserve, but I can tell he's pleased. The fracture is healing "uneventfully," he observes, meaning that nothing bad has happened. It occurs to me that medicine measures "events" in terms of the progression toward

illness, disability and death, rather than measuring the incre-
ments reversing that progression. But today I keep my obser-
vation to myself. It's enough to see that soon I will walk on
solid bone, a complete tibia that will cause the titanium
inside to be nothing more than an accessory.

He cancels the surgery and sends me home with a very
precise prescription: keep doing what you're doing.

With each friend I speculate on all of the possible explanations for the new bone growth: Perhaps it is simply the natural healing process, spurred months ago by the rod
replacement surgery? Or is it the yoga, lowering levels of the
stress hormones in my bloodstream and encouraging the for-
mation of the calcium callus? I consider it all: painkillers,
good orthopedists, acupuncture, tofu and meditating at five
in the morning, a fat man with a beard beaming energy, sheer
luck of the draw. Or, maybe, Will Rogers had it right: nothing
is as good for the inside of a man as the outside of a horse.

That plan Calvin and I hatched about me riding in the round pen, like the riders of Austria's famed Spanish Riding School, that was a good plan. Because, really, who would believe anything could happen when, on a warm Saturday afternoon a couple of months later, Harley is trotting calmly in the small pen, me sitting in the saddle without my stirrups to practice balance and ease the pressure off my bad leg? Doing the same old thing we know by rote now?

What are the odds? A long shot, for sure—that a child, perhaps four or five years old, who has never been to any barn before, is brought to this stable by her parents, friends of someone just passing through? And, further, that this child, unfamiliar with barn rules—how could she know there were rules?—should be left unattended by these parents, who are so very glad to see their friend, gosh, it's been such a long time? And no one would guess that this child should decide it would be fun to play pop-goes-the-weasel, with herself as the weasel, as the lady on the brown horsy goes by.

Who would even speculate that a child would hide on the lower railing and spring up to the side of the pen just as the brown horsy and the lady pass?

Who would see it coming when the brown horsy startles just slightly and takes one quick step to the side, as if to avoid the child, should she land in his way?

And who could imagine that, meanwhile, this popping girl would distract the lady for just a second—*See her dark hair*—but the very *same* second in which her brown horse steps to the side? And that this slight loss of balance would be enough to slip the lady from the saddle, so that she tumbles—almost in slow motion, everyone will note later—to the deep, sandy ground?

This fall would not be serious, like tipping from a barstool to land on a firm mattress. Except that—and here's the real believe-it-or-not—the horse halts as the lady spills from his back to the ground. It would be likely that the horse then would just move forward, out of the way of his fallen rider. But because the sides of the pen are rounded, the horse can't move forward, so he takes one step backward. And in making this step backward, the horse's hind hoof hits the scarred tissue of the lady's titanium leg, where the bone is still not united, where more than 50 percent of the blood supply has already been destroyed.

My nightmare real, again. *And when I am pinned.*

Harley's soft nose is in my face, his ears up, as if to say, What are you doing down there again? Calvin is right beside me. "Can you stand, luv? Are you hit?"

I grab onto his arm. *I don't want to look I don't want to look.* But I do, and there I am, amazingly, in one piece. The anklebone connected to the shinbone; the shinbone connected to the knee bone. Just like the song. The thick leather of my chaps running uninterrupted on both sides.

"Can you stand?" says Calvin in the tone he usually saves for skittish colts. I say I think so. Sore, but yes, I can. He pulls me up. "There, that a girl," he says.

And then there I am, on two feet, not bleeding.

What had seemed to hang as a moment suspended now breaks into fast forward. Calvin bellows, "What idjut is responsible for this? She could have been killed!" His face is very red, he looks very close to hitting something. Drew is yelling something too, the little girl starts to cry, Janice says, "I'll get some ice, Sam, come sit down"; Juan moves quickly into the pen to grab Harley's reins.

"Momento, por favor," I ask him. My voice shaky, feeling weak in the knees. I lean into Harley and hug his neck. "It's OK," I tell my brown horse. "It's not like before." I look at Juan. "I don't want him to be scared."

Juan nods. "Sí. Yo sé."

"You think I'm loca?"

"Sí, pero it's OK."

I arrange myself on the lawn chair Janice hastily prepares,

elevate and ice-pack my leg, and take the four Motrin Janice supplies to keep the swelling down. Drew brings my cell phone, "Call your doctor, just to be safe." He's right. I leave a message that begins, "I'm fine, but . . ."

The mother of the child brings her up to me to apologize. The girl's copper eyes are huge with fear and incomprehension, unsure still of the cause that created this explosive effect. "I'm fine, honey," I say to her softly, like telling a secret her mom can't hear, "but you and I just have to learn to be very, very aware around horses. They're so big."

She nods, then tucks her chin tight, not looking at me.

I reach a hand to touch her tiny arm. "That way we don't get into accidents. OK?"

The girl turns her big eyes to me once more. Should I tell her horses are dangerous? Will fear teach her anything that will save her from wounds and pain and confusion? Will it prevent her heart from breaking, ever?

Or will my words become one of the bricks in a wall she will eventually come to live inside? Will it make her recede into a careful world where even the mildest discomfort is avoided, a life in bubble wrap? Thirty years from now, will she be the kind of woman who always turns away from, rather than toward, all the not-for-sures, all the no-guarantees?

I would rather see her scarred and limping.

In this moment I see clearly the point to which that canyon trail led. I will no longer run away from my life, careening and oblivious, as equally blind to what is in front of me as I am to what is behind. The singular texture of each moment I will embrace as best I am able. I will run into my life with my eyes open and my hands outstretched.

EPILOGUE

There is a tiny guest house painted white, a cottage more like, at the end of a road about five miles up a canyon in Malibu. The house is on the down slope of a hillside covered in twisting, purple-flowered vines of vinca. It is the same canyon to which I first moved four years ago when I was married. There is a steep flight of stairs that leads from the road down to a deck, and to the front door. I always make sure to hold the railing going up and down. I move slowly still, but, some days, it doesn't hurt at all. Some days, I don't even limp.

On the deck I have potted trees and an asparagus fern that keeps trying to die on me. There is a table, covered with a bright mint-checked tablecloth, in the corner by the railing. That's where all my friends like to sit and take in the view of the mountains when they come to visit. Sometimes we have to duck and cover when the crazy flock of escaped green parrots flies overhead; they squawk and haggle with each other like street merchants. Edward says they have been up in these parts for years.

There is also a fleece-lined dog bed for Ming. Her age has finally caught up to her; she sleeps more than ever now when not being hassled and annoyed by Goshi, the Akita puppy Gurmukh gave me as a birthday gift. He weighs about eighty pounds now and is supposed to sleep in a large crate that is also on the deck. But most nights and all day he sleeps on my bed. I have lots of bookshelves, which is wonderful, and a glass-topped desk Renée gave me. The dust that keeps collecting there is a constant reminder that I'm still not a good housekeeper.

In the kitchen, my shelves are stocked full of food my mother insists on sending in her regular care packages from New Mexico. The refrigerator is covered with the cut-out comics she always includes.

By the handle of the freezer hangs my first and only blue ribbon, "First Place Pomona Chapter Schooling Show." It's kind of silly, really. There were only about five riders in the show, held in someone's backyard arena, so we were all guaranteed a first place in something. I couldn't squeeze into a pair of real hunt boots that day, because my leg is a little hard to fit—I keep saying when my ship comes in I'll splurge for a pair of custom-made. It didn't matter what I wore, at any rate. Harley walked, trotted, and cantered on cue. I was worried I would confuse the points where we were supposed to turn or circle, but, in the end, I remembered everything just fine. As we rode up the centerline of the arena toward the judge, Calvin was hooting and hollering and carrying on like we had just won a gold medal.

Only a few of my friends have noticed my little ribbon hanging on the refrigerator. But that's all right. I know it's there.

Each afternoon at about three I quit whatever I'm doing and head down the hill to the stable. Those paddock boots that were new three years ago now have cracks in the leather, and I think I'll need to get them resoled before long. For now Harley and I just ride in the arena, although he always looks up toward the area where the trail comes down, ears pricked tightly forward. It's probably the construction noise; they're building a bunch of new homes up there now. Still, sometimes I wonder what he sees. What he remembers.

The other day I didn't start my ride until nearly sunset, and a thick blanket of fog was rolling in off the Pacific. The fog grew more dense as we rode, blurring the shapes of things with its opal dust. As we cantered along the rail, a gust blew toward us and we were swallowed by the gray, wet mist. The ground disappeared for a moment, and all I could feel were four good legs beneath me, going forward.

ACKNOWLEDGMENTS

If Edward Albert Jr. had not saved my life, these words would not have been typed. There is no measure or expression adequate enough to thank you for all that you have done for me, Edward. Also, I want to extend my appreciation and respect to Matt, who endured painful and difficult times with me. I hold you and your family in my heart, always.

Many books and articles informed and influenced my thinking during the course of writing, among them Nan Goodman's *Shifting the Blame: Literature, Law, and the Theory of Accidents in Nineteenth-Century America*; *Target Risk*, by Gerald J. S. Wilde, Ph.D.; *Why We Hurt: The Natural History of Pain*, by Dr. Frank T. Vertosick Jr.; and the essay "Purebreds and Amazons: Saying Things with Horses in Late Nineteenth-Century France," by Kari Weil.

I am deeply indebted to the paramedics of the L.A. County Fire Department, the emergency team at UCLA Hospital, and to Dr. David Mesna and the orthopedic staff at Kaiser Permanente Hospital, Woodland Hills, California, for their top-rate care, calm explanations and, ultimately, their friendship. Acupuncturist

Steve Lee has the hands and spirit of a healer. Dr. Jared Strote, my resident expert, you write great e-mails. Thanks to everyone at Malibu Vista Ranch for caring for Harley when I couldn't.

I am very fortunate to have in my life loving friends who also happen to be deep thinkers and talented writers. I'm afraid I've impinged upon their generous natures more than once—raided their refrigerators, drank their wine and plucked their brains. I offer each of you my sincere gratitude: Mary Rakow and Lola Wiloughby, my stalwarts, and Colleen Burns, Jody Hauber, Karen Horn, Rochelle Low, Julianne Ortale, Candace Pearson, and Nancy Spiller, all members of the Los Angeles writing collective Hard Words, who wouldn't dream of letting me leave the house with my slip showing; Janet Fitch and Les Plesko, who know a thing or two about tough love; Mary Ellen Strote and Renée Vogel, who always keep their heads when I am losing mine; and Tina Griego, for everything. Beverly Olevin, Cassandra Clark and the incomparable Sandra Tsing Loh: Let's keep doing our voodoo.

Without the inspiration of my friends and mentors at the New York State Summer Writers' Institute, my life and my work would be much impoverished. Robert and Peg Boyers and Marc Woodworth, you have been my guides. I am grateful to Phillip Lopate and Jim Miller in particular for always raising the bar.

I can't offer enough thanks to my agent, Peter Matson, who helps me to put my ideas together. Jim Rutman, you are the best Grade 1 ever, and a good friend. Thank you Jennifer Barth, for your belief in my work, and for your patience.

Without Stephanie Tuck, Eleni Gage, Robin Sayers, Monica Corchran and the rest of the staff at *InStyle* magazine, Harley, the dogs and I would not have stayed afloat. You are great confidantes, and *you look fabulous*. Barb Harris, Peg Moline and my friends at *Shape* are never short on encouragement. Thanks too to Jeff O'Connell at *Muscle and Fitness*, Mike Carlson at *Men's Fitness* and Jim Rosenthal at *Flex*. Brains, brawn and always willing to buy lunch. What more could a girl ask?

Gurmukh Kaur Khalsa, Father Mike Heher, and William *Yoshin* Jodran *Sensei*: You each teach me what it means to walk a path. I will spend the rest of my life trying to live your examples.

My mother, Deanne, is and always has been perfect. I am proud to be your daughter. I miss my grandmother, Evelyn, who taught me to look for the meanings of things. Finally, I thank Richard Machowicz. You've taught me how to walk through life without crutches, in every sense.

Samantha Dunn
2001

ABOUT THE AUTHOR

SAMANTHA DUNN'S novel *Failing Paris*, was a finalist for the PEN/West award. Her writing has appeared in the *Los Angeles Times*, *InStyle*, *Shape*, *SELF*, and numerous other national publications. She lives in Southern California.

A GUIDE FOR READING GROUPS

As Samantha Dunn dares to examine the events leading up to her injury, she uncovers a wise line of questioning for us all. A provocative choice for reading groups, *Not by Accident* stirs conversations about self-awareness, turning points, and the process of mending a life. We hope that the following topics will enhance your discussion of this brave memoir. For information about our other reading group guides, visit us at www.henryholt.com.

1. Samantha is only able to awaken her spiritual self when her body becomes incapacitated. How do her physical injuries reflect her emotional ones? What was the eventual "cure"?

2. Instead of using conventional chapters, Samantha Dunn structured her book in three parts containing dozens of present-tense scenes. What is the effect of this storytelling approach? If you were to classify your life into three parts, what would the major turning points be?

3. *Not by Accident* is dedicated to Samantha's mother and grandmother. For better or worse, what did they teach Samantha about survival, and about being a woman?

4. In part three, Samantha is stopped by the police while driving Matt's truck. The officer says, "If you were my wife with a broken leg, I sure wouldn't let you drive around in a car like this. Tell your husband he needs to take better care of you." Samantha then mentally lists the sacrifices Matt made for her. Do you think the officer's assessment of Matt is too harsh?

5. Guru Dev calls Harley a guru, "that which brings you from darkness into the light." According to this definition, how is a guru different from a rescuer such as Edward Albert, who facilitated Samantha's life-saving trip to the hospital? How do these roles apply to Samantha's numeric spectrum of friendship? Describe some of your gurus and rescuers.

6. Discuss the evolution of Samantha's faith. Are there any similarities between the yogis and the Catholic priests she mentions?

7. Days before Samantha was scheduled for bone graft surgery (a procedure that might have been even more painful than her original injury) an X ray revealed that the operation wouldn't be necessary after all. To what do you attribute her seemingly miraculous growth of new bone? What is your opinion of the alternative treatments she tries?

8. In Samantha's thorough research on people labeled accident-prone, she encountered varied theories about the phenomenon, including trauma reenactment, masochism, risk-taking personalities, and left-handedness. What appears to have caused Samantha's lifetime of "accidents"?

9. Consider the aphorism Samantha heard from a friend: "God touches us with a feather to get our attention. Then, if we don't listen, he starts throwing bricks." What message do you think she took from this?

10. One of the book's most prominent characters is Harley, though conflicting attitudes toward him are presented through Samantha's mother, doctors, and friends. How did your perception of Harley shift throughout the book?

11. Samantha grew up without a father, and her beloved uncle died tragically. How did these events shape her future, and her attitudes toward the rest of her family?

12. Horseback riding is often thought of as a luxury. Though it was clearly a financial challenge for Samantha to have access to horses, riding was always essential to her. What made horseback riding a necessity rather than a luxury in her life? How does Samantha's relationship to horses differ from that of professional riders or those who breed their horses for profit?

13. Samantha refers to the many magazine articles she has written, but she also penned an acclaimed novel. Which

of her novelist skills are detectable in this work of non-fiction?

14. How do Samantha's voice and persona in the epilogue compare to those in the book's first paragraphs?

15. Throughout the book, Samantha explores the theme of facing fears and finding the courage to ride Harley again. What insight does she give us about putting tragedy in perspective?

16. Discuss your own experience with a similar event to that in the book. Did it affect you in ways that were similar to Samantha's metamorphosis?